REARRANGEMENTS

REARRANGEMENTS
THE COURCHENE PAPERS

Thomas J. Courchene

MOSAIC PRESS
Oakville-New York-London

Canadian Cataloguing in Publication Data

Courchene, Thomas J., 1940 -
Rearrangements

Includes bibliographical references.
ISBN 0-88962-507-7

1.   Canada - Constitutional law - Amendments.
2.   Canada - Economic policy - 1971-1991.*
3.   Canada - Politics and government - 1984-   .*
I. Title.

JL65 1991.C68 1991   342.71'03   C92-093153-7

Published by MOSAIC PRESS, P.O. Box 1032, Oakville, Ontario, L6J 5E9, Canada. Offices and warehouse at 1252 Speers Road, Units #1&2, Oakville, Ontario, L6L 5N9, Canada.

Mosaic Press acknowledges the assistance of the Canada Council and the Ontario Arts Council in support of its publishing programme.

Design by Ruth Schaffler
Typeset by Aztext

Printed and bound in Canada.

ISBN   0-88962-507-7 PAPER

MOSAIC PRESS:
In Canada:
Mosaic Press, 1252 Speers Road, Units 1&2, Oakville, Ontario L6L 5N9, Canada. P.O. Box 1032, Oakville, Ontario L6J 5E9.

In the United States:
Distributed to the trade in the United States by: National Book Network, Inc., 4720-A Boston Way, Lanham, MD 20706, USA.

In the U.K.:
John Calder (Publishers) Ltd., 9-15 Neal Street, London, WCZH 9TU, England.

To the memory of my father who, like countless other Canadians in small-town Canada, toiled long and hard and away from the limelight to build our country,

and

To my grandchildren (Andrew, Eric Matthew...) in the earnest hope that our generation will also build well.

ACKNOWLEDGEMENTS

Section 1 ("What Does Ontario Want? The Coming of Age of John P. Robarts' 'Confederation of Tomorrow' Conference") was my 1988 Robarts Lecture and was originally published by the Robarts Centre, York University, 1989.

Section 2 ("Forever Amber") appeared in David Smith, Peter MacKinnon and John Courtney (eds.) After Meech Lake: Lessons for the Future (Saskatoon: Fifth House Publishers), 1991, pp. 33-60 and as Reflections/Reflexions, #6, Institute of Intergovernmental Relations, Queen's University, 1990.

Section 3 ("The Community of the Canada's") appeared (in French) in the volume of background papers to the Belanger-Campeau Commission and (in English) as Reflections/Reflexions #8, Institute of Intergovernmental Relations, Queen's University, 1991.

Section 4 ("A First Nations' Province") appeared as an op-ed piece in the Globe and Mail (October 18, 1990).

Section 5 ("Global Competitiveness and the Canadian Federation") was prepared for a University of Toronto Conference (sponsored by the International Business and Trade Law Programme("Global Competition and Canadian Federalism" (September 1990). It has not been previously published.

Section 6 ("Grappling With Mobility: The Role of the State as a Regulator of Financial Institutions:) is reprinted from Diane Wilhelmy and Pierre Coulombe (eds.) Penser Globalement, Think Globally (Toronto: Institute of Public Administration of Canada), 1990, pp. 299-330.

Section 7 ("Zero Means Almost Nothing: Towards a Preferable Inflation and Macro Stance") is reproduced from the Queen's Quarterly Vol. 97, No. 4 (Winter, 1990) pp. 543-561.

Section 8 ("Canada 1992: Political Denouement or Economic Renaissance") is reproduced from R. Boadway, T. Courchene and D. Purvis (eds.) Economic Dimensions of Constitutional Change (Queen's: John Deutsch Institute) 1991, pp. 45-69.

Section 9 ("In Priase of Renewed Federalism") is excerpted from my C.D. Howe Institute Monograph of the same title (Toronto: C.D. Howe Institute) 1991, pp. 86-94.

We wish to express our gratitude to the publishers and Journals for granting reproduction privileges.

TABLE OF CONTENTS

PREFACE ix

INTRODUCTION xi

PART I - Political Evolution

1. What Does Ontario Want? The Coming of Age
   of John P. Robarts' 'Confederation of Tomorrow'
   Conference 1
2. Forever Amber 43
3. The Community of the Canadas 73
4. A First Nations Province 105

PART II - Global Imperatives

5. Global Competitiveness and the
   Canadian Federation 110
6. Grappling With Mobility: The Role of the
   State as a Regulator of Financial Institutions 147
7. Zero Means Almost Nothing: Towards a
   Preferable Inflation and Macro Stance 174

PART III - 1992: Canada in Play

8. Canada 1992: Political Denouement or
   Economic Renaissance 194
9. In Praise of Renewed Federalism 224

REFERENCES 229

PREFACE

This book of essays is the result of the work and ideas of four people - Marcel Côté of Secor (Montreal), Ed Cowan of Data Sound, Howard Aster of Mosaic Books and Art Stewart of Queen's School of Policy Studies. I am most grateful for their efforts and the confidence they have placed in my recent research. My debt to Cote is especially significant, not only for his integrative and generous introduction but also for our many policy discussions over the last few years.

Many others have also played an important role in influencing my research. Hopefully, most of these are acknowledged in the endnotes of the relevant essays. However, several individuals have been particularly instrumental - Western Ontario's John McDougall who spent the 1990-91 academic year at the School of Policy Studies and Bob Young who is with Queen's this year as a Visiting Scholar, my Queen's colleague Doug Purvis, U of T's Richard Simeon and, above all, C.D. Howe's Tom Kierans. Finally, since I have not yet made the transition to word processing, Sharon Alton of the School of Policy Studies is an integral part of the production of all of my research.

I also wish to express my gratitude to the journals and publishers who allowed me to reproduce these essays.

A short comment to the readers. There is a fair bit of repetition in these essays. Some of this is inevitable since they were intially written for quite different audiences. Despite this repetition, the decision was made to reproduce them intact, so that each of the essays is self-contained. Secondly, the march of events on both the constitutional and economic fronts proceeds relentlessly. As a result, events have eclipsed selected aspects of the essays. Again, the decision was made (and again I concurred) not to update the essays to take account of more recent developments.

Finally, my transition from economist to embracing aspects of political science and the Constitution is due primarily to the constant urging of Margie Courchene. She made this transition rather exciting because she also provided many of the ideas that are at the core of these essays.

Thomas J. Courchene
Kingston, December 1991

ix

Part I
Political Evolution

INTRODUCTION

by Marcel Côté

Few modern democratic countries are perched as perilously as Canada on the brink of self-destruction.

Political and economic pressures stemming from our great internal diversity are straining our federal institutions to the breaking point. The problems go far beyond Quebecers' dissatisfaction, although this remains at the forefront of the pressures for change. The aboriginals' demands for greater recognition and for self-government, the West's alienation from the political and economic power centers of Ontario and Quebec, the silent determination of the six small provinces - with 17% of the population of the country - to maintain the present, massive economic redistribution system anchored around the federal government - all these factors also create tensions that are compounding the issues facing the Canadian federal system.

It has now become evident to most Canadians that a profound rearrangement of our governance structure is necessary and inevitable. The constitutional issue which has dominated the political agenda for more than a decade is consuming federal politics. We are still far - probably - from a revolution. Hence, it is necessary to ask what rearrangements will ease these profound tensions?

Now is the time to listen to Tom Courchene. Here is a man with ideas, insights, new approaches all based on sound analysis and a thorough understanding of all available research. Equally important is this man's boundless intellectual energy and his fearlessness to take risks and offer new solutions.

Tom Courchene, trained as an economist, is now one of Canada's most influential social scientists. He is listened to by those involved in the development and review of public policies in Canada. Few other Canadian social scientist has had his papers so widely circulated in Canada and so carefully discussed and assessed. From his study in his home near Kingston, Ontario, has come a constant stream of papers that have dealt with the predicaments facing Canada. These papers stand out by the strength of their analysis, by the originality of their insights and, more importantly, by the depth and breadth of their comprehension of the various forces that today strain Canada's governance structure.

With the exception of the first essay, the collection of papers presented in this volume were written in 1990 and 1991. They provide Canadians with new insights into our constitutional quandary, analyses of the forces that are fueling the crisis and the various ways Canada can rearrange itself.

Rearrangements

The governance of this country has gone astray. We seem to be unable to address the challenges that the country faces, either in terms of our domestic imperatives or the emerging global realities. This inability provokes, in turn, two crises, one dealing with our constitutional federalism, the other with our economic performance. The two crises have now become embedded in our political debates.

Tom Courchene is able as few others can to separate these two cises by analyzing their causes and potential remedies and then integrating them in terms of policy proposals.

Rearrangements are essential in several domains:
- the relationship between citizen and state
- the relationship between the provinces and Ottawa
- the relationship between Canada and the global community.

Moreover, these rearrangements are not limited to the institutional domain. They have to involve attitudes. Not only do we need changes in our "state of mind" but also, and probably more important, we need changes in the "mind of state". The key factor in all of this is that globalization and the telecomputational revolution have ushered in a new order which has dramatically enhanced the role of private agents, whether citizens or corporations.

This new reality is viewed as an opportunity for the members of the European community who have been thinking and breathing internationalization for over three decades now. But not in Canada! Canadians and their governments have been accustomed to operating behind protective barriers and living off the return from resources. They now find themselves largely offside with freer trade and the collapse of resource prices. For many of us, these are traumatic times: the realization that "those were the good old days" is profoundly disturbing to an inward-looking, entitlement-seeking and government-trusting society.

The Essays

This collection of essays pursues two objectives. First, it brings together the Courchene Papers relevant to the present constitutional debate. Both scholars and policy makers will find this compendium most useful. The Papers fully explore all the pertinent issues and they are secured by the whole body of economic and political science literature relative to the public debate in Canada.

Second, it provides Canadians with a solid overview of the question we must address today. Courchene's approach is moderate and shows a great sensitivity to minorities' points of view. Furthermore, Courchene incorporates the constitutional issues into the global framework of stresses and tensions assailing contemporary nation states. In particular, students who are looking for a broad survey of the constitutional question will find here a rich lode of analysis that will satisfy most of their needs.

The General Structure of the Book

The ten essays presented here are organized in three sections. Part I, *"Political Evaluation"*, includes four essays focussing on the sources of the constitutional tensions and the consequences for Canada as a whole and its various regions. Part II, *"Global Imperatives"*, locates these changes in a global context. The analysis shifts to the economic side and deals with the impacts of globalization and the telecomputational revolution in the remaking of Canada. The three essays develop Courchene's thesis that changes will occur in the structure of the Canadian nation state, irrespective of the nationalist forces to which we usually point as the source of these tensions.

The final section, *"1992: Canada in Play"*, marries both perspectives, the political one developed in Part I and the economic one developed in Part II.

Political Evolution

What does Ontario want? The first essay plumbs the Ontario psyche on the constitutional issue. Courchene frames the inquiry on the background of the new Quebec, as defined by the 'Revolution tranquille' of the '60s and the Quebec Inc. phenomena of the '80s. This allows him to develop a highly provocative and insightful analysis of Ontario and Ontarians. Of particular interest is Courchene's call that Ontario appears embarked on its own quiet revolution - a projection that while novel from the perspective of early 1988 (when this essay was first written) now seems fully justified. This is highly typical of Courchene. He is quite willing to risk being wrong in order to make his work more forceful. As a technique, this seems to work in part because he is right much of the time and in part, even when he turns out to be wrong, the resulting insights remain extremely valuable.

"Forever Amber", the second essay, was written in the wake of the Meech Lake debate. It focuses on the constitutional and economic initiatives of the '80s. My personal reaction to this paper is two-fold. First, it does not seem hardly possible to believe that we Canadians packed as much into the decade of the '80s! Second, Courchene must have had a great deal of fun writing this essay. The title of the essay sets the tone. The language is colloquial and the tone is, if anything, disrespectful in terms of both policies and politicians. (This is particularly true of his treatment of the Tories for whom, in 1979, he was a candidate in the federal riding of London East).

"The Community of the Canadas", the third essay, is Courchene's seminal contribution both to the Belanger-Campeau Commission (where he was the only non-Quebec anglophone to appear in public hearings) and to the "future of Canada" debate. There are three cornerstones to his analysis. The first is that Quebec will get control over what he calls "demolinguistics" - the combination of language, culture, population and immigration - whether this occurs within Canada or without.

The second, is that the way to approach a meaningful response to Quebec's constitutional aspirations is via "concurrency with provincial paramountcy". Thus, Quebec will assert its paramountcy over most areas while the rest of the provinces will have the freedom either to centralize, or to follow Quebec's decentralism, or to rebalance. Third, if the provinces do want to take on more powers, this is only possible if they associate themselves into larger units. Hence, you arrive at the five "communities" of the Canadas - Canada East, Quebec, Ontario, Canada West and the First Nations. (Some might argue that Canada West aught to be two regions, not one. I am sure that Courchene would have to trouble with this - his goal is to argue that generalized decentralization, if desired, requires, at the very least, economic union and likely political union for the west and the east).

"The Communities of the Canadas" has generated substantial debate and discussion in the country because of its decentralist thrust. However, my interpretation (and I am sure Courchene's as well) is that the model is fully flexible. Indeed, the provisions of "the Communities of the Canadas" can be used to centralize power outside Quebec, should Canadians so wish.

The final essay in Part I was originally published in the Globe and Mail. What is surprising is that this idea did not surface earlier. Courchene draws our attention to the fact that what most of the First Nations aspire is a section 92 of their own (Section 92 deals with provincial powers). Indeed, one is surprised to find that most programs administered by the Department for Indian and Northern Affairs are more consistent with provincial than federal functions - roads, welfare, health, etc. Indeed, territorially the First Nations are somewhat administered as a province, but that administration is run out of Ottawa!

Global Imperatives

In Part II, the focus of the essays shifts to the realm of economics and, in particular, to the impact of globalization on the evolution of the conception of nation states. The fifth essay is typical of Courchene - a wide-sweeping survey of the literature brought insightfully and forcefully to bear on the issue in question. In this case the issue is the future of the nation states. Courchene's conclusion, and my own as well, is that nation states are proving to be too small to handle the big challenges, and too large to handle the small challenges. Two important conclusions derive from this. First, the age-old centralization-decentralization debate is becoming increasingly sterile since the key levers are increasingly being pulled by supra-national agencies or groupings, such as the EEC and GATT.

Second, much of what will pass as "sovereignty" in this conception of the evolving global order will relate to how a people "live and work and play". The implication of this for Quebec is that "Independence" may well be a Pyrrhic victory. For Quebec can obtain, within a reconstituted federation, the ability to determine how its society lives and works and plays. The other striking feature of this essay is that Canada in the millennium will be a very different country than the Canada of 1991, even if Meech or Post-Meech did not exist. Global forces are reshaping our country as much as the tensions generated by our own internal diversity. A final message of this essay is to ask the question whether or not Quebec's aspirations within Canada are consistent with the evolution of global economic forces and where, necessarily, we will have to treat? Courchene's answer is that they are fully consistent.

"Grappling with Mobility", the sixth essay, is really an "industry study". In a sense it is outside the constitutional renewal thrust of the rest of the essays. However, very quickly one realizes that, apart from the very fascinating survey of the globalization of finance, the analysis of the Canadian financial sector falls into the typical Canadian conception of "two nations warring in the bosom of a single state". Quebec has adopted the "collective" approach found in Japan and in continental Europe for its financial sector, an approach which is at odds with the "individualist" Anglo-American conception. Although Courchene does not generalize this conflict, this "collectionist vs. individualist" approach is also at the heart of language policy and overall industrial strategy not only in Canada but in North America. In this essay, Courchene comes down on the side of the Quebec model. In the broader sense, what the analysis reveals is that the tensions between Quebec and the rest of Canada run much deeper than language and culture.

The seventh essay, *"Zero Means Almost Nothing"*, is almost certain to antagonize the mainstream of the economics profession, let alone those who run Canada's fiscal and monetary policies. Courchene is highly critical of the Banks' price stability stance. This is an intriguing turnaround. In the 1970s and early 1980s, Courchene was labelled as Canada's foremost monetarist. In this essay, he opts for fixed exchange rates, along the lines of the European Monetary System. His argument is two fold. First, now that we have the Free Trade Agreement and our trading relationships are increasingly north-south rather than east-west, the optimal exchange rate arrangement is, a la Europe, a fixed rate to the U.S.

dollar. Second, as Courchene notes, the macro dysfunciton of the 1970s was runaway inflation. However, the macro dysfunction of the 1980s and 1990s is one of domestic aggregate savings shortfalls which, if anything, are a fiscal not monetary problem. His recommendation is not only for fixed exchange rates but as well a coordinated federal-provincial fiscal policy. As he notes, Ontario should have acted, fiscally, to take some steam out of its boom over the 1983-89 period. And had this essay been written six months later, Courchene would have decried that dramatic diversion between the federal and Ontario budgets (and he does in the next Essay). The challenge Courchene throws to Canadians and to policy makers at the Bank of Canada and at the Federal Finance Department is that the on-going overvaluation of the dollar is not only "hollowing out" Canadian industry but "Americanizing" our social programs. In the larger context of this volume, this essay is really another example of how international developments are (or ought to be) forcing all of us to rethink our domestic policies, again irrespective of our own constitutional tensions.

1992: Canada in Play
The two essays in the third part of this volume weave together the political and the economic threads into a forward looking vision of what a renewed Canada could be.

In *"Canada 1992: Political Denouement or Economic Renaissance"*, Courchene integrates the economic and constitutional imperatives. To put Canada back together in 1992 on a new constitutional basis without addressing the economic imperative will be, at best, a short term victory. Both issues have to be addressed. However, this essay goes well beyond this. The first part is really a summary of his recent C.D. Howe Institute publication, *In Praise of Renewed Federalism*, in which he argues that European-type political super-structure for Canada is probably not in the cards and, more importantly, that there are substantial costs for both Quebec and th rest of Canada to the rending of Canada. Later on, he asserts that the Ontario budget is a new wild card in the constitutional debate. Specifically, he speculates that Premier Rae will be forced to undergo a Mitterrand-type about turn. Backing off of public auto insurance was indeed a first step in the direction that Courchene predicted. But he also surmises, importantly, that Ontario is intent on implmenting a European-style social-democratic program (or should we say Quebec style). His conclusion is that this will inevitably result in a fundamental constitutional realignment, as traditionally "centralist" Ontario might emerge as the new "decentralist" in the federation.

Such a proposition is typical of Courchene's writing, not hesitating to pursue the analysis to its logical ending, however unusual or off-beat it may appear at first look.

The concluding piece, *"In Praise of Renewed Federalism"* (Chapter 9) is excerpted from Courchene's recent C.D. Howe book of the same title and is an appropriate up-beat way to conclude this volume. We Canadians have worked economic and political wonders within the constraints or should I say, flexibility, of the existing Constitution. Tom Courchene's message in this final essay is not only that we ought to celebrate our magnificent accomplishments but that we have ample instruments at our dispossal to rework our institutional design.

With the end of this Introduction, I now turn you over to the writings of Thomas J. Courchene. I trust you, like I, will revel in the insights and even more, in the incredible integration of the political, economic and constitutional factors that comes to the fore in his writings. Most important of all, however, these are the essays of a Canadian who truly understands and loves his country. Readers may disagree with his assumptions, or his conclusions, but they cannot disagree with his approach, namely that the hour of decision is upon us and we have to act now to ensure that the upper half of North America remains something special, economically, socially and culturally, rather than becoming simply northern America.

Marcel Côté,
Montreal, December 1991.

1. What Does Ontario Want?

The Coming of Age of John P. Robarts'
"Confederation of Tomorrow" Conference

Premier Joey Smallwood, at the Confederation of Tomorrow Conference:
I notice that Premier Frost is here today and I remember his
saying when he was in office as the Premier of this great province
at a Dominion-Provincial conference, saying something like
this. He said, "You have all read that we have had three thousand
new industries come to Ontario since the war." This was about
ten years after the war. They already had three thousand new
industries. He said, "You think this is wonderful, don't you?" -
looking around at the nine of us, the other premiers. "You think
this is wonderful. You don't realize the other side of it, all the
new schools we have to build and all of the housing and all of the
hospitals and all the new roads and paving and everything else".
I said, "Stop, you are breaking my heart". (Nov. 27, 1967,
Morning Session).

I. INTRODUCTION

Befitting the celebration of Canada's centenary, John P. Robarts'
"Confederation of Tomorrow" Conference reached out to Quebec in a
spirit of national reconciliation. The march of events was such that the
Conference timing became the envy of any and all public relations gurus.
Some of this timing was orchestrated. Robarts had just returned from the
disastrous week-long October, 1966, federal-provincial tax-structure

conference: "Well, I suppose the Conference is adjourned" were Prime Minister Pearson's closing words (Simeon, 1972, p.85) as premiers filed out in varying degrees of disappointment, disenchantment and, for the conference, disarray. More importantly, the Union Nationale's Daniel Johnson had, electorally, just nipped the Quiet Revolution in the bud and in the process reasserted Quebec's long-standing linguistic and constitutional demands. Assuming the role of mediator not only between Quebec and the provinces but also between Quebec and Ottawa, Robarts courageously signalled his attention in Ontario's Speech from the Throne (January 1967) to convene a November conference on the future of Confederation.

What was not orchestrated were the events between January and November. Expo 1967 instilled in Quebecers a new sense of pride of accomplishment and determination of purpose as Montreal played centre-stage to the world. Charles de Gaulle fueled Quebec nationalist sentiments with his "vive le Québec libre" from the ramparts of Montreal's city hall. And René Lévesque had just bolted the Liberal party to found the "mouvement souveraineté association" which eventually became the Parti Québécois. All told, not exactly a great way to commemorate one hundred years of nationhood, but equally clearly a fantastic prelude to the Conferation of Tomorrow conference.

Robarts' conference was unique in two other ways. First, it was basically an interprovincial affair. Ottawa was opposed from the outset, but eventually sent four official observers. As a result, the Confederation of Tomorrow conference was the first open (televised) conference of provincial premiers in Canadian history. Second, Robarts' express purpose for the Conference was to "give Danny, as he called Premier Daniel Johnson ... the biggest soap-box in Canada to tell the people of the country what he really wanted for his province" (Pepin, 1985, p.113). The success of and momentum generated by the Conference was such that Ottawa moved virtually immediately to take charge of the entire constitutional dossier. Ironically enough, at the ensuing federal-provincial conference in early 1968 it was the televised clash between Justice Minister Pierre Elliott Trudeau and Daniel Johnson that catapulted Trudeau into the Canadian limelight and, two months later, into the prime ministership.

With this as prologue, the starting part of my analysis is the assertion that, not without several surprises along the way, Meech Lake is the logical culmination of the Confederation of Tomorrow process.[1] Indeed, I shall go further: the combination of Bill 101, Meech Lake and Free Trade essentially gives Quebec sovereignty-association, albeit in a federal context.

But a funny thing happened on the way to all these federal- provincial forums. Quebec went through two dramatic paradigm shifts. From a family-oriented, clerical-dominated society, Quebec has now emerged as the most individualistic, secular and entrepreneurial province. Moreover, Quebecers are now the least political of Canadians. Contrast this with present-day Ontario. With Meech Lake promoting federalism and Free Trade promoting continentalism, many Ontario elites find themselves engaged in a profound and highly political process of "country warp". "Who speaks for Canada?" is their Meech Lake refrain as they fear that Ottawa has devolved internal sovereignty to the provinces. The "Sale of Canada Act" is their Free Trade lament as they fear that important aspects of our culture and identity will be caught up in the U.S. melting pot.[2] The irony here is that these same elites have been hoist on their own petard. By endorsing FIRA and the NEP as part of Trudeau's Second Coming (and in the process alienating the west and the Americans), Ontario set the stage for Free Trade. By being first off the bench in supporting Trudeau in the 1980 Constitutional debates and eventually isolating Quebec in the name of "renewed federalism", Ontario clearly set the stage for a Meech-Lake-type *rapprochement*.

There is a larger irony at play here. "What does Quebec want?" has come to be associated with Daniel Johnson's articulation of Quebec's demands and indeed with the entire Confederation of Tomorrow conference. With the coming of age of Robarts' conference, however, most if not all of the provinces are now asking "What does Ontario Want?"

In spite of the title of this lecture, the truth is that I do not really know the full answer to this question. Accordingly, I will take the easier route and focus on Ontario in relation to Quebec. Thus, the first part of what follows is devoted to a highly subjective and selective appraisal of the evolution of Quebec society. A focus on Ontario, equally subjective and selective, then follows. Sandwiched between these two are some attitudinal data relating to these two provinces.

II. MARKET NATIONALISM: QUEBEC'S DISQUIETING REVOLUTION

A. Le virage vers les marchés

My entry point into recent Quebec trends is the observation that, post-referendum, the Parti Québécois abandoned its socio-democratic agenda and adopted an economic one. Indeed it is probably not exaggerating to claim that, post-referendum, the P.Q. became the most market-oriented government in Canada. Selective evidence is not hard to come by. First, on the wage front, there is the high-profile rollback of civil service salaries — an intriguing policy indeed from the vantage point of the Quiet Revolution where the state was viewed as the key instrument to social and economic process and even more intriguing given that public sector workers were an integral element of the P.Q. support base. Less high profile, but equally significant, was the freezing of the minimum wage. From a pre-referendum situation where Quebec had the highest minimum wage on the continent, representing about 55 per cent of the average wage rate in the province, the minimum wage had fallen by the end of the PQ mandate to about 35 per cent of the average wage and no longer the highest minimum wage in Canada, let alone the continent.

A second, but related, area is Quebec's new emphasis on the efficiency and economic aspects of the entire social policy network. Based on accumulated evidence that the welfare rolls were swelling with able-to-work persons and that the multiplicity-of- programs impact on welfare recipients was creating veritable poverty traps (since the aggregate tax rate in the transition from welfare to work typically exceeded 100 per cent), the P.Q. released its impressive *Livre blanc sur la fiscalité*. In an environment where the rest of Canada had difficulty in progressing beyond the notion that the social policy network is a "sacred trust", the Quebec white paper, by arguing for integrating the welfare, expenditure and tax-transfer components into a rationalized system, called attention to the inevitable relationship between the social and economic sphere. Not only has the Bourassa government begun to act on this agenda, but other jurisdictions are surely going to move in the direction of re-integrating social and economic policy.[3]

A third area where the P.Q. government undertook significant action was in the shoring up of Quebec's corporate base. The initiatives here are well known: first, the QSSP (Quebec's Stock Savings Plan) which, while inaugurated just prior to the referendum, was fine-tuned after 1980 to direct the benefits principally to the PME (petites et moyennes enterprises); and, second, the Caisse de dépôt which, as the pension arm of the government and with assets now in the neighbourhood of $30 billion, began to direct some of its investments with an eye toward the long-term interests of the Quebec economy. Most other provinces have given serious thought to replicating one or both of these institutions.

Fourth, the P.Q. embarked on a thorough (and still on-going) process of financial deregulation which served to   enhance significantly the competitive advantage of two of its indigenous institutions - the mutual insurance companies and the caisses populaires(credit unions). In terms of the former, the P.Q. allowed the mutuals to form downstream holding companies in order to branch out into other financial pillars. One result of this was that Claude Castonguay's Laurentian Group has grown by leaps and bounds (including substantial incursions into English Canada like the takeover of Eaton-Bay Finance and into both the U.K. and American markets) and became Canada's first financial institution to operate in all four pillars - banking, trusts, insurance and securities.

Similar legislation allowed co-operatives to tap the equity markets for capital - in effect to become a hybrid stock-cooperative enterprise. The result has been that the Caisses populaires (or the Desjardins Mouvement) has raised equity capital in Toronto and New York among other places and now has interests or operations in nearly 20 foreign countries. Moreover, with nearly 20 subsidiaries under its wing and heading toward $40 billion in assets, the Desjardins mouvement is the only other financial institution in Canada that currently operates in all four pillars. Not bad for a credit union!

The fifth element is the P.Q.'s embracing of free trade. That this sets Quebec offside vis-à-vis Ontario is too obvious to merit further comment.

Finally, there is marked and dramatic evidence that there has been a fundamental shift in the attitudes of Quebecers. At one point, Quebec had more MBA candidates than the remainder of Canada combined. More generally, the entrepreneurship of Quebecers has now been well documented. Later in the paper I shall present results of survey research related to the differing Quebec-Ontario attitudes.

B. An Indépendentiste Perspective

Why would the PQ do all this? One answer, which is the position of the new PQ leader Jacques Parizeau (and most of the above initiatives were Parizeau initiatives!), is that "market nationalism" is the only viable route to independence. The "analysis" would go as follows. In its quest for independence, the PQ made a huge mistake by legislating Bill 101 prior to the holding of the referendum. Once the Québécois acquired cultural and linguistic sovereignty (but without the knowledge that the *Constitution Act 1982* and the Supreme Court would eventually water down Bill 101's provisions!), the referendum became primarily an economic issue. And the underlying economics simply were not there. Hence, to Parizeau, Lévesque, and Co., the message was clear: get the economics on side in anticipation of a future referendum. To do this it would be essential to:

- build a much stronger corporate base;
- begin to put Quebec's fiscal house in order;
- develop a self-sustaining financial-institution network;
- decrease dependency on and economic ties to Ottawa and the rest of Canada (e.g. opt for free trade).
- encourage self-reliance and an outward-looking mentality.

Not surprisingly, perhaps, this *was* the P.Q. agenda, post- referendum.

C. An Economic Nationalist Perspective

While this *indépendantiste* interpretation is *consistent* with the evolution of recent Quebec policy, I do not think that it is the correct interpretation. Rather, my hypothesis is that the recent emphasis on markets and entrepreneurship is a natural extension of the economic nationalism that touched off the Quiet Revolution.

This process of evolutionary economic determinism would go as follows. From the Quiet Revolution, I would select three elements, all interrelated. The first is the process of secularization, the high profile aspect of which was to transfer all aspects of social and education policy from the church to the state (and epitomized by the creation of a provincial Ministry of Education). The second, alluded to earlier, was the conception that further social and economic progress for Quebecers would require the active participation of the state - both as socio-economic legislator and as entrepreneur. Enter the period of active "state capitalism". From this, the third almost followed directly - the nationalization of Quebec Hydro, wrapped up in Lévesque's "maîtres chez nous" rhetoric. Nationalizing Hydro accomplished a multitude of goals, not the least of which was the provision of a significant opportunity for French-speaking Quebecers to occupy the upper management echelons of a major corporation. Quebec Hydro remains to this day absolutely critical to the development prospects for Quebec. Witness the $40 billion of electricity sales that Quebec has already negotiated, pre-Free Trade, with New England. Moreover, Lavalin and SNC, both world-class engineering firms, are examples of leading-edge enterprises spun off from Hydro's activities.

(As an instructive aside, one can contrast this with the operations of Ontario Hydro. Were Ontario to split off the production/engineering/ research components from the distribution network, the former would probably qualify as one of the world's largest engineering firms. Freed of its narrow hydro focus, it would have an enormous contribution in terms of ensuring that Ontario became leading edge across a wide range of technology fronts. Instead, however, hydro remains basically inward looking. Not only does this imply that the corporation becomes "engineering driven" rather than "distribution driven" (as reflected until very recently by the implicit if not explicit policy of denying "micro hydros" access to the system), but also that the internal drive is toward self-sufficiency across the board. The best recent example of this relates to the construction of Darlington - the amount of cement in Darlington is close to twenty times that of the C.N. Tower, yet hydro poured it all by itself! In contrast, one can rest assured that when Quebec Hydro embarks on its next construction phase, an integral part of the operation will be to contract out activity with an eye to spinning off world-class firms. In microcosm, this is the general thrust of the ensuing analysis.)

The salient features of the Quiet Revolution - such as the modernization and enhancement in the socio-economic sphere and the nation-building activities of the state as reflected in the spate of new crown corporations including the Caisse de dépôt and the Société générale de financement on the financial side - have been well documented elsewhere. I shall limit my focus here to the observation that the best and the brightest of the young Québécois flocked to the civil service. One result was that Quebec came to possess the most professional provincial civil service, which arguably remains true to this day. Moreover, because of Quebec's opting out policies, its civil service acquired expertise over a range of areas much broader than those of the other provinces. This became very evident in the discussions over Canada's public pension system where Quebec's input not only influenced the structure of the CPP but then the province opted for its own QPP, replete with the Caisse de dépôt. Moreover, under pressure from the B and B Commission, perhaps from Robarts' Conference as well, and certainly reflecting the interests of the Trudeau Liberals, the federal government conveniently opened its doors to Québécois in the form of a bilingual federal civil service. (The *Constitution Act, 1982* aside, Ottawa is frequently "conveniently" available when Quebec calls, a large part of which is the fact that, except for short periods like Diefenbaker's first mandate and the Clark interregnum, Quebecers manage to ensure that a majority, normally an overwhelming majority, of their MP's are on the government side!)

Under this economic nationalist interpretation, Bill 101 was not so much a cultural and linguistic measure as it was an economic one - French as the language of work. With the civil service no longer able to absorb the new wave of graduating Québécois, Bill 101 ensured that they now had easier access to the upper echelons and to the board rooms of Canadian and multinational enterprises operating in Quebec. Business schools rather than law and public administration began to attract young Québécois.

Then came the Referendum. Support for separatism was probably already on the wane. But the victory of the "NO" forces had a massive cathartic impact on Quebecers. Virtually immediately, independence became a non-issue. So did further politicization of major policy issues. Culturally and linguistically confident, in firm control over the functions of state, and now in senior management positions in large enterprises, Quebecers took the logical next step in the process of gaining greater mastery over their economic destiny, namely seeking equity control of small and medium-sized enterprises and ensuring that selected key institutions facilitated this new venture. Enter the series of initiatives introduced by the Parti Quebecois. State capitalism was giving way to peoples' capitalism.

In the context of this economic nationalism approach to recent Quebec history, it is highly significant that one of the first initiatives of Bourassa's Second Coming was to commission three blueprints for the economic future of Quebec. These were not ordinary task forces: they were headed by cabinet ministers or elected members with expertise in economic portfolios. The resulting trilogy of reports - Pierre Fortier (Minister of Financial Institutions and Privatization) on privatization; Paul Gobeil (Treasury Board Minister) on the role of government and more generally on the delivery of socio-economic programs; and Reed Scowen (at the time, economic advisor to Bourassa) on deregulation - represents in my view, the most market-oriented approach to socio-economic policy ever promulgated by any government in the Western world.[4] No other provincial government could have possibly produced such comprehensive blueprints (and certainly not Ontario!). Quebec was and is clearly marching to a new drummer. More to the point, the fact that the Bourassa is essentially continuing with the economic agenda initiated, post-referendum, by the P.Q. lends credence to the economic nationalism thrust. Indeed, earlier this year in the context of introducing further financial deregulation, Financial Institutions Minister Pierre Fortier said he was pursuing a policy of "economic nationalism" similar to that initiated by the Parti Québécois (Aubin, 1988). Phrased differently, even if one can make a case that these new initiatives are consistent with laying the groundwork for some future referendum on independence, the continuity of policy, post- 1980, suggests that the economic nationalism perspective is the preferred interpretation.

D. Analytical Reflections

At this juncture, it is instructive to focus somewhat more analytically on this remarkable turn of events. First of all, the implications for Ontario are remarkably different as between the Quiet Revolution and what I refer to as the new "disquieting revolution". In terms of the former, Quebec was engaged essentially in a process of modernization, a "rattrapage" as it were. Ontarians were free to view these events with their chosen degree of interest or disinterest. Not so with the new revolution. Since Quebec is effectively engaging international markets and the world economy, Ontarians can no longer ignore these developments. For many of these issues, Ontario has two polar choices - to follow Quebec's lead or to call upon Ottawa to stifle these Quebec initiatives. However, in areas like financial deregulation Ontario really has no alternative but to follow Quebec's lead.

Second, the role of the state in Quebec has not so much been diminished as transformed. *L'État entrepreneur* has given way to *l'État catalyseur*. Thus, the essence of Quebec's new political economy is that the principal avenue by which Quebec will secure its long term economic viability is a dynamic outward-looking private sector owned and controlled by Québécois (and Quebecers) but aided and abetted by the state.

Third, this new emphasis on the private sector, on entrepreneurial activity and on markets falls easily within Quebec's traditional "nationalist" paradigm. As Ramsay Cook (1986) notes in another context:

Nationalism...is about ethnic survival and growth. It is also about self-interest and power...Consequently, nationalism struggles are not only about home rule but also, perhaps even primarily, *about who should rule at home.* (pp. 12-13 emphasis added).

Quebec's new political economy is indeed about "who should rule at home". Hence my designation of this paradigm shift as "market nationalism". In the broader Canadian context, and particularly in relation to the Free Trade debate, the implications of "market nationalism" are refreshing indeed. The popular wisdom, especially in Ontario, is that to be in favour of things Canadian is synonymous with being against the Free Trade Agreement. Quebec is actively demonstrating that an emphasis on looking outward and an emphasis on markets can embody nationalist values every bit as much as an emphasis on turning inward and on intervention. Amen!

Fourth, further evidence that the Quiet Revolution's emphasis on the state and that market nationalism's emphasis on the private sector are part of the same evolutionary continuum is that many of Quebec's leading businessmen and entrepreneurs today were in the *public sector* during the Quiet Revolution (or, more generally, prior to the market nationalism thrust). Focussing on only a few names that would be familiar to Ontarians - Laurentian's Claude Castonguay, National Bank's Michel Belanger, Provigo's Pierre Lortie and others such as Andre Saumier — were all civil servants during the Quiet Revolution or more generally prior to the referendum. Moreover, given that these names are probably as familiar to Ontarians as their own business leaders indicates that they are in effect household names in Quebec. In part, this explains the incredible pace of change in Quebec. In many ways the homogeneity of interest in the province, whether cast along language or culture or economic lines, implies that Quebec society has "family" characteristics in the sense that a convergence of opinion leaders on an issue spreads quickly through the society, especially when the leaders are in effect not only saying "do as I say", but also "do as I do".

This leads directly to (or rather explains) yet another significant feature of the new Quebec - the commonality of interest between business and government, in sharp contrast to the "two solitudes" in Ontario. A few years ago, in the context of an argument that Canada had to become more Japanese and less American in terms of the role of government in the economy, my response was that I did not believe that we were condemned to be relegated to the economic little leagues because our post-aboriginal settlers came from Europe rather than Japan. Clearly I was wrong. Jacques Cartier was a Samurai!

Sixth, one result of this is that there has been little shift in the thrust of policy from the post-referendum Lévesque regime to Bourassa's Liberals. Contrast this to the national arena where most of the agenda of Trudeau's Second Coming has been overturned (although not yet legislated) by the Mulroney Tories. I suppose that it would be too much to expect that the CBC would embark on *The Champions: Part IV* where this theme would be highlighted.

One might argue that the dramatic increase in entrepreneurial activity in Quebec is more revolutionary than evolutionary. After all, Durham referred to the "inert and careless competitors of the French race" and historians have entrenched this cultural interpretation by referring to French Canadians as the "eternal losers" in the economic sphere. However, following Paquet (1987) one can define the "entrepreneurial environment" in terms of two components — "ethos" (the ensemble of values and norms by which individual agents approach the marketplace and the institutional environment) and "opportunities". Paquet rejects, indirectly, this cultural interpretation by rejecting, directly, the prevailing myth that French Canadians lacked entrepreneurship.[5] Rather, the environment, both in terms of ethos and opportunities, was historically hostile toward entrepreneurship. One need not recall the numerous ways in which both the opportunities and the ethos constrained the exercise of entrepreneurship by French Canadians in the economic sphere. But it flowered in other spheres, one impressive result of which is the flourishing nature, against all odds, of a linguistically, culturally, and soon perhaps, constitutionally, distinct society in a sea of anglos, as the saying goes.

Entrepreneurship in the economic sphere was not absent, but the hostile environment (opportunity set) was such that it frequently took the form of emigration — opting for an environment more favourable to the pursuit of market-related goals. If one describes entrepreneurship as a seizing upon opportunities (or, more relevantly, reacting to the lack of opportunity) and/or bearing risk or uncertainty, emigration surely qualifies as market- related entrepreneurship.

Given this interpretation, underlying the current wave of Québécois entrepreneurship is a dramatic change, not in any deep- rooted cultural or societal values, but in the *entrepreneurial environment,* initially in terms of the opportunity set (as described earlier) and more recently in terms of the entrepreneurial ethos. It is in this sense that the overall process can be viewed as evolutionary.

The final point arising from viewing market nationalism as the natural successor to the Quiet Revolution in terms of progressively enabling Québécois to acquire greater control of their own destiny relates to P.Q. leader Jacques Parizeau's assertion that free trade will lead eventually to separation. In my view, this is more in the way of myth than reality. Part of the reality is that Quebec needs free trade in order to maintain its population base. The gradual post-war transfer of economic power from Montreal to Toronto implies that it would be extremely difficult for Montreal to regain its former role as a national production and distribution centre. Moreover, it has a substantial transportation disadvantage relative to Ontario in attempting to capture western markets. Thus, the only meaningful alternative is to look toward the markets that are nearer and that are larger. Hence, the obvious emphasis is on free trade. Without free trade, Quebec will be increasingly hard pressed to hold the outward-looking, entrepreneurial-oriented generation graduating from its universities. This was an essential part of the message in a recent book by former P.Q. Minister Bernard Landry. In other words, now that market nationalism has taken hold, the failure of the free trade agenda is likely to resurrect independence sentiments, not the reverse.

This has been a glowing overview of recent trends in Quebec. No doubt, too glowing. Quebec industry still has a long way to go before it can match the diversity, stability and prosperity of the golden horseshoe. Moreover, the above story is largely a *Montreal* story, not a Quebec story. Some of Quebec's regions such as the Gaspésie still remain among the poorest in Canada. Intriguingly, what allows Quebec to focus its attention on Montreal, on leading-edge industries and more generally on Québécois entrepreneurship is that to a large degree the federal government is looking after these lagging regions. Once again Ottawa is conveniently on side!

What is more intriguing, however, is that most Canadians would probably view these developments as finally bringing Quebec fully on side with the values and mentality of Ontario. Reality is quite different. While Quebec's current aspirations may have resonated well with Robarts' Ontario, they are well off-side the goals and aspirations of most Ontarians today and certainly off-side those of the Ontario government. To this I now turn.

III. QUEBEC vs ONTARIO: ATTITUDINAL DIFFERENCES

As a bridge between the above analysis of Quebec and the later focus on Ontario, it is instructive to present some evidence relating to the earlier thrust that individual self-confidence and entrepreneurship are replacing both the Church and the state as the driving force underlying Quebec society. In this context, I am very grateful to Hay Management Consultants for granting permission to reproduce some comparative attitudinal survey data collected as part of their Opinion Leader Research Program (OLRP).

The OLRP analysis refers to the new "ideology" surfacing in Quebec as the "Quebec Renaissance". In more detail (and fully consistent with the above analysis):

The new philosophy which so impressed us was primarily economic and political but it had some important social dimensions. It was not cultural. Central to the Renaissance were three important redefinitions of roles in Quebec. First, the role of government should be smaller while the influence of the private sector should increase. Second, the most important segment of a more powerful private sector will be medium and small businesses. Third, individuals should take greater responsibility for their lives and well-being rather than relying on either the state or large companies" (p.49)

Charts 1 through 4 present evidence in support of these propositions. From Chart 1, roughly 90% of Quebec opinion leaders (businessmen, academics, civil servants, etc.) anticipate that Canadians will become more self-reliant and entrepreneurial rather than looking to government and large companies for support. The corresponding percentage for Ontario opinion leaders is approximately 50 per cent. In terms of political forecasts (Chart 2) the evidence is nearly as striking: Quebec opinion leaders anticipate, relative to their counterparts in Ontario, that government will put more emphasis on economic policy than on social policy and that the latter will increasingly be redesigned to ensure compatibility with economic needs. The economic forecasts (Chart 3) reveal that Quebec opinion leaders are more optimistic about Canada's trade, technology and competitiveness than are Ontario leaders, although in this case the opinion leaders from the rest of Canada are nearly as optimistic as those from Quebec.

These three charts reflect forecasts or likely trends. Chart 4, however, focusses on *preferences*. Again the evidence is clear. Relative to Ontario, Quebec opinion leaders favour less government intervention (73% to 53%.) and favour de-emphasizing social programs in terms of policies that encourage growth (68% to 43%).

Finally, Table 1 focusses in more detail on a broad range of economic, political and social issues. The data here do not isolate Ontario. However, the previous evidence suggests strongly that the Quebec-Ontario differences would be greater than the reported data for Quebec and "others". Table 1 is instructive for another reason. It refers to research undertaken in 1985 and published by Hay Management Consultants in 1986. The previous four charts related to research undertaken in 1986 and published in 1987. Thus, the underlying trends and preferences reflected in Table 1 were widely held *prior* to Bourassa's Second Coming in 1985, which of course is the thrust of the analysis of the previous section.

CHART 1

Forecast: Canadians will become more self-reliant and entrepreneurial rather than looking to governments and large companies for security.

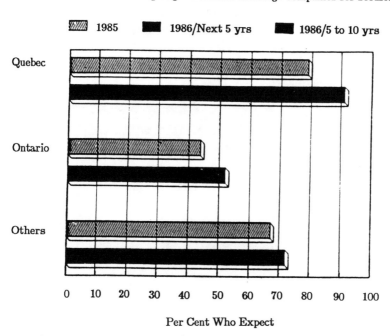

Per Cent Who Expect

Source: Hay Management Consultants, Opinion Leader Research Program, 1987

CHART 2
Political Forecasts

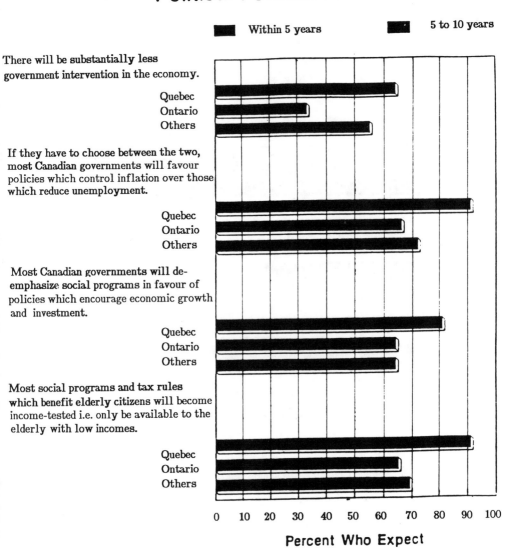

Source: Hay Management Consultants, Op.Cit.

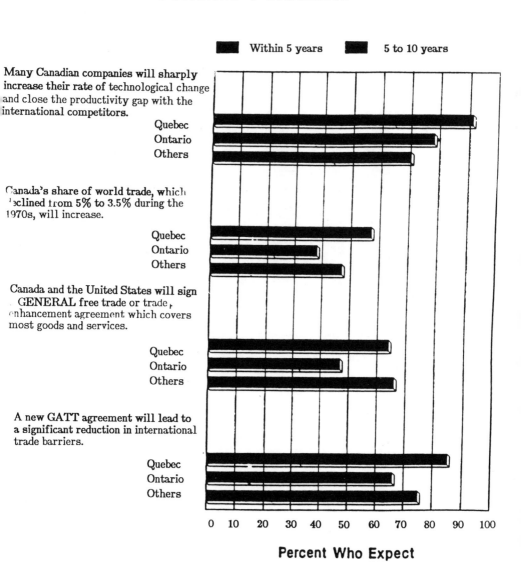

CHART 3

Economic Forecasts

◼ Within 5 years   ◼ 5 to 10 years

Many Canadian companies will sharply
increase their rate of technological change
and close the productivity gap with the
international competitors.

Quebec
Ontario
Others

Canada's share of world trade, which
declined from 5% to 3.5% during the
1970s, will increase.

Quebec
Ontario
Others

Canada and the United States will sign
GENERAL free trade or trade
enhancement agreement which covers
most goods and services.

Quebec
Ontario
Others

A new GATT agreement will lead to
a significant reduction in international
trade barriers.

Quebec
Ontario
Others

0   10   20   30   40   50   60   70   80   90   100

Percent Who Expect

Source: Hay Management Consultants, Op.Cit.

CHART   4

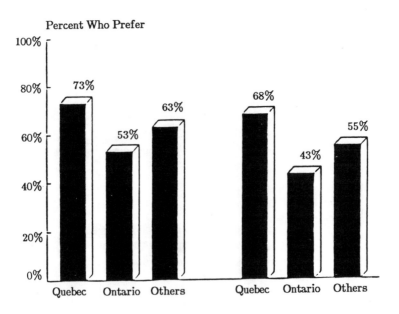

Percent Who Prefer

Should there be substantially
less government intervention in
the economy?

Should Canadian governments de-emphasize
social programs in favour of policies which
encourage economic growth and investment?

Source: Hay Management Consultants, Op.Cit.

TABLE 1

Economic, Political and Social Forecasts

EXPECTATION	QUEBEC	OTHERS
Economic		
Global economic growth flat or negative for next decade	18%	45%
Canada's share of world trade increasing	57%	37%
General free trade pact with United States	69%	49%
Inflation rising to 10% or more	7%	27%
Serious depletion of forest and/or agricultural resources	36%	57%
New Cooperation between labour and management	48%	36%
Political		
Substantial reduction in government intervention	52%	40%
Inflation with higher priority than unemployment on policy agenda	78%	64%
New tax incentives for investment in the private sector	90%	72%
New policies to increase investment in new technologies	82%	64%
Social		
Increasing self-reliance and entrepreneurism less dependence on government	79%	59%
High stress to increase suicide, crime and drug use.	28%	57%
Worker morale destroyed by technological change & restructuring	43%	64%
Preference		
Should there be a substantial reduction in government intervention (Percent Yes)	79%	59%

Source: Hay Management Consultants, Opinion Leader Research Program, 1986.

Prior to taking leave of these opinion-leader trends, it is useful to provide some further backdrop relating to the rise of the "individual" in Quebec. As the Hay study notes:

- By 1984 Quebec had the lowest fertility rate in Canada (prior to World War II it had the highest);
- Quebec has the highest ratio of working age population to non-working age population, (i.e. lowest dependency ratio), whereas 50 years ago it had the highest ratio;
- Over 1 in 3 Quebecers between the ages of 18 and 24 is enroled in a post-secondary institution - a rate 5% higher than Ontario. This no doubt reflects the role of CEGEPs.

Moreover, given that Quebec is probably more advanced in terms of the whole range of issues relating to sexual equality rights, it may not be surprising that these factors combine to provide an environment which favours reduced government expenditures and an enhanced role for individual self-reliance.

Finally, it might be argued that the attitudes of opinion leaders are way off-side relative to attitudes of "average citizens". However, in the annual CROP-CPQ Quebec poll in the same time frame (Cloutier, 1986), citizens in Quebec expressed views to the effect that unions, governments, the media and the Church already had enough or too much power in society, but that private companies do not have enough. Here are a few other results of the poll:

- business leaders inspire as much confidence as religious leaders and more than ever before;
- 76 per cent of the population want business people to participate actively in the big discussions of the day.
- 48 per cent think that the government should give business management more power in coming amendments to the labour laws.

While comparative data are not available for Ontario, I would have trouble imagining Ontarians holding business in this high regard. In Quebec, however, the evidence is mounting that business is the new religion.

IV. WHAT DOES ONTARIO WANT?

A. The Way We Were

As backdrop to the analysis of modern-day Ontario and Ontarians, it is essential to develop some perspective of Ontario's role and self-image, historically, in the federation. Accordingly, in what follows I shall attempt to outline some "stylized facts" or "defining characteristics" that pertain to our province.

First, Ontario is so prosperous and diversified economically, so powerful politically and so dominant culturally that, historically, national policy debits frequently had little choice but to be cast in a pro-Ontario light. This is not so much a statement about Ontarians as it is about the economic geography of Ontario within Canada. While Ontario's dominance has been diminishing in certain areas over time (e.g., televised federal-provincial conferences with equal billing to the ten premiers certainly encroaches on Ontario's traditional ability to pursue, quietly or otherwise, its influence in the corridors of power), it is nonetheless the case that this position of pre-eminence has conditioned the Ontario psyche. From this follows several further sylized facts.

Second, since Ontario could generally count on the federal government furthering the province's interests, Ontario has been (and still is) in favour of a strong central government. Politically, Ottawa must retain emergency powers, such as the declaratory power. On the industrial side a strong central government was also desirable because Rideau Street came to be viewed as an extension of Bay Street. One has only to cite major initiatives like the National Policy, the Auto Pact, the National Energy Program, and nuclear policy, to recognize that Ontario industry has frequently been more interested in an effective pipeline to Ottawa than to Queen's Park.

The third aspect is a generalization of the second. Probably moreso than other Canadians, Ontarians tended to direct their political activities and loyalties toward the federal rather than the provincial government. This is obviously the case with reference to Quebec and the West. It is less obvious when the comparison is with the Atlantic region. However, whereas Ontarians looked to Ottawa to legislate in the national interest, which was generally in Ontario's interest, the Atlantic provinces' interest in a strong central government has traditionally been one of *countering*, via equalization or other regional programs, the pro-Ontario or pro-centre perception or reality of federal government initiatives.

Fourth, and relatedly, the management of the big levers of economic stabilization has always kept a close eye on the Ontario economy. This is clearly evident in current Bank of Canada policy. Maintaining short-term real interest rates two full percentage points above U.S. rates is, I believe, a highly inappropriate policy given that our economy is more capital intensive than the U.S. economy. However, the inflationary concerns that are driving this policy are obviously designed to prevent the overheating of the golden triangle, where unemployment is enviably under 5%. Needless to say, there are many other regions or provinces in the country where this unemployment-inflation trade-off is distinctly less enviable. Newfoundlanders would clearly favour an interest- rate policy that placed more concern on the reality that their unemployment rate tends to be closer to 20 per cent. Since there can be but one thrust to monetary policy, this essentially boils down to an Ontario thrust. Note that this ties in closely with the previous point in that the peripheral regions of the country typically argue for "compensation" from Ottawa as a result of the directing of federal stabilization policy to the industrial heartland. Having said this, now that the implications of the Bank's interest rate policy are threatening to drive the dollar toward the mid-80-cent mark, the key Ontario-based industrial interests are swinging into action - the CMA, the CFIB, the BCNI and the CLC — and their voices will be heard!

Fifth, while Ontarians and their government obviously desire sufficient influence to protect their own interests, if given the choice they would much rather exercise this influence by blocking any offending federal or sister-province legislation than by acquiring further provincial powers. In this sense, the Ontario of today is not a "province rights" advocate, especially if this implies a substantial diminution of key federal powers. Thus Ontario did not take up Ottawa's invitiation to "opt out" of the same range of policies as did Quebec. Likewise, on several occasions during the post-war period Ontario threatened to mount its own personal income tax system. In my view these threats were intended principally as powerful bargaining chips to attempt to force Ottawa to alter its policy thrust. On the two most recent occasions this tactic worked very well. Circa 1970, Ontario gained the right to have a say in federal tax reform, including the ability to initiate its own tax credits. And in the early 1980's the threat worked equally well in that Ottawa largely backed off those aspects of the MacEachen 1981 budget that the Ontario government found unpalatable. To have opted for its own personal income tax would have likely precipitated full-blown tax decentralization as other provinces followed Ontario's lead. Not only would the result have been a diminished ability on Ottawa's part to conduct effective stabilization and distribution policy, but it would have served to erode substantially internal free trade across the provinces.

This leads directly to the sixth point — Ontario's historical position with respect to free trade. With the National Policy firmly in place, Ontario's interests were more in the direction of freeing internal trade than in freeing international trade. That this was in sharp contrast to Western Canadian aspirations is not only well known and well articulated, but it is also indelibly etched somewhere in the subconscious of those of us who were born and raised on the prairies. Analytically, internal free trade (or a Canadian economic union as it is usually referred to) would represent the *natural extension* and, at long last, *the full implementation of Macdonald's National Policy*. Effective external barriers and the absence of internal barriers would effectively enshrine Ontario hegemony within Canada. As will be detailed later, it is hardly surprising that when Ontario's economic position became threatened, this internal-common-market thrust became Ontario's front line of attack.

The seventh defining characteristic is that Ontario, despite its privileged economic position or perhaps because of it, was never (until recently) an innovator in social policy. In terms of medicare, for example, Pearson's Ottawa simply made Ontario an offer that, eventually, it could not refuse. On the other hand, Ontario was more receptive to the federal initiative with respect to welfare (the Canada Assistance Plan). But these were not Ontario initiatives. In general, there is little of the social policy path-breaking in Ontario that characterized Saskatchewan and later Quebec. Where Ontario did lead, it either had little choice (e.g. pension regulation, resulting from the court decision that it was a provincial matter and Ontario was the core province) or it acted because it faced the problem before other provinces (e.g. various urban issues).

It is intriguing to question why this is so. One answer is that Ontarians are basically conservative. This cannot be the entire answer, although it is probably important. Another is that overall economic performance of the province, and more importantly, the diversity of the economic base which made the province relatively cycle proof, obviated much of the need that surfaced in sister provinces. I would like to suggest a third and far more strategic reason: It is one thing for Saskatchewan or Quebec to innovate on the social policy front. It is quite another if Ontario assumes social policy leadership. In the former case, New Brunswick, for example, looks on with interest, assessing whether or not it desires, or is fiscally able, to match Saskatchewan's initiative. In the latter case, the name of the game alters substantially. Ottawa is pulled into the social policy arena because the issue is now as much a "regional disparities" issue as it is an issue of individual provincial spending preferences. Ontario recognized full well that assuming the lead in this area would substantially complicate the nature of intergovernmental transfers and, more importantly, Ontario and its taxpayers would end up paying for the lion's share of extending any new social policy initiatives beyond the province. This is of much more than passing interest since there is little question that the Ontario of today has become far and away the social policy leader. More on this later.

This list of "defining characteristics" is not intended to be exhaustive. For example, one could easily add a significant cultural dimension (indeed revolution) by observing that the United Empire Loyalist tradition in the province has largely been overwhelmed by post-war immigration. Toronto may still be largely white, but the anglo-saxon and protestant aspects of the WASP tradition have given way to a multicultural and even Catholic orientation. And so on. However, in terms of the ensuing analysis, the above enumeration of stylized facts will probably suffice.

B. Managing the Cartel

In his book, *The Politics of Federalism: Ontario's Relationship With the Federal Government, 1867-1942* (1981) York historian Chris Armstrong concludes:

> The people of Ontario...have always considered themselves to be 'real' Canadians and assumed that their wishes are the wishes of the nation collectively. Any apparent conflict between national and provincial objectives may be dissolved by the conviction that the interests of Ontario are the interests of Canada. (p.238)

As the title of the book indicates, Armstrong's comments apply to pre-World War II Ontario. A major thrust of what follows is that they also provide a key to understanding Ontario's behaviour over the last decade. Intriguingly, however, the Ontario of Drew and Robarts effectively managed Ontario's priviledged position within the federation to ensure that what was good for Canada was also good for Ontario.

Generalizing somewhat, Ontario over the post-war period was quite sensitive of its economic pre-eminence in the federation and managed cleverly, even graciously, to carve out compromises within the federation where failure to do so would have impinged on its own interests. The "Confederation of Tomorrow" conference is one obvious example. I know that others have come to view this as a magnanimous gesture on Robarts' part. And in part it no doubt was. However, the economist in me suggests that altruism drives few people and even fewer institutions! The reality was that Ontario's cosy niche would clearly be threatened unless some attempt were made to accommodate the "new" Quebec. Obviously, not all accommodations would be acceptable to Ontario. But *some* accommodation was essential. In terms of the above "defining characteristics", the trade-off here for Ontario was evident — maintaining a strong central government vs. accepting some devolution of power to maintain internal harmony, particularly when failure to do the latter might, as noted above, impinge on Ontario's ability to pursue its own interests. Intriguingly, "opting out" acquires a new rationale in this context. Allowing Quebec to opt out of programs such as the CPP/QPP, the personal income tax system and a variety of socio-economic programs represented a creative compromise — Quebec obtained greater room to manoeuvre while the rest of the country was able to design a far more centralized system. As long as Ontario did not follow Quebec's lead, the remaining provinces would probably not opt out either. Elsewhere, I have argued that "opting out" should be viewed as a solution rather than a problem in terms of our federation. In the present context, I would take the argument further: opting out represented a clever compromise which maintained (and heightened) centralist tendencies for nine provinces and at the same time allowed Quebec more flexibility in areas that were perceived to be important to it but at the same time were not "threatening" to Ontario. Thus, this was an essential part of Ontario's (Canada's) ability to manage the federation in ways that allowed its own interests to remain front and centre.

Another variation on this theme relates to Ontario's willingness to endorse the transfer aspects of fiscal federalism. Ontario was never a great fan of an overblown system of intergovernmental transfers, since it recognized that Ontario taxpayers would foot a large portion of the bill. Nonetheless, Ontario did go along with equalization and with regional development initiatives, both of which were driven by Ontario's superior economic status. These programs eventually became so much a part of the glue that bind us together as Canadians that they became enshrined in the *Constitution Act 1982* (s.36). Focussing only on equalization, again Ontario's willingness to go along with these initiatives can be cast in terms of a "nation-building" perspective. But self-interest was never very far from the surface. First, as the *quid quo pro* for the inauguration of the equalization program in 1957, the Ontario government would henceforth receive the full amount of taxes collected within the provinces from the three equalized revenue sources (personal income tax, corporate income taxes and succession duties) rather than, previously, some national-average value of such revenues. Second, this was the heyday of Keynesian philosophy and Ontario's "generosity" on the equalization front was accompanied by the knowledge that the second-round spending impacts of equalization payments would end up benefiting one or another of Ontario's industries.

These were heady days indeed for Ontario. The province was in the economic and political driver's seat and the perceived magnaminity of its overtures (via Ottawa) to Quebec and the rest of Canada took on a bit of the surreal for Ontarians. Ontario was indeed adopting a "pan-Canadian" vision (albeit largely self- interest driven). More importantly, in the eyes of many Ontarians the province was becoming the moral conscience of the nation, an "alternative" federal government as it were. What was far less clear to the average Ontarian was that this probably had very little to do with the (Armstrong) proposition that "the interests of Ontario are the interests of Canada". Rather, it had everything to do with Ontario's ability to wheel, deal and compromise and in general to manage its privileged position to ensure that Canada's interests coincided with Ontario's interests.

By way of summary to this point, Ontario up until the early 1970's basked in the economic and political glow of its position within the federation. There was no challenge domestically to its economic dominance and the world economy was evolving in an expansive and tranquil fashion. Ontario industry had an influential and direct pipeline to

Ottawa. Maintaining this comfortable pew required a few concessions on Ontario's part: some attention had to be directed to the aspirations of Canada's regions and some accommodation had to be made to ensure that Quebec would not destabilize the Ontario position. Ontario took advantage of those increases in provincial powers that could be used to further its own interests but, by and large, Ottawa was serving the province well and it was important for Ontario that the key economic and political levers remained as a federal trust. Moreover, I believe Ontario recognized that it was important not to go too far in terms of social policy reform because this would set off a chain reaction across the provinces with Ontario being the ultimate "payee".

All in all, it is probably fair to say that Ontario entered the decade of the seventies with its economy and underlying philosophy within Canada fully intact. Toryism ruled within and toryism was an apt description of the manner in which Ontario and Ontarians approached their fellow Canadians. *How then, fifteen years later, does Ontario now find itself so off-side with Canada and Canadians?*

Alternatively, as the heading of this section indicates, one can cast the dominant Ontario position within Canada in terms of what economists refer to as a "common agency" problem or, more familiarly, as a cartel problem. While the analogy is admittedly strained, some insight can nonetheless be gained comparing Ontario's position to that of Saudia Arabia within the OPEC cartel. Under favourable external economic conditions, the Saudis can keep the cartel together by (a) setting the overall parameters, (b) allowing the other cartel members to enjoy reasonable flexibility within the overall parameters and (c) collecting the residual rents as the pre-eminent power. The arrangements break down if external conditions erode (i.e. if the world is awash in non-OPEC oil) or if the other partners begin to run afoul of the rules of the game (e.g. "cheat" on their quotas). In the latter case, the Saudis hold the ultimate weapon: their production cost advantage allows them to rev up their production, drive down prices and in the process deny rents to most other cartel members.

Ontario is in a "similar" position. Under the conditions of the 1950's and 1960's, Ontario did play a crucial role in setting the overall parameters of Canadian policy. Ontario kept the other provinces on side by a series of compromises and side-payments (including the acceptance of the Borden line for Western energy, for example) and by affording them considerable room to manoever (including allowing some "province building"). And there were ample residual economic rents.

However, beginning in the early 1970's and culminating in the early 1980's, this arrangement came largely unstuck. First, the external economic environment turned hostile. For the first time in the post-war period Ontario's invincibility on the economic front was challenged.

Moreover, the partners to the traditional coalition found new economic and political strength in rising resource prices and began to press their own agenda, in effect challenging Ontario's role as the dominant player. Backed into a corner as it were, Ontario responded by pressing for a legislative agenda that essentially attempted, in Armstrong's (1981, p. 238) words, to "impose its version of Canada upon the rest of the nation". While I have doubtless carried this cartel analogy too far, the remainder of the paper will focus on why and how Ontario got backed into this corner and the consequences of its "Ontario first" agenda.

C. Drifting into Country Warp

First, the centre-periphery conception of Canada that fostered a common Ontario-Quebec viewpoint across many fronts began to erode. On the political side, Quebecers increasingly began to follow a nationalist political agenda. Not much that Ontario could do here, except for a missed opportunity for a meaningful initiative in the mid-1970s when all three Ontario parties were on side in terms of accomodating aspects of the French language in Ontario. On the economic/industrial side the link was also eroding. As Toronto began eclipsing Montreal as the nation's production and distribution hub (and Montreal was retreating from a national centre to a regional one), Quebec industry began more and more to look toward Quebec City for industrial leadership. And Ottawa's role vis-à-vis Quebec became progressively one of backstopping industrial decline via commercial policy (tariffs, quotas) and regional incentives. Again, not much that Ontario could do about this. Nonetheless, the interests of the centre began to diverge sharply.

Second, and far more important, was the fact that Ontario, like all industrial economies in the seventies, was whiplashed by the march of events in the global economy. The inflationary spiral, which was triggered by the U.S. financing of Vietnam and which eventually resulted in the break up of the Bretton Woods fixed exchange rate system, when combined with the 1973-74 oil shock plunged the industrialized world into recession. But this was only a precursor for the Great Stagflation of the early 1980's, again triggered by a massive energy price spike. Occurring simultaneously, and not unrelated, was the revolution in computational and telecommunications technology. The result was the world's most significant process of Schumpeterian "creative destruction" as nations everywhere restructured, reorganized, and recapitalized their industry to accommodate the new world economic order. Canada and Ontario lagged considerably in this process of renewal largely because the 1980-82 recession was so much more severe in Canada than elsewhere in the industrialized world. (In turn, this was largely due to the fact that, thanks to inappropriate macro policy, we had not yet digested the impact of the first energy crisis when the second one hit. But this is a separate story).

In global terms the result of all this was the emergence of the industrial superiority of the Pacific Rim, and eventually (although not causally unless one introduces the role of the U.S. budget deficit) the emergence of the massive trade imbalances of the Americans and the corresponding rise of U.S. protectionism. For present purposes, the essential point is that leading up to the early 1980's Ontario had every reason to feel that its industrial and economic base was being threatened.

The third point is that the domestic impact of the energy shock was to shift the economic centre of gravity in Canada to the West. Inevitably, Canada became embroiled in an intense internal income distribution or redistribution struggle over the ownership of the mushrooming energy rents. Ontario was impacted on all fronts. Among its concerns or desires were the following:

- preferential domestic energy prices to feed an already faltering manufacturing sector;
- concern that energy exports would drive up the exchange rate to an extent that its manufacturing sector became even less competitive;
- concern that Alberta was not bearing its appropriate share of the funding of federal-provincial transfers and, particularly, of equalization;
- concern that Ontario industry would not have adequate access to the Alberta mega-projects and more generally to energy-related procurement.
- concern that Alberta energy revenues would be deployed to attract industry from Ontario.

The last two concerns, which relate to the internal economic union issue, were exacerbated by the federal mega-projects task force. Basing its analysis on the continuation of rapidly escalating energy prices, the implicit thrust of the task force was that the future for Ontario manufacturing lay *not* with continuing to penetrate the U.S. market but rather with supplying the projected $210 billion of impending mega projects. No surprise, then, that the internal economic union issue would surface as a key Ontario demand.

The fourth challenge threatening Ontario was the emerging nature of fiscal federalism - the intergovernmental tax-transfer system. Ontario's view was that, as a result of the 1977 fiscal arrangements (which block-funded the established programs, i.e. health and post-secondary education), the Ontario Treasury suffered a revenue hit in the order of $2 billion dollars over 1977-82 in terms of what revenue growth would have been in the absence of the new arrangements. As the 1982 arrangements approached, Ottawa introduced a new concern, fiscal imbalance, namely the concept that the federal deficit was already too high relative to the aggregate fiscal position of the provinces (or, really, Alberta's surplus). The net result was another $2 billion hit in transfer growth over the 1982-87 period. Ontario fared no better on the equalization front. As a result of mushrooming of energy rents, Ontario qualified under the formula for roughly $1.5 billion of equalization payments over the 1977-82 period. Ontario's position on this was reminiscent of the Robarts' years, namely that Ontario should not be eligible for equalization. Surely the program was "over-equalizing" if Ontario became a beneficiary. In return for being willing to give up their equalization entitlements, Ontario argued that the formula ought to be changed and, in particular, since energy rents were the cause of rising equalization flows to the have-not provinces, Alberta should bear a more appropriate share of program funding. (In passing, one should note that this was a valid position *prior* to the NEP, but hardly afterward since the NEP represented a massive federal revenue grab in the energy sector). In any event, Ottawa did pass legislation which retroactively stripped Ontario of its equalization entitlements, but it did not incorporate Ontario's thrust in terms of reforming equalization.

Ontario's growing sense of "moral outrage" with respect to all of this is extremely well documented in terms of a series of three background papers appended to the 1980, 1981 and 1982 Ontario budgets. These papers are very thorough, well-researched, forcefully articulated and progressively more hard-hitting as the realization sinks in that Ontario had effectively lost completely across this whole range of issues.

All in all, small wonder that Ontario and Ontario interests felt threatened by these series of dramatic developments. More importantly, by and large they were beyond Ontario's control. If Ontario wished to pursue its self interest, it would have to do so via Ottawa. In turn, if the Canadian agenda was not perceived to be in the interests of Ontario, then Ontario would have little choice but to use its influence and power to argue that the Ontario agenda was in the interest of Canada. And it did!

D. What's Good for General Motors is Good for the USA

1. The NEP

In terms of the sequence of events leading to Ontario's isolating both Quebec and the West, my story begins with Premier Davis' break with the Clark Tories and their energy policy. Even prior to negotiations on energy between the Clark and Lougheed governments, Ontario signalled its clear intentions by issuing a position paper on energy which, among other things, argued that "the federal government must use its influence and constitutional authority to direct oil and natural gas revenue flows in accordance with the agreed national objectives" (Simpson, 1980, p. 192).

This implicit call for the use of the "declaratory power" was followed, once the outlines of the Ottawa-Alberta agreement began to take shape, by Premier Davis' sharp denunciation of the Clark Government's policies:

> There is no honest consensus that significant oil price increases, by themselves, lead effectively to reduced consumption. The only thing we know is that a massive increase in the price of oil can stall economic activity and slash employment growth...
>
> ...our intense frustration and alarm about what appears to be a seemingly unrelenting commitment to chase an artificial, erratic and soaring world price — a price set by interests and circumstances foreign to Canada and our economic realities.
>
> ...the oil-pricing proposal ... appears ... to be an excessive and imprudent response to the claims of the producing provinces and the petroleum industry" (reproduced from Simpson, 1980, pp. 198-99.)

To be sure, Premier Davis was on vacation for most of the ensuing election campaign, but he and his views were featured prominently in Liberal election advertising.

Moreover, Trudeau campaigned through Ontario with roughly the same message: "It's as though the [Crosbie] budget was written without knowledge of the importance of energy costs to Ontario's economy" (Simpson, p. 350). The seeds of the National Energy Program were clearly being sown. And during one of the final campaign swings through southwestern Ontario, Trudeau articulated elements of a new Canadian economic nationalism, including a much- invigorated FIRA. The receptiveness of Ontarians to this message was such that the essential elements of the nationalist-centralist NEP were now in place.

The NEP became policy in the fall of 1980. It was a massive political and economic attack on the energy producing provinces. Far and away, it represented to date the most expensive mistake, in terms both of efficiency and national unity, in post-war fiscal history. Not only were the West's energy rents confiscated by the rest of Canada but the set of generous exploration incentives literally forced all exploration out of the West and into the $6 billion fiasco of Canada Lands activity. This was half of it. The other half was an excercise in nationalism and protectionism — the Canadian ownership provisions, the export taxes, the infamous "back-in" provisions for projects in the Canada lands and the discriminatory incentives based on the proportion of Canadian ownership. Combined with the new FIRA provisions, it is hardly surprising that the Americans were outraged.

Ontario may not have been the author of the NEP, but the program would not have materialized without very substantial Ontario support.

Indirectly, however, Ontario *is* the author of the Free Trade Agreement. By being willing to discriminate against the Americans when they themselves were already rapidly drifting into a protectionist mentality meant that there was absolutely no sympathy for exempting Canada from any U.S. protectionist measures. The result was that the Canada-US status quo no longer appeared tenable and the business community took the view that it had little choice but to hitch itself to the free trade bandwagon. As important, in terms of the domestic debate, was the decision to include energy in the FTA. This was a brilliant tactical manoeuvre on Mulroney's part. In one fell swoop, Ontario's ability to speak out nationally against the FTA was substantially circumscribed. What residual ability was available, Ontario Industry Minister Monte Kwinter eroded when he declared last fall that in terms of the FTA the interests of Ontarians are the interests of Canadians. But the West has ample evidence of what Ontario's interests were (and are) in the energy sphere. Indeed, the FTA will ensure that Ontario interests can never perpetrate another NEP on the West.[6] In this context, it is instructive to note that the FTA is part and parcel of the more general Alberta demand for a triple-E Senate (equal, elected, effective). A triple-E Senate would enhance the ability of the west to block federal legislation that would undermine its interests. In terms of the energy sector, this is precisely what the FTA does and this is why, in some sections of the west, the Senate and the FTA are viewed as a package. In any event, from the western perspective, the FTA is every bit as much about Ontarian hegemony as it is about continentalism. Former Alberta Premier Peter Lougheed expressed it best when he proclaimed that the energy provisions of the FTA are "our autopact".

This is an incredible turn of events. On probably the most important economic discussion in memory to face Canada, the voice of Ontario is not only way off side her sister provinces, but any attempt by Ontario to take its message beyond the province is likely to solidify support for the FTA. Moreover, even in the areas of culture and sovereignty, which apparently play well to many Canadians, Ontario's voice is relatively weak as exemplified recently by the intense debate over who should get the all-news T.V. license.

There still remains the ballot box, however, and it is clear that it is here that Canadian will make their ultimate decision with respect to the FTA. And it is here that Ontario's power is still secure. Nonetheless, the point I want to underscore is that it is hard to imagine the Ontario of Robarts ever painting itself so narrowly and awkwardly into a corner. To be fair, however, Robarts did not face these same circumstances.

2. The 1980-82 Constitutional Debates

Whereas the NEP was more akin to an internal power struggle within the federation (although it obviously underscores Ontario's belief in a strong central government), Ontario's support of Trudeau's 1980-82 constitutional process can be rationalized almost entirely in terms of Ontario's "defining characteristics" and its role in the federation. The critically important point to recognize is that what was novel about this round of constitutional debates was the introduction of the concept of the Canadian economic union (henceforth, CEU). As I have argued elsewhere (1984) the focus on the CEU changed the nature of the bargaining process almost immediately. Most of the provinces had long been viewing the patriation process as the vehicle by which to enhance provincial powers. This was especially the case in the spring of 1980, given the victory of the NO forces in the referendum and Trudeau's promise of a "renewed federalism". But the CEU dramatically altered all of this. At base, the CEU was such a centralizing concept and it was so well received by Canadians that the provinces suddenly realized they would be lucky to get out of the process with their *existing* powers intact, let alone any enhanced powers.

Almost immediately Ontario threw its support behind the federal position. History will probably record this Ontario initiative as being far-sighted and pan-Canadian. And in part it surely was. However, the vantage point in this paper is to focus on the process by which Ontario has managed to isolate herself from the Canadian community. One need not look much farther than the decision to support Trudeau in the constitutional process. It is hard to imagine a series of initiatives that would conform more closely to Ontario's "defining characteristics". First of all, in an important sense, the Charter is centralizing. As Alan Cairns has noted: "The consequence (of the Charter), and a very clear purpose, was to set limits to the diversities of treatment by provincial governments, and thus to strengthen Canadian as distinct from provincial identities" (1979, p.354). More recently, Cairns added: "the language of rights is a Canadian language, not a provincial language" (1984). While most Canadians presumably welcome the Charter, in terms of provinces it clearly resonates most closely with an Ontario conception of the federation.

Second, as initially formulated, the 1980 constitutional provisions embodied almost no additional powers to the provinces. This also fits very well into the Ontario conception of the federation and it stood in sharp contrast to the provincial-rights version that Trudeau offered the provinces in 1978 (and that they rejected!).

Finally, Ontario obviously welcomed the emphasis on the Canadian economic union. Recall that this was the time frame of the projected 210 billion dollars of proposed mega projects. Implementation of a full-blown CEU would ensure access to these projects for Ontario's industry. If this could be combined with an overall "buy Canadian" preference, then the benefits to Ontario would be even more substantial. Indeed, it is hard to find a period in post-war Canada where the removal of internal barriers would be more advantageous to Ontario than this 1980-82 period. Thus, Ontario took the view that constitutional renewal in the wake of the Quebec referendum required the implementation of a Canadian common market. Industry and Tourism Minister Larry Grossman spelled this out in an article in *Policy Options* in the fall of 1980 and in early 1981 his Ministry issued a formal position paper on enhancing internal mobility. In both of these documents, there is a call for an overall "Canadian" preference, particularly in relation to the mega projects.

While it is difficult to disagree with attempts to enhance the free movement of goods, services, labour and capital across provincial boundaries, it is not difficult to see that a free domestic market and a "buy Canadian" preference is a very effective "Ontario first" policy. Predictably, most of the provinces reacted very negatively to the CEU concept, arguing that it "could only protect further the economic rights' of Ontarians" (Hudon, 1983, p.141).

In the final analysis, there was not much left of the CEU concept, since Ottawa traded important aspects of it away in order to get support from the remaining provinces (except Quebec of course) for its overall constitutional package. Indeed, when political scientists focus on the November, 1981, constitutional Accord they typically pay scant attention to the CEU provisions. And it may well be that Ontario would have jumped on the constitutional bandwagon even without these internal market provisions.

In any event, the final result was clear: By agreeing to the Constitutional Accord, Ontario was not only willing to isolate Quebec from the Canadian constitutional family but as well to support measures which in effect served to diminish Quebec's powers. One can of course argue that the "ends justified the means". After all the constitution is home now and Canadians do have a Charter of Rights and Freedoms. And I suppose that Ontarians can reconcile the fact that flags flew at half-mast in Quebec when the *Constitution Act 1982* was proclaimed by noting that this was the action of a separatist government. Nonetheless, it is worth recalling that Ontario's role in isolating Quebec constitutionally is a far cry from Robarts' gesture in giving "Danny" the "biggest soap-box in Canada to tell the people of Quebec what he really wanted for his province".

It was inevitable that some Meech-Lake-type rapproachment would surface. And I congratulate Premier David Petersen for the role he played in the process and continues to play in bringing the Meech Lake Accord to fruition. I recognize, however, that there is substantial opposition to the Accord among Ontario elites and perhaps among ordinary Ontarians as well. After all, Meech Lake "federalizes" Canada and as such does not square well with Ontario's "defining characteristics". I will only focus on one issue here, namely the "distinct society" provision. I have maintained all along (Courchene, 1987) that this clause has very little to do with individual rights or sexual equality rights. Rather its role, to the extent that an interpretive clause has a role, is more in the nature of ensuring that Quebec maintains flexibility to mount the sorts of policies outlined in the first part of this paper (e.g. the Quebec Stock Savings Plan, the activities of the Caisse de dépôt and the regulation of its non-bank financial sector). Had the Trudeau or Davis-Grossman concept of a full-blown Canadian economic union been implemented in the *Constitution Act, 1982* it is questionable whether Quebec would be able to maintain the constitutional freedom to design its socio-economic regulatory and institutional structure to suit its own needs. In any event, the issue confronting Canadians and particularly Ontarians is whether or not Meech Lake is too high a price to pay to bring Quebec fully into the Canadian constitutional family. My view is that it is not. More importantly, perhaps, if Meech Lake fails, the price the next time around, if indeed there is a next time, will certainly be higher.

Having thus managed to alienate both Quebec and the energy producing provinces, the immediate problem for Ontarians and indeed all Canadians was how to deal with the devastating effects of the Great Stagflation. As matter of fact, the Ontario recession was short lived compared to the rest of Canada, thanks to the dramatic rebound of the North American auto industry. For the peripheries, however, the recession was only the beginning of their problems. Raw material prices and energy prices in particular collapsed. World wheat prices fell by nearly a dollar when the U.S. began to "outsubsidize" the EEC. And American protectionism created substantial uncertainty relating to the export access of fish and lumber. Hence, by the mid-1980's Ontario was back in the *economic* driver's seat. Indeed, one would probably have to go back several decades to find a situation comparable to the mid-1980s dominant economic position of Ontario in the federation. However, the big difference is that, despite its tremendous economic clout, Ontario is no longer in the *political* driver's seat. This should surprise no one, given Ontario's recent initiatives. Moreover, both Meech Lake and Free Trade, if enacted, will ensure that Ontario will never regain the power that it was once able to wield in the federation. And, as if to add insult to injury, the generally accepted perception of Mulroney's election strategy is to carve out a Quebec/West axis!

One might have expected that, given its prosperity, Ontario would reach out to support some of the stagnating regions. For example, given the growing concern in Ontario with respect to acid rain, some agreement could surely have been worked out sooner for Ontario Hydro to burn more low-sulphur western coal rather than the environmentally disturbing Pennsylvania coal. But something very unusual was taking place in Ontario. The province began progressively to look inward. The Ontario government abandoned its economic agenda and opted for one that highlighted social democracy. Roughly simultaneously, Ontario industry, or at least the Toronto business elites, gave up on the government of Ontario. In my view, this process had its origins in Ontario's general support for the economic policies associated with Trudeau's Second Coming. But it surely crystalized around the Free Trade issue. Enter Ontario's Quiet Revolution.

E. Ontario's Quiet Revolution

The comparison between Ontario and Quebec today could not be more stark. Bourassa's Liberals are pursuing an economic agenda. Peterson's Liberals are pursuing a social agenda. Moreover, business and government in Ontario are off in their own solitudes whereas in Quebec they are, in Japanese fashion, following a common agenda.

Why has this occured? Again, I obviously do not have the full answer. I would suggest, however, that at least part of the answer lies in one or more of the following three hypotheses. The first is that Ontario is (or at least perceives itself to be) wealthy enough to follow a social agenda. Thanks to the fiscal conservatism of the Davis Tories, beginning back in the late 1970's, Ontario came out of the Great Stagflation in better fiscal shape than any other government in Canada. Moreover, as long as Ontario industry is humming along at such a record pace, the revenue inflows allow for considerable flexibility on the social front. The argument would presumably be that the combination of the roll-backs in federal transfers (alluded to earlier) and the preoccupation with an economic agenda during much of the energy crisis years has resulted in some inevitable back-sliding in terms of social-policy goals and that now is time to engage in some catch-up. In its strict form this argument would suggest that the recent focus is likely to be temporary.

The advantageous Ontario fiscal position, relative to other governments, also underlies the remaining two hypotheses. The second hypothesis is political. The most obvious element here is the Liberal-NDP accord, namely that a agenda with an emphasis on social democracy was (and is) the price of wresting power from the Tory dynasty. It would be folly to deny the importance of this element. But I think that there is more to this "political" scenario. It is important to recall that the Tory dynasty was anything but "open". By this I mean that Drew and Robarts and Davis were pros when it came to changing policy directions *within* the Conservative party. These were not quiet revolutions: they were *silent* revolutions. But Premier Davis carried this one step too far when he unloaded the separate school issue on his party and on the province. Not only has this politicized the Ontario citizency, but it ensures that the policy process will henceforth be far more open.

Relatedly, the Liberals probably have little choice but to carry on with this openess. As Viv Nelles so aptly phrased it — the Liberals were initially a government by accident, then they were a government by acclamation and their challenge now is to govern. Despite their massive electoral victory, they need to plant some roots to develop a more permanent constituency and to do this they have opted for a rather open government or at least a government that is making extensive use of avenues such as legislative hearings. They may or may not succeed in this process of seeking consensus, but the fallout from the separate school issue and their own interests in building a constituency dictate that they will probably give it a good try.

This has been a rather tortuous way to come to the main point, namely that a more open system in an environment where there are three viable parties almost of necessity tilts the political rhetoric, if not the actual agenda, to the left of centre. Moreover, the emphasis on individual and collective rights and freedoms arising from the Charter has politicized the citizenry and mobilized special interests. This complicates governance in its own right at the same time that it speaks to openess. To the extent that this scenario is correct, the focus on a social agenda is not likely to be so temporary.

Finally, the third hypothesis is that Ontarians are indeed engaged in a process of redefining themselves. More than a decade of wrestling with either Quebec's challenges or Quebec's aspirations has left English Canadians both weary and exasperated. And clearly this is putting it in the mildest possible form. Moreover, as a result of all of this internal focus, Quebecers (or at least Québécois) have emerged with a new confidence and awareness of who they are in relation to themselves, to their province and to their country. Westerners, still reeling from the reality of internal power politics - obviously the NEP but as well decisions like the awarding of the F-18 contract - may not exude confidence but they surely have a better awareness of their priorities in terms of an economic (free trade) and political (triple E Senate) agenda, both of which constrain the influence of the centre. In contrast, Ontarians emerged from this process more confused about who they are and more divided in terms of what they want.

I would suggest that, in the context of the rise of the centralist-nationalist spirit of Trudeau's Second Coming, significant elements of Ontario society sought identity in the most traditional Canadian way - to be unlike the Americans and in particular to disassociate themselves from Reaganism. In the run- up to the 1980 U.S. elections, I recall being astonished that it was difficult to find any pro-Reagan articles on the *op ed* pages of my daily papers. And if Ontarians had concerns prior to Reagan's election, the Reagan agenda no doubt confirmed them - a return to a version of "rugged individualism"; supply-side economics and tax breaks for the rich; an unwinding even an uncaring in terms of certain social programs; a dramatic decrease in unionization; the rise of the moral majority; a decreased emphasis on the environment; and so on. In part, then, the emphasis on a social agenda may represent a conscious decision by Ontarians to set themselves apart from their neighbours to the South. In Jeffrey Simpson's words (1987), it may represents a conscious buying into the "Peace, Order and Good Government" rhetoric of the Canadian constitution rather than the "Life, Liberty and the Pursuit of Happiness" which underlies the American Creed. When combined with the already existing pressures for greater movement on the social front, the resulting coalition becomes a significant force, particularly if the underlying assumption is that economic or business interests, off in their own solitude, are quite capable of fending for themselves.

To the extent that there is something to this view, it is obvious that the election of the Mulroney Tories represented a severe blow to this coalition. A greater role for the interplay of market forces, a greater degree of economic integration with the U.S., and the perception, if not the reality, of a reduced role for the central government all combine to undermine an agenda that focuses on social issues on the assumption that the pre-existing economic fabric remains intact.

To be sure, such concerns are not limited to Ontarians. But Ontario is the only province with the luxury of having a viable (even if short-term) alternative approach, namely looking inward, focussing on domestic free trade and allowing Ontario industry to continue to extract rents from the rest of Canada. For a while this approach was cleverly clothed in GATT raiment until the recent GATT ruling on wines, etc., unfrocked it. Unfortunately, the reality is that this re-assertion of the notion that what is in Ontario's interest is in the interest of Canada no longer washes across the system. Nor does it wash with the Ontario business establishment. But, as noted earlier, there still is the ballot box...

In any event, Ontario's agenda is almost entirely a social policy agenda - rent controls, housing policy, equal pay for equal work of equal value, indexing of pensions, revamping insurance, Sunday shopping, day care, etc. Moreover, as Ontario Treasurer Robert Nixon's recent budget clearly revealed this is a very expensive agenda. The contrast between this agenda and that recommended by Premier Peterson's economic advisory council a week or so before the Ontario budget could hardly be more dramatic. The one significant overlap, and where Ontario is showing some signs of moving from a social to a socio-economic or even to an economic agenda, relates to the role of R and D, post-secondary centres of excellence and more generally an emphasis on human capital.

The underlying issue is *not* that Ontario is addressing important social priorities. This is, and always will be, a noble goal and indeed a measure of a civilized society. Rather, the issue is why these goals appear to be pursued primarily or in some cases only in social terms and not within the context of an integrated socio-economic framework. For most of Ontario's social priorities, it would have been possible to design alternative programs more selective in terms of the target group, more incentive-compatible with economic priorities and less costly in terms of budgetary implications. Robert Nixon's recent budget is consistent with a view that either free trade will falter at the ballot box or that Ontario will be the principal beneficiary of the fiscal and economic surplus that will result from the FTA. What it is not consistent with is Ontario's announced position that free trade threatens its economic future.

Contrast this to the novel proposal in the last Quebec budget which would provide substantial earnings supplementation (structured to take account of family size) in order to ensure that persons on welfare or UI have a substantial incentive to re-enter the labour force if opportunities exist. This is not only good social policy, it is good economic policy. More generally, with appropriate policy design, equity and efficiency are typically complementary not competing goals.

In any event, I am confident that the march of economic events will compel Ontarians to move sharply and quickly toward an economic agenda. What I am far less confident about is that this is going to be an easy transition. In particular, if Ontario's current agenda is largely driven by a conscious desire for a more activist state in pursuit of social democracy (along Quebec's Quiet Revolution lines), then the gulf to be broached is substantial indeed.

V. Implications

In sorting out what all of this might imply for the future I will focus in turn on Ontario, Quebec and Ottawa.

The incredibly divisive policies of Trudeau's Second Coming are remaking Canada both politically and economically. Mulroney's Tories might be accused of attempting to overturn too much of the Trudeau agenda, but any successor government would have been driven to substantial initiatives in the name of restoring our national fabric. Since certain Ontario elites played such a major role in the nationalist-centralist thrust of policy in this era and since Ontario effectively had a veto in terms of isolating Quebec constitutionally, it is hardly surprising that this same group of Ontarians find themselves way off-side in terms of the Mulroney agenda.

What is surprising, at least to the mainstream of my profession, is the stance of the average Ontarian toward free trade: not only is Ontario's existing prosperity linked to U.S. trade but the available evidence at least as I read it is that Ontarians will be the ultimate beneficiary of the FTA.

Part of this puzzle may be explained by the attitudinal surveys which indicate that Ontario opinion leaders are not near as willing as those in Quebec (nor those in other provinces) to adapt to the new world economic order. Moreover, the above analysis argued that Ontarians, internally, may well be politically engaged in their own quiet revolution, where the emphasis is on a social rather than an economic agenda. Another part of the explanation is that Ontarians would much prefer the "good old days", as it were, when Canada conformed in large measure to Ontario's "defining characteristics". However, what may have been possible prior to 1980 appears to be out of the question now and Ontarians ought to be clever enough to reason why. Continuing with the earlier analogy, what is good for General Motors is no longer good for the USA!

In terms of Quebec, my earlier view that the combination of Bill 101, Meech Lake and the FTA effectively confers sovereignty association in the province will, I think, prove accurate. Quebec will continue to innovate both domestically and internationally across a wide range of fronts, particularly when its current economic boom begins to unwind. And the rest of Canada will probably not dare to interfere. This realization has bothered me throughout this paper. Perhaps I have got the whole thing wrong: perhaps it is Quebec, not Ontario, that holds the real power in the federation. For example, Canadians continue to argue about what share of energy rents ought to accrue to Ottawa. But the sizeable energy-related rents will, in the future, likely accrue to Quebec. Since Quebec's exports of electricity are priced between 2 and 3 times domestic rates, these exports (currently negotiated at $40 billion to the year 2,000, but likely to escalate substantially) clearly embody very substantial economic rents. As currently formulated, Canada's equalization formula ignores these rents and Quebec qualifies for roughly 50% of all equalization payments. Despite the support of the economics profession, the Economic Council of Canada, clearly Ontario, and the Parliamentary Committee on the fiscal arrangements (1981), I am reasonably confident that Canada will find it difficult to alter the equalization formula to take account of Quebec's hydro rents.

Be that as it may, in terms of the near future the failure to approve Meech Lake and Free Trade may have dramatic implications in Quebec. In terms of the former, Pierre Trudeau was no doubt correct when he noted that, at the time the Quebec Government launched the Meech Lake initiative, only about 5 per cent of Quebecers had any interest in the issue. However, in the interim interest has heightened significantly, in part because of the vocal opposition of Ontario elites and of course because of Trudeau himself. In the public-lecture version this paper (April, 1988) I nontheless argued that the failure of the Meech-Lake exercise would, of and by itself, be of limited immediate consequence to the de-politicized, outward-looking, acquisitive Quebecers. I also noted that the reaction of the Quebec government would be another matter: at some future date, but not tomorrow, the overturning of Meech Lake may come to haunt Canadians with a vengeance. I still adhere to this view provided that Free Trade is enacted. But if the FTA also fails then an overturning of Meech Lake will take on much greater significance. Without an FTA, I would argue that, contrary to the prevailing wisdom, the English in Quebec are probably in for a very much harder time if Meech Lake fails than if it passes, and this for "defensive" not aggressive reasons.

This brings me to the free trade issue. The FTA is vital to Quebec particularly since it resonates so well with the goals and aspirations of the "new" Quebec. In this sense Free Trade is clearly the most explosive issue Ontarians have had to grapple with in memory. It is one thing if the Americans veto the FTA. It is quite another if, via the ballot box, Ontarians do! An integral part of the above analysis was to present the backdrop relating to how Ontario managed to manouver itself into this "wicked problem" syndrome.

Finally, the current agenda is not without very substantial risks to the federal government. First Ontario's social agenda clearly will cause Ottawa major headaches. Now that Ontario has emerged as the social policy leader in the federation, Ottawa will surely be besieged by a chorus of demands from "have not" provinces for additional funds to ensure that their citizens have "equal opportunities" in terms of section 36 of the *Constitution Act, 1982*. Moreover, Ottawa and in particular Finance Minister Michael Wilson, must still be reeling from the after-shock of the Ontario budget. Part of the rationale for the tax reform exercise was to bring corporate and personal income tax rates in line with the U.S. tax reform. Much of this was Ontario-oriented since it is the manufacturing sector (unlike the resource sector) that is potentially highly mobile. For Treasurer Nixon to move in and take up a considerable chunk of the vacated federal tax room on the income tax side not only undermines the entire federal tax-reform process, but as noted above reflects Ontario's abandonment of an economic agenda. It is obvious that Nixon has generated much joy in Michigan and Quebec.

The Ontario budget also deserves comment in terms of the more general context of Ontario's newly re-constituted economic dominance in the federation. Specifically, the issue has to do with the fact that the Bank of Canada's arsenal is currently deployed to keep the lid on inflation in the golden horseshoe. Given the impact that the resulting higher interest rates are having on the much-less-economically-advantaged regions of the country, one would have thought that Ontario would take these concerns to heart in setting its budget parameters. Rather, the opposite occurred. By spending, rather than saving, its fiscal dividend and, more generally, by stimulating absorption Ontario put even greater pressure on the Bank of Canada to utilize high interest rates to control Ontario's now-heightened inflationary tendencies. This too is a far cry from the Ontario of Robarts, but it no doubt reflects the range of current tensions in the federation.

Re-focussing on Ottawa, the federal government is involved in a very delicate game by targeting its policy initiatives (with hindsight although perhaps not with foresight) toward the "province rights" areas - Quebec and the West. To the extent that this implies that Ottawa is becoming more of a broker across regional and provincial interests, this poses a problem for Ontario in terms of its "defining characteristics". But it also poses a problem for Ottawa. Ontario's power and influence *will* be exercised within the federation in one way or another. A central government conforming more to a confederal than to a federal mold will surely tend to ensure that Ontarians begin progressively to articulate their interests through Queen's Park (and with a different agenda!). For example, the on-going controversy between Ottawa and Ontario as to whether the province can levy a "flat tax" would effectively be solved by Ontario implementing its own personal income tax. Phrased differently, if the federal government comes to be perceived by Ontarians as not adequately reflecting the interests of Ontario, the end result will be a much stronger Queen's Park, a much more decentralized federation and, by definition, a much weaker central government. While this is essentially diametrically opposed to Ontario's preferred conception of the federation, it is nonetheless an eminently viable alternative for the province and, as such, ought to give all federal politicians all kinds of pause for thought. Moreover, even some of the "province-rights" provinces would have second thoughts about this scenario.

Herein lies the dilemma as Canadians enter what will surely be one of the most turbulent years of our history in attempting to grapple with Free Trade and to a lesser extent Meech Lake. Harking back to the introduction, it is unfortunate that that there is not another "Confederation of Tomorrow" conference on the horizon. It is not clear who would assume the mantle of the new John Robarts but it is clear that one of the issues that would occupy centre- stage would be "What does Ontario want?"[7]

Endnotes

* It is a pleasure to thank Tom Kierans for his role in this paper. The general thrust as well as the title arose out of a series of discussions over the past few months. In terms of attempting to sort out what Ontario is, or might be, all about, I am also indebted to York's Canadian policy community, which surely can lay claim to be Canada's finest. In particular, it is a pleasure to express thanks to historians Viv Nelles, Chris Armstrong, Ramsay Cook and Jack Saywell. Much of what "rings true" in this paper reflects their contribution. Finally, I would like to thank UWOs Andrew Sancton for suggesting the term "market nationalism" to describe Quebec's on-going revolution. However, given the highly subjective nature of the analysis, I am sure that all these individuals are relieved that I exempt them completely from any responsibility for the views that follow.

1. Whether either or both of Robarts and Daniel Johnson would endorse Meech Lake is intriguing, but not particularly germane to the issue I wish to explore. For what it is worth, however, my view is that Robarts would react positively to Meech Lake. As co-chairman (with Jean-Luc Pepin) of the Task Force on Canadian Unity, Robarts and the Task Force stated: "Let us put our conviction strongly: Quebec is distinctive and should, within a viable Canada, have the powers necessary to protect and develop its distinctive character; any political solution short of this would lead to the rupture of Canada" (Pepin-Robarts Report, 1979, p. 87). Not only is this very close to the "distinct society" clause but the overall thrust of the Pepin-Robarts Report may well have influenced the Meech Lake Accord.

2. It is probably appropriate to apprize readers that I wholeheartedly supported both Meech Lake (1987c) and Free Trade (1988b).

3. Indeed, between the time of delivery (April, 1988) and publication of this paper, Ontario has released its task force report on the welfare system (Ontario Ministry of Community and Social Services, 1988) which recommends significant changes in the direction of integrating social and economic policies.

4. Consider the following provisions. In terms of the delivery of health services, the Gobeil Report recommends:

    - decentralization of the management of institutions, including collective agreements;
    - the possibility of assigning management of hospitals to outside firms;
    - more extensive contracting out;
    - the creation of HMOs (health maintenance organizations) along capitation rather than free-for-service lines;
    - new types of institutions for the elderly;
    - use of the income tax system to finance health costs.

Similar sweeping recommendations are made for income security (e.g. a negative income tax) and post-secondary education (e.g. implementation of a voucher system). The Scowen Report opts for thorough deregulation in the social and economic sphere. The Fortier Report recommends that, apart from Quebec Hydro, most of the so-called "strategic" crown corporations be privatized. For more detail see Courchene (1987a) or preferably the reports themselves.

5.   The remainder of this paragraph and the following are lifted from Courchene (1987b).

6.   But this does not mean that Ottawa will not use the tax-transfer system to access enhanced energy rents if there is another energy price spike. Indeed, one can confidently predict that it will.

7.   A bit of a postscript. Two significant events related directly to this paper have occurred since final editing. The first is the return of the Mulroney Tories, and the second is the Supreme Court decision on language and Premier Bourassa's subsequent invoking of the not-withstanding clause. The former is fully in line with the above analysis while the latter may appear to raise some consistency issues. Effectively, Quebec gave Canada free trade. Had the Tories captured only 42 instead of 63 of the 75 Quebec seats (still a comfortable majority of Quebec seats), Mulroney would not have had his majority and free trade would likely have been stymied. Suffice it to say that a decade ago this route to achieving free trade would not have ranked high in terms of likely scenarios.

The language issue is more difficult to reconcile. Among the intriguing questions is: why is Quebec confident enough to vote en masse for continental free trade but not confident enough to tolerate bilingual signs? Fathoming this question is well beyond the scope of the present paper. Two related observations are relevant, however. The first is that underlying the shift toward individualism and the markets was, and is, a collective confidence and security that the Quebec language and culture are safeguarded via Bill 101 and various other policies and measures. A perceived or real unwinding of this security blanket would serve to chip away at the foundations underlying "le virage vers les marchés." The second is that, once the Supreme Court reported, it was almost inevitable that Bourassa would invoke the notwithstanding clause, irrespective of which option he chose to pursue. To do otherwise would be to admit that language and cultural policy for Quebec could be determined outside the province.

The irony in all this is that the "suggested" Supreme Court compromise (bilingual signs emphasizing French) was a perfectly viable option for Bourassa in 1985 or 1987, but not once the Supreme Court had lent its imprimatur.   Obviously this is not meant to be an evaluation of these recent events, only how they relate to the above analysis.

2. Forever Amber

I. INTRODUCTION

With the victory of the NO forces in 1980 and with Trudeau's promise of "le fédéralisme renouvelé", Canadians and our governments had every expectation that the constitutional signals were finally flashing green. And in an important sense they were. In 1982, nine provinces and Ottawa found a way through the constitutional intersection. And with the historic 1987 compromise, the way was set to bring Quebec across the constitutional threshold as well. But apparently this is not the Canadian way. We seem to have an incredible ability to ensure that the future of our federation remains continually in the balance. Thus, with "assistance" from all players we engineered Meech Lake through a highly sophisticated kamikaze exercise. Then, in those heady days in Quebec immediately following the Meech debacle, it appeared the signals were flashing red: the momentum and the societal cohesion in Quebec pointed toward a quick exit. However, this is apparently not the Quebec way either. Kanesatake and Kahnawake burst Quebec's sovereignty euphoria, at least for the near term, and combined with the recession and internal politics associated with Quebec's parliamentary committee imply that Quebec will not likely be able to forge a unified non-partisan position. Hence, as we enter the 1990s we are back, albeit with a more complicated agenda and process, at our familiar constitutional crossroad. Moreover, the signals are also looking increasingly familiar: forever amber.

With this as backdrop, the purpose of this paper is to review the 1980s constitutional record both in its own right and in terms of what it might portend for the 1990s. I am giving a very broad definition to the "constitutional record", specifically those forces internal or external that impinge on federal-provincial, interprovincial or citizen-state relationships. The principal background material is an appendix table that records and assesses selected events in the 1980s in terms of their implications for this triad of relationships.

In more detail, part II focuses on the domestic political agenda and its impact on the institutional and constitutional framework. The analysis will be conducted in terms of the three political "mandates" in the 1980s - Trudeau's Second Coming and the two Mulroney administrations. Necessarily, this will draw on existing treatises, e.g. Milne (1986) and Simeon and Robinson (1990). Part III then deals very briefly with the way in which developments in the global economy are likely to influence the evolution of Canadian federalism. In the concluding section these various forces brought together in order to isolate selected challenges and choices facing us in the 1990s.

II. DOMESTIC POLITICS AND THE CONSTITUTIONAL FRAMEWORK

A. Trudeau's Second Coming

From the perspective of the 1977 block-funding of the established programs and the Liberals' very generous constitutional proposals of 1978 (which, incredibly, the provinces rejected), Trudeau's Second Coming represented nothing less than a complete philosophical reversal. In Trudeau's own words, from a CTV Christmas, 1981, interview:

I think that the turn of the pendulum or the swing back of the pendulum [toward centralism] happened probably sometime between '78 and '81. I don't like to be too partisan, but I think that we had that short period of the Conservative party that was preaching the community of communities and I think it brought forth rather clearly when even Mr. Clark couldn't reach an agreement with Alberta, after he'd given up Loto Canada, after he'd given away the offshore and after he'd been making many other promises to decentralize to that community of communities, I think it became obvious to more and more people that that was going too far and then I began to feel that I had support for stopping the pendulum (Milne, 1986, p. 23).

And stop the pendulum he did. Virtually the entire Liberal agenda - the NEP, the intentions to strengthen FIRA[1] and Canadian ownership, *the Constitution Act, 1982*, the termination of the revenue guarantee and the "re-conditioning" of post-secondary education transfers, the 1984 Canada Health Act, etc. - can be interpreted as deliberate initiatives designed to strengthen the federal presence, power and visibility not only vis-à-vis the provinces and regions but also with respect to the forces of "assimilation and integration" emanating from south of the border.   .

Whether one refers to this as "defensive expansionism" following Aitkin (1959) or as the Liberals' "new federalism" (Milne, 1986) or the "nationalist-centralist-interventionist agenda" (Courchene, 1989 and Chapter 1, *this volume*), the implications were profound. At the highest level of generalization, by alienating the regions and provinces (the west with the NEP and the Canada Health Act, and Quebec with the Constitution), the Americans (intended changes in FIRA and the discriminatory features of the NEP) and the business community (galloping deficits and the fear that Canada would, for its anti-US policies, be caught in any U.S. protectionist wave), Pierre Trudeau became, indirectly at least, the "author" of both Meech Lake and Free Trade. Phrased differently, it was virtually inevitable that the Trudeau agenda would trigger powerful countervailing forces. And for the constellation of interests associated with the FTA, the Trudeau policies were overturned with a vengeance, i.e. well-nigh "constitutionalized" in the Canada-US free-trade agreement. But other aspects of the "new federalism" have been anything but overturned. Foremost among these is the Charter which, as Alan Cairns has noted, has not only "democratized" the constitution (by "entitling" new groups such as natives, the disabled, linguistic minorities, women, multicultural groups) but as well has created a "non-territorial" or pan-Canadian component to constitutional federalism:

> At a more profound political level...the Charter was an attempt to enhance and extend the meaning of being Canadian and thus to strengthen identification with the national community on which Ottawa ultimately depends for support. ...The resultant rights and freedoms were to be country-wide in scope, enforced by a national supreme court, and entrenched in a national Constitution beyond the reach of fleeting legislative majorities at either level of government. The *consequence, and a very clear purpose, was to set limits to the diversities of treatment by provincial governments, and thus to strengthen Canadian as against provincial identities*. Rights must not be dependent on the particular place where an individual chooses to reside (Cairns, 1979, p. 354, emphasis added);
>
> The language of rights is a Canadian language not a provincial language. If the Charter takes root over time the citizenry will be progressively Canadianized (Cairns, 1984).

The challenge the Charter poses to the traditional operations of Canadian federalism was highlighted by my colleague John Whyte when he noted that, in a charter-based society, citizen-state relations become "systematized, centralized, uniform, constant, unilateral and direct" while in a federal system they are "diverse, filtered, diluted, subject to mediation and complicated" (cited in Simeon and Robinson, 1990, pp. 281-2).

Ironically, however, the Charter is fundamentally offside with respect to the Liberal agenda (although perhaps not with Trudeau's personal philosophy). It is inherently "republicanizing" in the sense of undermining aspects of the essence of parliamentary government by introducing a checks-and-balances component (the courts) fully into our governing machinery. More intriguingly, it is inherently "Americanizing" in the important sense of moving us closer to embracing aspects of the individualism underlying the American Creed.[2] Seymour Martin Lipset was correct, in my view, when in a recent *McLean's* interview he argued that the Charter, not the FTA, has the greater potential for bringing us into the American orbit and ambit. Evidence of this can be found in the Charter-influenced position adopted by Premiers Wells, Filmon and McKenna in the countdown to Meech to the effect that no province should have special powers.[3] This is quintessentially American, not Canadian, since asymmetric powers have long characterized our federation and important aspects of asymmetry are central to the *Constitution Act, 1867*.

Meech Lake may have been the first attempt to adjust to the insertion of the Charter into our governance structure. But it will not be the last and before full accommodation is achieved the Charter will have touched deeply many aspects of the Canadian psyche including, for example, executive federalism (Courchene, 1990e). On this score, David Milne raises an issue or puzzle that promises to be an academic gold mine for historians and political scientists alike: Why should an essentially conservative people, with little inclination to distrust governments on principle, have decided to bypass governments and entrust so many of its rights, especially language rights, to judges and not to politicians? (Milne, 1986, p. 52).

1. The Canadian Economic Union as Catalyst

What was the conceptual and/or operational catalyst that triggered this 1980-84 agenda? The answer, I think, was Chrétien's 1980 "Pink Paper" *(Securing the Canadian Economic Union in the Constitution)*.

To attempt to demonstrate this, it is critical to recognize that what was novel about the 1980-82 constitutional round was the inclusion of the concept of the Canadian economic union (henceforth, CEU). Almost immediately, the nature of the bargaining process altered dramatically. Most of the provinces had long been viewing the patriation process as the vehicle by which to enhance their powers. This was especially the case in the spring of 1980, given the victory of the NO forces in the referendum and Trudeau's promise of a "renewed federalism". But the CEU had such potential for centralization (see Simeon (1982-83)) and it was so well received by Canadians that the provinces suddenly realized that they would be lucky to escape from the process with their *existing* powers intact, let alone any enhanced powers.

The provinces found themselves in a truly awkward position: to argue their side they had in effect to challenge the free flow of goods, services, capital and people across provincial boundaries. Not surprisingly, Trudeau made full use of the provinces' dilemma. On the opening day of the televised constitutional conference in the fall of 1980, after each premier has his say, it was the Prime Ministers' turn:

...if we look at the agenda...there are eight items of the twelve where the provinces are either attempting to increase their powers or to reduce the federal ones, and this...in the most decentralized federal form of government in the world. Now against these eight items...where the provinces are asking for more power for themselves there is one item, the one called Powers over the Economy [effectively, the CEU issue] where, respectfully we are not asking for more powers for ourselves, the federal Canadian government, we are just asking that the constitution reflect what all of us wish and many of you said you wished—to have in Canada a common economic market (Trudeau, 1980, p. 95).

Critical to the constitutional process was that Ontario immediately threw its support behind the federal proposals. History may record this as a nation-building, Canada-first initiative on Ontario's part. However, it is also the case that the introduction of a thorough-going CEU was very much an "Ontario first" policy (Hudon, 1983; Courchene, 1989). Recall that this was the very time frame of the projected $210 billion of mega-projects, many of them energy related. A full-blown CEU (e.g., no purchasing preferences on the part of the Alberta government) would ensure full access by Ontario industry to these projects. Moreover, if this could in addition be combined with an overall "buy Canadian" preference, then the benefits to Ontario would be even more significant. Hence, it is perhaps not surprising that Ontario's Industry and Tourism Minister, Larry Grossman, argued just this (i.e. a CEU and a "buy-Canadian" preference) in *Policy Options* in the fall of 1980 and his department issued a formal Ontario position paper (the so-called "Purple Paper") to this effect in 1981. In effect, this would represent at long last the full realization and culmination of Macdonald's 1879 National Policy. And the timing could not be more opportune. Moreover, this Ontario-Ottawa symbiosis meant, for example, that intentions designed to put more teeth into FIRA would find Ontario government support, and so on.

To be sure, the CEU acted principally as a catalyst in all of this, since Trudeau agreed to *enshrine impediments* to the CEU (preferential hiring for Newfoundland's offshore and the right to mount indirect taxes in respect of natural resources for the west) and, more generally, backed off the implementation of provisions like enhancing the trade and commerce power in order to cement the constitutional accord in the fall of 1981.[4] Nonetheless, in the context of the 1980-82 environment, the so-called "people's package" (economic rights via the CEU and political rights via the Charter) provided a powerful rationale not only for the constitutional process but also for the entire "new federalism" agenda. For example, Milne offers the following comments with respect to the NEP:

> ...if the object of the Trudeau government's constitutional strat-
> egy was to throw up guarantees and symbols against separatism
> and regionalism that would only subtly consolidate federal
> power, its National Energy Program was more directly and
> boldly centralist. Steeped on an intoxicating nationalist rhetoric
> that challenged both foreign multinationals and "selfish" provin-
> cialism in the name of Canadian "patrimony", energy security,
> and pricing fairness, the policy's primary purpose was the
> strengthening of the federal state. Just as it had done during the
> battle over the constitution, the government served up national-
> ism as a powerful doctrine for rebuilding federal power. Once
> again, the theory was advanced that the "people's" interests
> could only be furthered by promoting the Canadian state, by
> celebrating Canada as it might be expressed through federal
> instruments and agencies (Milne, 1986, p. 70).

The link can also be made in the fiscal federalism area as well. Under the guise of a "fiscal imbalance" (i.e., the federal government was shouldering too large a share of aggregate government deficits), Ottawa pared back the value of the EPF grants by the two-tax points that were part of the 1977 block-funding arrangements (and were designed to compen-sate for the termination of the revenue guarantee). At roughly the same time Ottawa moved, again unilaterally, to "re-condition" the 1977 EPF transfers and began to argue that the provinces were "underfunding" post-secondary education. This approach of going over the heads of the provinces and appealing directly to Canadians reached its apex with the 1984 Canada Health Act: in effect, the federal government adopted the role of "guarantor" and, in some areas, ultimate arbitrator for aspects of the provincially-run, health-care programs (Courchene, 1984).

Finally, the Liberal's approach to bilingualism and biculturalism whereby English and French speaking Canadians can feel at home anywhere in Canada resonates much more with the CEU and the Charter than it does with the "collective-rights" approach to language and culture espoused by successive Quebec governments.

However one interprets this constellation of initiatives, it is clear that they represented a dramatic shift in both the traditional attitudes and traditional structures of the federation. As Breton (1985) notes, parliamentary government à la Canada accommodates and even encourages these massive pendulum swings. Enter the Mulroney Tories.

B. Mulroney I: National Reconciliation

On September 4, 1984, Canadians resoundingly rejected the "new federalism", admittedly with some help from Prime Minister John Turner. As impressive as the magnitude of the Tory sweep (211 out of 282 or 3/4 of the seats) was its generality (at least 70 per cent in each region) (Simeon and Robinson, 1990, p. 301). While "national reconciliation" lay at the core of the Tory's campaign message (*loc. cit.*), it is probably more appropriate to portray the message as an attempt at "rebalancing" the federation and, in particular, re-accommodating some traditional elites - business, the Americans and, above all, the provinces.

1. Rekindling Cooperative Federalism

From Mulroney's Sept Iles campaign speech (August 6, 1984):
> Our task is to breathe a new spirit into federalism...A
> Progressive Conservative government will be guided by
> the principle of respect for provincial authority (Simeon
> and Robinson, 1990, pp. 301-2).

From the vantage point of 1980-84, this is, however, really breathing the "old" spirit back into federalism, namely that federalism is first and foremost a relationship among and between governments. This aside, Mulroney certainly acted quickly on this commitment. Interstate (or executive) federalism flourished. Comparing the first year of the Mulroney mandate with the 1980-84 annual average reveals a dramatic increase in "federal-provincial diplomacy": first ministers' meetings (13 vs. 5), ministers' meetings (353 vs. 82), deputy ministers meetings (72 vs. 45) for an overall total of 438 vs. 132 (Milne, 1986, p. 222).

In terms of substance, rather than process, the Mulroney Tories negotiated both the Atlantic Accord and the Western Accord during their first year in office. The Atlantic Accord was particularly illustrative of the new environment: "Despite a unanimous decision from the Supreme Court in March 1984 awarding Ottawa the exclusive right to exploit and develop the offshore, the Mulroney government less than a year later granted to Newfoundland equal management powers, a decisive say on the mode of development on the offshore, and all rights to apply royalties and taxes 'as if these resources were on land, within the province'" (Milne, 1986, p. 99).[5] Likewise, while the Western Accord may not have "gutted" the NEP, it did mark a "retreat of federal interests in the energy field, a reversal of the older policy of slanting federal energy policy towards Ottawa's own narrower state interests, and a joint intergovernmental decision to return oil and gas to the more or less normal operation of the market place." (*Ibid*, p. 112).

The FTA has been viewed as driving the final nail in the NEP philosophy, since it effectively "enshrines" market prices and, therefore, prevents the diversion of western energy rents via "made-in-Canada" prices. True. But it does not protect energy rents from the operations of the federal tax-transfer system. Not much political capital is spent in deregulating energy prices in the context of collapsed resource prices, as was the case for the 1985 Western Accord and even the FTA. The real challenge will come if and when energy prices spiral again. At the time of writing, oil is touching $40 a barrel. Should the price continue at this level, all the old pressures for rent-sharing will be rekindled.

Other initiatives that qualify as resurrecting cooperative federalism would include ACOA (Atlantic Canada Opportunities Agency) and WDO (Western Diversification Office), both of which represented an increased provincial/regional say in development initiatives.

2. The FTA

The overt anti-Americanism of the 1980-84 era (sabre-rattling on FIRA, see footnote 1, and the NEP) became much more problematical in the mid-1980s when the Americans began to run record balance-of-payments deficits. Protectionist sentiment mounted, particularly in Congress, and the fear was that for our earlier sins we would not be exempt from any American turning inward. Hard evidence was not long in coming - steel, fish, softwood lumber, shakes and shingles, UI, etc. Moreover, with the dollar dipping at one point below 70 cents, Canadian business was making important inroads in the U.S. market and free trade would "lock in" this market access. The fact that Europe 1992 was already launched and the fears (in this time frame) that it might become "fortress Europe" implied that, alone of the G7, Canada would not have access to a "domestic" market of at least 100 million. Finally, but not exhaustively, the Macdonald Commission's strong endorsement for a Canada-U.S. free-trade agreement found a ready audience both in terms of substance and timing. Relaxing the FIRA provisions was a first step, but the window of opportunity opened for something much more grandiose - the FTA.

In terms of the Tories' policy of "national reconciliation", the FTA was a natural. In one feel swoop, Mulroney catered to all of the parties who felt aggrieved by Trudeau's 1980-84 agenda - business, the Americans and the provinces, particularly Quebec (the Constitution) and the west (the NEP). Moreover, the Quebec-West/ business axis was fully in line with the Tories political base. To be sure, Ontario was offside but Mulroney cleverly isolated this province by including energy in the FTA: Alberta's support for the FTA stiffened in full knowledge that the FTA would prevent Ontario from ever again unloading an NEP on the west. Thus, whereas Trudeau went over the heads of business and the provinces to the people in implementing his agenda, the FTA reverses all of this - Mulroney went over the heads of Canadians and appealed directly to business and provincial elites. The result was Canada's first recent election fought on "class lines", with Turner positioning himself and his party fully within the 1980-84 conception and with the traditional "class-party", the NDP, intriguingly relegated to the sidelines.

3. Meech Lake and Tax Reform

The high point of Mulroney's reconciliation efforts during his first mandate was surely the 1977 Meech Lake Accord. Euphoria prevailed for a while and the Accord was viewed as an historic compromise not just with respect to 1982 but as well 1867. Since interest centers less in its origins than in its denouement, discussion will come later.

The Tories launched into a thorough tax reform mid-way through their mandate. Some of this (base broadening and lowering marginal rates for income taxation) was triggered by the U.S. tax reform. The remainder, essentially the GST, was designed not only to replace the federal manufacturers' sales tax but as well to shift taxation from income to consumption. For electoral purposes, the Tories split up the overall package, in effect loading all of the "goodies" (lower rates, base broadening, conversion of exemptions to credits) into the first round and leaving the GST to be implemented in their next mandate. Foresight, let alone hindsight, questioned the political wisdom of a two-stage implementation procedure (Carmichael, 1988; Courchene, 1988a).

C. Mulroney II: Drifting into Country Warp

On November, 1988, the Mulroney Tories won the free trade election and by year's end Mulroney and Reagan initialled the FTA. Thus, as of January 1, 1989, the Tories were in a very unique position: the single issue of the election was now behind them and they had a full term in front of them with no electoral commitments. To this point, nearly two years later, they have enunciated no new agenda (this is due in early 1991) and they have instead presided over an unbelievable unwinding of their pre-existing agenda, replete with profound implications for federal- provincial, interprovincial and citizen-state relations, not to mention for the Tories themselves with the popular support for the Prime Minister running roughly at the level of the prime rate.

1. The Denouement of Meech

The rise and fall of Meech is far too complex to be dealt with in any comprehensive manner in the present context.[6] A few comments must suffice. Obviously, the election of Wells, Filmon, and McKenna - premiers who did not sign the Accord and two of whom (except Filmon) campaigned against the Accord - complicated matters. So did Bourassa's recourse to the notwithstanding clause in the context of the sign-language legislation (Bill 178). Immediately, Filmon joined Wells and McKenna in opposition to the Accord. However, in my view, what eventually stymied the Accord, and what has catapulted Canada into a profound constitutional crisis, was the victory of the Trudeau vision (essentially, the Charter) over the Mulroney vision that constitutional amendment falls solely in the domain of executive federalism. To be fair, this amending procedure is also the legacy of 1982.

The conflict involved both substance and process. In terms of the latter, I have already noted that the democratization of the constitution via the charter and the consequent "entitling" of Canadians (individuals and selected groups) increasingly discredited an amendment procedure limited to eleven (male) first ministers. Perhaps the most revealing incident in the whole process was the lavish praise from fellow premiers and the Prime Minister showered on Ontario's David Peterson (in the televised "second" Accord in the late hours of June 9, 1990) for "magnanimously" offering Ontario Senate seats to clinch the "new" accord, while individual Ontarians were, on the whole, adding this initiative to the list of reasons for punishing Peterson at the polls. The Charter had more than taken root in English Canada. It was redefining what English Canada was all about and this redefinition did not include "eleven men...around a table trading legislative, judicial and executive powers as if engaged in a gentlemanly game of poker" (Deborah Coyne, cited in the Joint House/Senate Committee Report, 1987, p. 130).[7] In a sense, Meech Lake was hoist on its own petard. The essence of Meech was asymmetrical treatment for Quebec (the distinct-society clause) embedded in a symmetric ratification formula. Under the "equality" thrust of the Charter some provinces simply exercised their equality or symmetry right to defeat the Accord.

In the final analysis, it was Elijah Harper and the Natives that drove the final nail into Meech Lake, but multicultural or women's groups in English-speaking Canada would had done the same had they the opportunity. All first ministers have now recognized that the Meech process was seriously flawed.

Substance is far more complicated. Quebec's Meech Lake demands were couched more in symbol than in substance. Given the humiliation attached with the rejection of this approach, the next set of Quebec will surely be steeped in substance and will embody a conception of Canada in terms of decentralization that will go well beyond what most English Canadians deem acceptable. This is particularly the case given that the current mood outside Quebec runs exactly in the opposite direction -

towards a uniform application of the Charter throughout the land and, hence, toward a *rescinding* the notwithstanding clause. However, while concerns about the post-Meech-Lake scenarios are admittedly uppermost in some quarters, there are other concerns contributing to the general malaise in the population.

2. Fiscal-Driven Decentralization

Despite the fact that many non-Quebec Canadians tend to look to Ottawa to play a greater role, the reality of the last few years is that the federal deficit and debt burden is driving Canada into unprecedented decentralization. Leading the way here is the current two-year freeze in established programs' financing (EPF) after which the EPF growth will be GNP minus 3 per cent. Since the financing of EPF is a combination of tax transfers and cash transfers, what this means is that the tax transfer component will progressively account for more of the total transfer. Indeed, estimates suggest that cash transfers to Quebec will fall to zero before 2,000 and those for the rest of the provinces sometime before 2010.[8] Thus the roughly $8 billion of federal cash transfers will eventually fall to zero. This can be viewed as decentralizing on three counts. First, if the provinces maintain service levels by increasing their taxes, the share of provincial to federal taxes increases. Second, if the provinces react by cutting back these programs or redesigning them, this is also decentralizing in the sense that these "national" programs will progressively be designed provincially. The third reason is closely related to the second: when the federal cash transfer falls to zero, how does or can Ottawa insist on any standards at all? Less dramatic, but nonetheless significant, are the selected freezes on the Canada Assistance Plan (for the "have" provinces) and the UI strictures (which, for the poorer provinces, will transfer unfortunate citizens from "federally financed" UI to jointly-financed welfare).

All of this focuses on "expenditure-shifting" as it were. On the revenue side, the GST invades the sales tax area traditionally viewed by the provinces as their home turf. Intriguingly, there have been two polar responses to this. On the one hand, Quebec will integrate its sales tax with the GST (and will collect it for Ottawa and presumably will, at Ottawa's expense, employ Quebecers rather than "feds") and thus will take advantage of the broader base to lower its sales tax rate. On the other hand, the western provinces at the Western Premiers meeting in Lloydminster in July, 1990, have argued that the resulting revenue constraints may require that they develop, à la Quebec, their own, separate, personal income tax system (Western Finance Ministers, 1990). While this initiative has been viewed as a flexing of western muscle in the post-Meech era, it is significant to note that the twenty page document espousing a separate PIT made no mention at all of Meech. Rather it was driven by the issues and concerns raised above.

In any event, whereas the 1980-84 squeeze on intergovernmental transfers was part of an overall framework to increase federal visibility and enhance national standards, the current squeeze is fiscal-driven (and presumably unintended) and if anything will lead in the direction of increased and/or enforced provincial autonomy over the design and delivery of the social envelope.

3. FTA Implications

Somewhat related to this are two implications arising from the FTA. The first of these has to do with the political economy of east-west transfers under increasing north-south integration. As long as trade flowed largely east-west, with Ontario the principal north-south conduit, the second-round spending impacts of interregional transfers generally came to rest somewhere in Ontario. Under full north-south integration for all of Canada's regions, this may no longer be the case. Some of the regional payments imbalances with the centre will, now, shift south with the result that the second-round impacts of regional transfers may no longer come to rest in Ontario but rather in North Carolina or California. At a political level, this will surely erode support for these transfers, particularly those that privilege "place" rather than people.

This may or may not be viewed as decentralizing, but what is clear is that sheltering significant regions of the country from market forces is going to become progressively more difficult both economically and politically.

The second implication relates to north-south integration itself. What this means is that the provinces and regions will now pay more attention to their competitive position vis-à-vis their cross-border regions. Thus, the provinces will take umbrage at federal policies that for whatever reason place their economies at a disadvantage, north-south. The result may be that the provinces will demand more say in economic policy affecting their region and may imply that wage behaviour across regions will become more diverse, perhaps even to the point of having wages for federal employees based more on regional than national scales.

In economic parlance, all of this can be restated as follows: the optimal currency area is no longer the nation but the cross-border regional economies. One implication is that as north-south integration proceeds the appropriate exchange-rate policy will be one that favours fixity over flexibility. To delve into this is any detail (Courchene 1990g and Chapter 6, *this volume*) would take me too far afield. Suffice it to say that Quebec Chamber of Commerce (1990) submission to the Quebec Parliamentary

Commission on the provinces' political and constitutional futures devotes considerable time to rethinking the framework for the conduct of monetary policy.

4. Institutions in Decline

Never has the popularity of a governing party fallen so low. This in itself is raising some major concerns about the nature of representative government. In this progressively information age, where direct democracy (e.g. referenda) is now increasingly feasible and when five years is easily equivalent to several mandates earlier in this century, should there not exist mechanisms for triggering elections or at least mechanisms such as referenda where, say, the government must achieve some minimum level of support (e.g. 25%) to forestall an election? What this would mean is that the nature of "responsible government" would become two- fold: in the normal course of events it would be defined as usual (support of elective representatives) but in abnormal times the "responsibility" would also have to carry over to citizens. What generates these concerns is, of course, the GST debate. Here we have the incredibly ironic situation where the unelected Senate is attempting to reflect the democratic will of the *people* (not the elected representatives). To be sure, this does run counter to parliamentary democracy, but it does not run counter to the Constitution nor to a more general interpretation of democracy. If the Senate has any moral role in the legislative process, it is precisely at times when a government with 15% national support is attempting to push through a significant measure that roughly 80% of Canadians are against.

However, for purposes of this paper, the real issue is not the low popularity of the Tories but rather the incredible degree of cynicism that has developed with respect to our traditional institutions of national governance - the House, the Senate, national parties, executive federalism, etc. Some of this began in Mulroney's first mandate (the F-18 contract) and was certainly advanced in the more recent budget where Via Rail cuts and military closures were concentrated (perhaps unavoidably, but the issue is perception not reality) in provinces that opposed either or both of Meech Lake and free trade (N.B., Nfld. and Manitoba). More recent still, appointment of the eight special Senators runs directly counter to the aspirations of the west for Senate reform. This is particularly the case for Alberta, the principal Triple-E advocate, since the packing of the Senate is viewed by them as designed to unload the GST on Alberta. One not surprising result is the move toward regional parties, parties that *will* vote their regional (not national party) interests - Reform in Alberta, Bloc Québéçois in Quebec and COR in New Brunswick, for example, Note that a decline in the role of national parties and the rise in regional parties is somewhat similar to the earlier suggestion for more direct democracy since the allegiances of the new parties are to the regions they represent and they would bolt from any "governing coalition" on an issue of such importance as the GST.

The second result is that Mulroney Tories have by now almost completely unwound any "national reconciliation". In terms of the impending constitutional challenges, the timing could not be worse since there is literally no one in the system now who has the moral support to speak for English (or non-Quebec) Canada.[9]

5. Native Issues

With Elijah Harper in Manitoba and with the fallout from Oka/Mercier, aboriginal rights have now been catapulted to the top of the constitutional agenda, at least for English Canada. As my colleague John McDougall has noted, Canadians are finally coming to the realization that land is to the natives what language is to the Québéçois. However, there is a worrisome undertone to all of this, namely that English Canada might be privileging aboriginal rights as an instrument in the on-going Quebec-Canada clash. In this regard, Premier Rae's very strong commitment to meaningful negotiations on aboriginal issues is particularly welcome.

What all of this means is that it will be extremely difficult for English Canada to even contemplate consideration of a new set of constitutional demands from Quebec unless, among other items, aboriginal rights and issues are an integral part of the package. Meech Lake spelled the end, at least for the foreseeable future, of incremental (single-issue) constitutional change. I doubt whether Quebec realizes this or is willing to accept this - yet another challenge for the 1990s in terms of our constitutional future.

III. Global Determinism

Thus far, the thrust of the paper has been, implicitly, that the forces driving future change in federal-provincial, interprovincial or citizen-state relationships are *internal* forces. This is far too narrow a conception. Indeed, I would suggest that the forces of globalization will have more impact on the triad of relationships in the millenium than will internal factors.

Drawing very briefly from other work I have done (1990b), it seems to me that globalization and the telecomputational revolution will affect the role of national governments in at least four ways. Two of these relate to a transfer "upward" of some of the traditional functions of national governments. The first is the growing importance of transnational corporations. Unlike the old multinational corporations which entered countries subject to a host of "commitments", transnationals enter under "national treatment" conditions. Moreover, it is the transnationals (i.e. the private sector not the public sector) that are now driving globalization. This has enormous implications. For example, one can no longer meaningfully speak of a "national" production economy. Production is international and this poses major concerns for national welfare states since they were, in general, geared to "national" production machines. Second, and related, national governments are increasingly finding that activities that used to be done at the national level now have to be passed "upward", partly as countervail to the globalizing transnationals. The Bank for International Settlements (BIS) capital-adequacy rules for financial institutions are a good example. This tendency toward international regulations and international standards is bound to expand and multiply.

The two other forces pass "power" downwards. First, the information revolution is privileging citizens. They are garnering enormous power as a result and this complicates old-style governance (for unitary or federal state alike). Second, and more intriguing, globalization is spreading across the world through a network of "international cities". Nothing much has changed over the last decade in the relationship between Ottawa and Bonn, except that now it is Berlin. But much has altered in the relationship between Toronto and Frankfort. Yet our international cities (Toronto, Montreal and Vancouver) are "constitutionless". They are creatures of their respective provincial governments. This poses problems because Saskatchewan's international city is not in the province and the Maritimes international city (Boston/New York) is not even in the country.

I shall limit myself to only one implication from all of this. In the face of a diminished role in the economic and regulatory sphere for national governments, citizens will increasingly view "sovereignty" as the ability to influence how they live and work and play. One can argue whether or not this is the city or provincial government level, but under the existing distribution of powers, it is *not* the national level. Are "distinct societies" the way of the future?

What all of this brings to mind is the McLuhan vision of the "global village", or the "think globally, act locally" slogan of environmentalists. With the emphasis on markets, with the information revolution empowering citizens and with national governments attempting to "federalize", internationally, it is difficult not to view all of this as inherently decentralizing.

IV. Conclusion: The 1990s and the Constitution

No other decade in our history has had such a profound influence on our national psyche. From the perspective of 1980, we are almost unrecognizable as a society. The institutions and the compromises that brought us through our first century are now no longer in vogue, let alone tolerated. Meech Lake and its distinct society clause is the best example of all of this. In an important sense it was rooted in the spirit of the *Constitution Act, 1867* - a society struggling to maintain its identity in the face of a "sea of anglos" and seeking to secure this through a lot of symbol and a slight extension of existing substance. Implicit, if not explicit, in the Meech Lake process was an olive branch (indeed, a carte blanche) offered by Quebec to EBQ (Everybody but Quebec) - please take advantage of this opportunity to restructure yourselves in your likeness and image so you too can mount a bulwark, should you wish, against the sea of Americans. Where Meech Lake went off the rails is that EBQ never responded to this challenge. There was a period earlier this year when Premiers Filmon, Wells and McKenna could have utilized their potential Meech Lake veto, *not* to subject Quebec to this or that condition, but rather to extract a new deal in EBQ. For reasons elaborated earlier, this did not materialize. The fact remains that Quebec was, and still is, profoundly indifferent as to how EBQ restructures itself internally, provided only that Quebec acquires certain powers.

My personal view, and really the conclusion of this paper, is that this remains the real constitutional opportunity for the 1990s. No province would be happier if this would occur than Quebec. Thus, the real challenge facing EBQ is not so much to focus on what Quebec wants, but rather to focus on what the rest of us, collectively and individually, want from Canada. If we could settle on this first, then whether or not our goals are consistent with Quebec's would be clear cut. If they were, then integration between EBQ and Quebec might still be complicated in practice, but not in principle. It is in this sense that the ball is now in our court.

If the above analysis serves as a guide, however, the prospects are not good. In 1980, EBQ was incredibly apprehensive of a Quebec referendum. No longer. Setting the "we've had enough" arguments aside, there are several reasons why this is the case. Foremost among these is the FTA. The prospects of a breakup in 1980 could have been devastating in economic terms: Ontario would have been forced, literally, to plead to be the 51st state. Not so now, since we have guaranteed access to the U.S. market. But this works in "boomerang" fashion as well: with guaranteed access to the U.S., why cater to *any* Quebec proposals since, in the event of a break-up, we can always mount some sort of free-trade agreement with Quebec. Everybody in the world is doing this. Thus, the economics of a potential break-up is no longer the critical issue that it was in 1980 for EBQ (more correctly, for Ontario and the West since an independent Quebec would pose significant problems for Atlantic Canada).

Having thus set aside the economic issue for EBQ, the major change ushered in by the events of the 1980s is that EBQ has come an enormous way in terms of defining itself: we are a "Charter" nation. As I have elaborated above, at base this is quintessentially American. However, it is appropriate and important to recognize that our *value system* through which the Charter is interpreted remains, thus far at least, quite different from the American Creed. But, it is also the case that "life, liberty and the pursuit of happiness" resonates better with the Charter and the FTA than does "peace, order and good government". Phrased somewhat differently, whereas Canada was traditionally "goal oriented" while the U.S. was more "means oriented", the Charter is driving us quite dramatically in the direction of "due process" (means), perhaps at the expense of goals. Put yet another way, Quebec's approach embodies a collective rights agenda which is not only inherently goal-oriented and resonates well with "traditional" Canadian ways (crown corporations, "place" prosperity, equalization, etc.) but runs directly counter to any individualist or due-process mentality. In turn, this emphasis on due process or appropriate process is unwinding the legitimacy of the Commons, the Senate and particularly executive federalism and is finding recourse in regional parties and punishing leaders like Peterson who were actively engaged in "traditional" processes like executive federalism.

One can of course argue that the solution lies in electing a new "group" or in implementing new institutions such as a Triple-E Senate. I do not wish to argue that these are not potential solutions. But it is also critical to recognize that Canada has embarked on a wholly novel and exciting venture, namely integrating a charter society with a parliamentary society. At the underlying philosophical level, the Charter is, as yet, inconsistent with our traditional notion of Parliamentary government and is surely inconsistent in its process dimension with executive federalism and particularly with the executive-federalism amending procedure. Accommodating these institutional/philosophical conflicts is challenging enough without having them overlaid with proposals from Quebec which will surely be seen as seeking special status. But this is our fate in the 1990's.

Two final comments are in order. The first is that under the influence of the charter and the amending formulas (particularly in Meech but also in the *Constitution Act 1982*), there is a view emerging in EBQ that the appropriate conception of constitutional federalism is one that has identical powers across all provinces, i.e., symmetrical federalism. Apart from the fact that this represents an incredibly reconstructionist view of our 120 years of history, it may be a recipe for disaster. Quebec will argue for, and in my view requires, some powers that would be patently foolish to give to all other provinces. Consider manpower or human-capital policy. It may have gone unnoticed, but Quebec has long had substantial control in this area and in any set of proposals it will probably want even more

control. How does EBQ respond? Symmetry is a non-starter: no one
would suggest that my home province, Saskatchewan, ought to have its
own, independent, human capital policy. One logical response to symmetry is for the west and Atlantic to merge themselves into "regional"
provinces: a human capital policy for Canada west and Atlantic Canada
may make sense, but not along existing provincial lines. Thus, if
symmetry is to prevail it implies a realignment such that the new provinces
have a sufficient economic and population base to meaningfully utilize
such powers. Premier McKenna's recent proposal for, effectively, Maritime economic union might be best viewed in this context.

However, this degree of change is unlikely in the near future. Elsewhere (1990b and Chapter 3, *this volume*), I have argued that there is an
alternative approach to the symmetry issue. Allow all provinces equal
powers (symmetry in principle) but then let EBQ utilize section 94[10] of the
constitution to "pass upward" some of these powers, either to Ottawa or
to an EBQ "super level" (i.e. in asymmetry in fact). This is "opting in",
in contrast to the Quebec's "opting out" which generated much of our
existing asymmetry and which is (apparently) no longer acceptable. I
believe that this is more than a gimmick: it incorporates a conscious
exercise in constitution-making on the part of EBQ and, as important, this
procedure is rooted, not in some novel recommendation, but right in the
original BNA Act.

The second observation relates to Quebec. EBQ will have substantial
trouble with the request for greater powers on the part of Quebec. After
all, isn't this the province that went through not one, but two, societal
revolutions since 1960 - the Quiet Revolution and what I have referred to
as "market nationalism" (1989 and Chapter 1, *this volume*)? Moreover,
Quebec has gone its own way in terms of tax policy, financial institutions,
the role of the "caisse", and laws relating to language and culture. And
now, thanks largely to Quebec, we have the FTA. So the question in EBQ
becomes: given that Quebec has been able to do *all of this under the
existing constitution*, how can they be dissatisfied? Do they not already
have a version of sovereignty association, albeit within the constitutional
framework? Are not any additional demands really disguised demands for
separation, in which case they will be never-ending?

These are indeed critical questions. I have no answers but I do have
some responses. First of all, the fact that Quebec was excluded from 1982
was not a major issue for Quebecers (as distinct from their government),
at that time. They were engaged elsewhere, developing their entrepreneurial class and information networks in French. Even at the time of
Meech Lake, much less than 10% of Quebecers had any interest in the
substance or process. (Moreover, Quebecers paid much *less* attention to
the substance of Meech Lake than did the rest of Canadians). The Quebec

Government was concerned, however, and I think the reason was that the Charter- cum-constitution had potential for not only restricting future Quebec accomplishments on the cultural-socio-economic front but as well for rolling back *existing* accomplishments. With hindsight, even if Quebec was excluded from 1982, it would have been useful to "grandfather" the sorts of initiatives that they had been undertaking unless they ran directly counter to the Charter. This has always been my personal rationale for supporting Meech - enshrining the "distinct society" clause would allow Quebec to continue its dramatic post-1960 evolution. It is in this sense that Meech was really more about symbol than substance, since it was not immediately evident, even to Quebecers, *where* and *how* the *Constitution Act 1982* would bite.

But EBQ rejected this symbolism. Now the name of the game has altered dramatically. Quebec is forced to restate its case *in terms of substance*. This is going to be difficult for Quebec. The tendency will clearly be to cast the net quite broadly. Added to this is the fact that Quebec will not want to place itself once again in the Meech Lake position where there is no fallback position. Thus, unlike in Meech Lake, Quebec will *not* table a set of *minimal* demands.

My second general comment is that Quebec was humiliated by the Meech Lake process. In 1980, Quebec said yes to Canada. In EBQ's "referendum" (Meech Lake), EBQ said no to Quebec. Earlier, I noted that the FTA among other things implied that EBQ would be less concerned (than in 1980) with an independent Quebec. The reverse is also true. The remarkable "épanouissement" of the Quebec business sector during the 1980s engendered a sense of confidence across all Quebecers that they could "go it alone" if EBQ was unresponsive to their concerns.

My last comment in this context is at the heart of the pending Quebec-EBQ impasse. The next round of Quebec proposals will be driven largely from a business/economic/global perspective, with of course due recognition to language and culture. The co-chairmen of the parliamentary committee are (for the Liberals) Michel Belanger, retiring chairman of the National Bank and (for the P.Q.) Jean Campeau, retiring chairman of the Caisse de dépôt, by far the largest investment fund in the country. They may have differing political ideologies when it comes to the appropriate "constitutional" setting for Quebec within North America, but they are unlikely to differ much in terms of the nature of the measures required to ensure that Quebec remains viable economically in the FTA and global context. Moreover, Bourassa's own statement on June 23, 1990, was that Quebec would not embark on any venture that would endanger the economic livelihood of Quebecors. Hence, what will emanate from Quebec in the new year is an economics-driven agenda.

However, unless things change markedly, our response will be a *socio-political response,* conditional largely by the values of the Charter.[11]   Canadians are caught in a time warp.   English Canada and particularly Ontario, is only now going through its own "Quiet Revolution".   Quebec knows where it wants to go and is determined to get there, Canada notwithstanding.   EBQ is still wrestling with where it wants to go. Part of the problem here is that EBQ, and particularly Ontario, has always been so well-positioned economically that the sorts of global economic concerns that influence Quebec elites have never permeated the minds of Ontario citizens.   And if they did, this is what Ottawa is for, isn't it? Queen's Park plays nowhere near the role for Ontario-based business that Quebec-city plays for Quebec-based business.

In any event, the underlying message is that it would be a tragedy of monumental magnitude to reject an economics-driven package from Quebec on the basis of socio-political concerns only to realize a decade or so down the road that British Columbia, too, wants a similar package of "distinct society" proposals because it is fully Rim oriented and, perhaps, largely Pacific Rim peopled.

In lieu of a formal conclusion, I want simply to reiterate some of the major forces that will be at play in the 1990s.   First and foremost, we must be aware of the way that global forces are shaping not only Canada but all nation states.   I may be wrong to suggest that these forces imply a declining role for national governments and an increasing degree of consumer and citizen "sovereignty", but I am not wrong to suggest that it is utter folly to swim against the globalization tide.   In this context, EBQ may aspire to a stronger role for the federal government, but if this is the case it must be a *different* role than Ottawa has traditionally played.   And it behooves EBQ to begin defining this new role now.   Second, Quebec and Ontario (and perhaps EBQ as well) are at quite different phases of socio/political/ economic philosophy.   Quebec has had its cultural or Quiet Revolution whereas Ontario is only beginning.   The challenge here is, somehow, to see the future through all of this when evaluating any new constitutional proposals.   Third, even if the Charter may be "Americanizing", the fact is that Canadians not only have a markedly different value system than the Americans but this is an integral part of what defines us as a society.   Yet much of this value system has been conditioned over the years by the role of Quebec in the federation - regional policy, equalization, multiculturalism. Both the FTA and globalization are exerting enormous pressure on this value system.   Before we jettison Quebec (and its likely outlandish demands, come next spring) we should be sure that we have put in place some mechanisms to anchor these values.

This leads me to the final point of the paper.   Observers of the Quebec scene have a reasonable bead on the nature of the demands that will emanate from that province over the next year or so - control over manpower, telecommunications, language, culture, perhaps R and D, plus a significant "disentanglement" in terms of overlapping functions, etc. On the surface, the issues in play in EBQ will be "symmetry", the Charter and centralization/ decentralization. However, in order that these proposals can be fully addressed EBQ must begin the admittedly difficult process of sorting out its own cultural/economic priorities vis-à-vis Quebec, the Americans and the rest of the world and the reference point for all of this must be the year 2,000 or beyond and not 1990 or 1991. Quebec is conveniently providing the window of opportunity for precisely this exercise.

Endnotes

* This paper was prepared for and presented at the University of Saskatchewan Conference "After Meech Lake," sponsored by the College of Law and the Department of Political Studies, Saskatoon, 1-3 November 1990. It is a pleasure to acknowledge the many conversations with, and comments from, John McDougall in the preparation of this paper. Robert Young also contributed valuable suggestions.

1. It may seem ironic that although FIRA was established in 1973, it did not become a high-profile bilateral issue until 1982. As Leyton Brown (1985, p. 33) notes:

    FIRA and the NEP came to be referred to in a single breath for three reasons: first, because of FIRA's apparent association with the NEP; second, because of the cumulative effect of FIRA's recent regulatory practices; and third, because the Canadian government's announced intention of broadening and expanding FIRA's powers in a fashion the United States saw as discriminatory.

    These "intentions" were advanced in the 14 April 1980 Throne Speech and included expanding FIRA's powers to publicize foreign takeover bids, to seek Canadian counterbidders, and to conduct performance reviews of existing foreign-owned companies (Ibid, p. 41). Canada eventually backed off these intentions.

2. One important aspect of this is the degree to which the Canadian Supreme Court relies on U.S. decisions in adjudicating cases under the Charter. (See Manfredi, 1990.)

3. The intent is not to argue that the trend toward provincial equality stems from the Charter. Clearly, the emergence of the principle of equality of provinces can be traced to such events as the return of control over public lands to the western provinces, the evolution of the various amending formula toward equality and the movement toward a "Triple E" Senate. Milne (1990) traces this evolution of provincial symmetry. The point in the text is that the Charter enhanced this vision of equality, particularly in terms of the opposition to the distinct society clause in Meech.

4. Presumably in order to rectify this, one year to the day after the November 1981, Constitutional Accord, Trudeau launched the *Royal Commission on the Economic Union and Development Prospects for Canada.* While this (Macdonald) Commission's final report did endorse the notion of a Canadian economic union, it did anything but embrace the 1980-84 nationalist, centralist-interventist agenda. Opting for free trade ran directly counter to economic nationalism and the focus on "people prosperity" rather than "place prosperity" ran counter to the notion of a centralist-interventionist federal government. This is further evidence to the effect that the Trudeau agenda had generated powerful countervailing forces.

5. To be fair, Trudeau's "Second Coming" also took Atlantic Canada's concerns into account. Section 36 of the *Constitution Act, 1982* enshrined equalization as well as provisions for equalizing regional opportunities. Moreover, the 1982 Nova Scotia energy accord went some direction toward recognizing Nova Scotia's interests, but nowhere near as far as the Atlantic Accord, especially after taking account of the 1984 Supreme Court decision.

6. For further discussion, see Watts and Brown (1990, Chapter 1- 3).

7. This provides yet another perspective from which to assess the "rolling of the dice" analogy utilized by Mulroney in the dying moments of Meech.

8. Quebec has long received extra personal-income-tax points in lieu of cash transfers for post-secondary education funding. Thus, its cash transfers fall to zero before cash transfers to other provinces.

9. It is not obvious that the federal government could, even in the best of times, legally or constitutionally speak for English Canada since it also represents Quebec. As one commentator put it recently, Ottawa

speaks for ten provinces and each provincial government can speak for only one. Thus, there is no formal or legal constitutional institution that can speak for EBQ (everybody but Quebec).

10. Section 94 reads as follows:

> 94. Notwithstanding anything in this Act, the Parliament of Canada may make Provision for the Uniformity of all or any of the Laws relative to Property and Civil Rights in Ontario, Nova Scotia, and New Brunswick, and of the Procedure or all or any of the Courts in Those Three Provinces, and from and after the passing of any Act in that Behalf the Power of the Parliament of Canada to make Laws in relation to any Matter comprised in any such Act shall, notwithstanding anything in this Act, be unrestricted; but any Act of the Parliament of Canada making Provision for such Uniformity shall not have any effect in any Province unless and until it is adopted and enacted as law by the legislation thereof.

Frank Scott argues that the role of this provision was to allow the original non-Quebec provinces (and future non-Quebec provinces as well) to "centralize" if and when conditions became more favourable. (See LaSelva, 1983).

11. To be sure, there may be issues on which a socio-political response is fully appropriate. However, what I have in mind here is, for example, an adherence on the part of EBQ to a strong role for Ottawa (in the face of a decentralized Quebec agenda) when the thrust of global forces is *also* decentralizing.

Appendix Table:
Political/Economic Factors
Conditioning the 1980s Constitutional Climate

Date	March of Events		Federal/Provincial Implications	Interprovincial Implications	Implications for Citizen/State Relationships
	Political	Economic			
Panel A: Trudeau's Second Coming					
Dawn of 1980s	Clark Interregnum	Resource Boom	Clark Tories willing to accommodate west in terms of Energy Prices. (Decentralization)	Economic centre of gravity moving west.	Demands rising to share Alberta's rents.
Feb. 1980	Trudeau's second coming		Appeal to Canadians, not provinces. Campaign against Clark's decentralist/privatization agenda.	Ontario lowers boom on Alberta. Premier Davis' words (not premier himself) feature prominently in Liberal campaign.	Final campaign swing through Ontario reveals nationalist/interventionist philosophy. Beginning of rift between business and Ontario government.
April 1980	FIRA proposals in Throne Speech		Beginning of economic nationalism.	Another Ontario First policy. (Canadians do not have enough confidence to invest outside Ontario).	Increasing concern by business about anti-U.S. policy.
May 1980	"No" forces win Referendum		Trudeau promises "le fédéralisme renouvelé."	Provinces anticipate enhanced powers under renewed federalism.	Canadians breathe sigh of relief.
Summer 1980	1980-82 constitutional negotiations begin		"Economic Union" (Internal Common Market) provision very centralizing. Provinces caught by surprise.	Provinces view Ontario's support of Trudeau's package to be Ontario First policy (Economic union gives Ontario access to Energy projects). Ontario also argues for protecting domestic market from foreigners.	"Peoples package" (Charter and Economic Union) appeals to Canadians. Represents the beginning of people vs. provinces clash that eventually rises to fore at end of decade.
Fall 1980	NEP (Budget)	NEP	Ottawa pre-empts western energy rents and transfers them to Canadians via lower-than-world prices. Diverts activity (via subsidies) from west to "Canada lands."	Viewed by west as an Ontario-Ottawa conspiracy. Strengthens west (Alberta)–Quebec axis, since Quebec supports west's position.	Raises issue of whether Canada is about people or provinces. Business community very concerned about anti-American aspects of NEP as well as interventionism (e.g., the "back-in" and the Canadian content provisions). Business concerned further by MacEachen's 1981 Budget and its retroactive provisions.

Appendix Table (continued)

Date	March of Events — Political	March of Events — Economic	Federal/Provincial Implications	Interprovincial Implications	Implications for Citizen/State Relationships
1981	Neo-conservatism (Reagan, 1981; Thatcher, 1979)		Canada way off side vis-à-vis rest of world.	Resonates more with Canada west than with Ontario (especially in light of NEP).	Astonishing degree of antagonism towards Reagan philosophy, at least as reflected in *Globe and Mail* op. ed. pages.
April 1981	Re-election of PQ		Stage is set for clash over the constitution.	Quebec's embracing of an economic agenda will create substantial problems for other provinces (e.g., financial deregulation).	PQ drops sovereignty, pushes economic agenda. Beginning of Quebec's embracing of the international economy, which culminates in overwhelming free trade support in 1988 election.
Fall 1981-Spring 1982	Midnight Accord and *Constitution Act, 1982*		The "gang of ten" isolates Quebec and patriates the constitution. The west is brought in by a resource taxation amendment and the Notwithstanding Clause. Newfoundland obtains provisions for preferential hiring for off-shore employment. Thus, the "economic union" beginnings of the 1980-82 constitution process are sacrificed to repatriate the constitution, replete with the Charter. Quebec invokes notwithstanding clause for all its legislation and withdraws from all further constitutional conferences.	Amending formula for most items is 7 provinces and 50 percent of population plus federal government. Quebec "loses" veto here. However, for certain items, unanimity is required. This advances the concept of provincial equality (symmetry).	The constitution is "democratized." Aboriginals, linguistic minorities, multicultural groups, women (gender equality) have rights enshrined via Charter. Most significant constitutional change since Confederation. Flags fly at half-mast in Quebec City, but Quebec citizens largely indifferent, pursuing "market nationalism."
1981+		1981-82 recession and then auto-led recovery in Ontario and collapse of energy and raw material prices.	Interest rates peak at over 20 percent in depths of recession. Federal deficit mushrooms. The 6 and 5 program initiated. Ottawa pares back transfers to provinces.	Ontario again king of the castle. Reverses 1970s and early 1980s where resource provinces acquired power. West falls upon hard times.	Severity of recession increases citizen attachment to transfer system.
1984	Canada Health Act		Arguably, the apex of Trudeau centralization. Ottawa will control standards and aspects of medicare. Unanimous commons support, despite opposition of several provinces.	Several provinces incensed. Lays groundwork for spending power provision in Meech Lake.	Triumph for "national programs." Citizens ignore constitution and look to Ottawa, not provinces, for maintenance of social programs.

Appendix Table (continued)

Date	March of Events		Federal/Provincial Implications	Interprovincial Implications	Implications for Citizen/State Relationships
	Political	Economic			
1984+		Record U.S. Twin Deficits (Fiscal and trade)	Concern over fiscal deficits does not spread to Canada. Will create problems later. Fall in Canadian dollar enhances our penetration of U.S. markets. - Fuels U.S. protectionism vs. Canada.	Ontario "spends" fiscal dividend unlike Alberta in '70s which banked its fiscal dividend in the Heritage Fund. Later, this forced the Bank of Canada to use high interest rates across Canada to control "Ontario" inflation.	Record balance of payments deficits leads to protectionist sentiment in U.S. Trading status quo in danger particularly in light of U.S. view of FIRA and NEP.
Panel B: Mulroney I.					
Sept. 1984	Mulroney Election		Business agenda (deficits and patching up relations with the Americans) and reconciliation agenda (with west in terms of NEP and with Quebec in terms of 1982 constitution). Focus switches away from citizen interests toward provincial interests. Overall agenda is decentralist.	Development of Quebec-west Axis. But Tories also have 70 percent of seats in each region. Arguably, Mulroney government proves to be least responsive to Ontario's concerns in this century.	Citizen-state relationships alter dramatically. Tory concern is more with provinces (federalism) than with citizens. And at citizen level, interest centres on business rather than the "ordinary citizen" (as in Canada Health Act). Turner's patronage appointments are major factor in election. Voters anticipate new approach from Tories who deliver, initially, with the appointment of Stephen Lewis as UN ambassador.
1985	Western and Atlantic Accords		Resurrection of cooperative federalism.	Resource provinces gain greater control.	Little reaction, since easy to move to market pricing when resource prices are depressed.
1985-87	Abortive Aboriginal Constitutional Deliberations		Negotiations on an amendment for aboriginal self-government break down.	Quebec not at constitutional table.	Citizen involvement and concern minimal. Aboriginal loss here will reverberate on Meech Lake, although through unanticipated channels (Elijah Harper in Manitoba).
1987	Meech Lake Accord		Unexpected unanimous agreement on integrating Quebec fully in the constitutional family. Viewed by Ottawa as historic compromise, not only with respect to 1982, but 1867 as well.	Initially, highpoint of Mulroney's reconciliation efforts. Atmosphere among premiers close to euphoria. Three year ratification process proves too long to ensure passage. Several provinces initiate hearings.	Initial citizen reaction positive, but not euphoric. As process proceeds, Charter enshrined groups (women, aboriginals, multicultural groups, etc.) gain strength and challenge the legitimacy of a ratification procedure that rests solely within the realm of executive federalism.

Appendix Table (continued)

Date	March of Events		Federal/Provincial Implications	Interprovincial Implications	Implications for Citizen/State Relationships
	Political	Economic			
1987+	FTA and 1988 Election		Tories sign FTA with U.S. 1988 election on FTA won, thanks to overwhelming Quebec support. Opposed by Ontario, PEI and Manitoba, although business interests deliver much of Ontario in 1988 election. The western provinces, historical free-trade advocates, very lukewarm to FTA, except Alberta. Reflected in election results. FTA transfers aspects of Canadian sovereignty upward to FTA tribunals. As of 1 January 1989, Tories have a full mandate with no electoral commitments.	For Quebec, FTA is just one more step in direction of "market nationalism." Alberta views FTA as guarantee against NEP.	1988 election fought on "class" lines. BCNI very active and successful, particularly in Ontario. Surprisingly, NDP not a factor in this "class" conflict. Individual Canadians express concern about social programs. (Viewed as essential component of glue that binds our polity).

Panel C: Mulroney II.

Date	March of Events		Federal/Provincial Implications	Interprovincial Implications	Implications for Citizen/State Relationships
	Political	Economic			
1 Jan. 1989		FTA	Emphasis on markets is "decentralizing" in the important sense that all levels of government are constrained. Although the FTA applies largely to the federal government, the provinces will eventually be equally bound. The Supreme Court is likely to be quite intolerant of interprovincial barriers now that there is Canada-U.S. free trade.	Support for the east-west transfer system will likely decline now that economic integration along north-south lines will increase. In the limit, as north-south integration proceeds, the Canadian regions will likely become less integrated east-west.	The "life, liberty and pursuit of happiness" of the U.S. Constitution resonates more with the FTA than the "peace, order and good government" rhetoric of the Canadian constitution. Thus, the FTA (by emphasizing markets) and the Charter (by introducing the Courts into our Parliamentary system) introduce powerful "Americanizing" influences into Canadian politics and governance. The challenge is to maintain a Canadian polity in the presence of a north-south economy.
1987-89	Election of new premiers		New Brunswick (McKenna, Oct. 87), Newfoundland (Wells, April 1989) and Manitoba (Filmon, April 1988) have new premiers. Since they were not signatories to Meech Lake, they do not feel bound by the agreement.	Beginning of provincial split over Meech.	Individual Canadians delighted to find new avenues for combatting Meech Lake. Premier Wells, in particular, is literally overwhelmed by anti-Meech Lake "support" from non-Newfoundland Canadians.

Appendix Table (continued)

Date	March of Events		Federal/Provincial Implications	Interprovincial Implications	Implications for Citizen/State Relationships
	Political	Economic			
1989-1990	Erosion of National Reconciliation		Tories begin process of alienating almost everyone. 1989 budget punishes anti-free-trade provinces (PEI and Manitoba) and anti-Meech Lake province (NB) in terms of military base cuts and Via Rail cuts.	7-3 split develops over Meech.	National debates, such as that over the FTA, inevitably generate opposition. These measures, however, introduced a conception of cynicism, if not vengefulness, on the part of the Mulroney Tories. Opposition is particularly strong in the west (particularly Alberta) which promotes both Senate reform and the Reform Party.
Dec. 1989+	Bill 178 and the use of the Notwithstanding Clause		In wake of Supreme Court judgment, Bourassa utilizes notwithstanding clause, to promote use of French in terms of commercial signs. Mulroney and other original Meech signatories hold firm to Meech Accord. Begin to speak of "disaster" scenarios if Meech fails.	Reaction in rest of Canada stuns Quebec. Manitoba, for example, rethinks Meech policy. Somewhat later, i.e., over Charest Report "Bloc Québécois" is launched, supported passively at least by the Montreal business community.	For citizens, Meech becomes a lightning rod for all manner of concerns about Mulroney Tories. Anti-French sympathies materialize, particularly in Ontario. More substantively, many Canadians and some premiers adopt positions that all Canadians and all provinces ought to be treated equally. Influence of Charter is evident here.
23 June 1990	Meech Lake Fails		"Second Meech Accord" falls apart under pressure from Manitoba (Elijah Harper) and Newfoundland. However, supposed negative capital markets implications of Meech do not materialize. Both Michael Wilson and Premier Bourassa move to calm international capital.	Tumultuous St. Jean Baptiste Day Parade in Quebec. Later, Bloc Québécois sweeps by-election. Quebec constitutes two commissions to propose new constitutional arrangements. Suggests that in future it will deal with "Canada" only on a one-to-one basis. But who speaks for Canada? Ottawa and provinces contemplate their own constitutional commissions.	In a sense, triumph for Charter and "symmetrical" federalism.
Summer 1990	Oka/Mercier		Deflates sovereignty balloon. Raises general question of role of aboriginals in any Quebec constitutional alternative. Catapults native rights into forefront.	Focus is on Quebec, but substantial implications for other provinces since most aboriginal claims are outside Quebec. In general, citizens outside Quebec more tolerant of Native demands.	Extremely complicated impasse, but probably the case that citizens outside Quebec become less tolerant of Quebec demands, constitutional or otherwise.

Appendix Table (continued)

Date	March of Events		Federal/Provincial Implications	Interprovincial Implications	Implications for Citizen/State Relationships
	Political	Economic			
1990-		Monetary Policy	High interest rates and an overvalued dollar lead initially to charges that the rest of Canada is fighting the Ontario-triggered inflation. Later, even Ontario suffers from tight money.	Quebec Chamber of Commerce report to the Quebec parliamentary commission on the constitution argues for substantial changes in the structure of the Bank of Canada.	Business increasingly concerned that the overvalued Canadian dollar is converting the FTA opportunity into an economic nightmare.
1990		GST and Senate Appointments	Ottawa pushes GST in spite of overwhelming opposition from provinces and Canadians. Quebec finally comes on side in anticipation that it can collect and administer the federal tax. Senate threatens to withhold approval. Mulroney begins stacking Senate.	Packing of Senate stymies Senate reform process. Quebec-west axis weakens as Quebec supports GST.	Incredible cynicism pervades country. Senate appointments deflate western hopes for a reformed Senate.
1990-		Globalization	Ongoing globalization has substantial ramifications for the future of national governments. Powers transferred "upwards" to transnational governmental bodies and to supra-national governmental bodies and "downwards" to consumers via the information revolution and an emphasis on markets.	Emphasis on markets likely to make regional transfers more difficult in future. Regions likely to become more independent of each other.	As globalization erodes role of national governments, citizens likely to pay more attention to community governments. How one organizes the way in which one lives and works and plays is about all that remains in terms of sovereignty. And for this the local governments are as important as national governments.
Dawn of 1990s			No obvious leader anywhere in English Canada that can command national respect. Spells trouble for dealing with pending Quebec proposals. For the first time in constitutional debates the federal government finds itself as a player rather than an umpire since a more decentralized federation is among the range of possibilities.	Quebec again withdraws from first ministers' conferences. Bob Rae wins Ontario election. Citizen reaction to Meech Lake and executive federalism? Beginning of new approach to politics and policies?	Major conflicts developing. Non-Quebec citizens increasingly influenced by Charter and its implications for equal treatment across citizens and provinces. Particularly concerned about the existence of notwithstanding clause. But western premiers, for example, are demanding greater powers. Is federalism a system for "provinces" (Mulroney) or "people" (Trudeau and Charter)? In either of these, the Atlantic provinces are the most vulnerable. Not surprisingly, NB Premier McKenna is now promoting closer economic integration for the three Maritime provinces.

3. The Community of the Canadas

I. INTRODUCTION

After my initial surprise and, I would admit, pleasure in being included among the "experts" requested to submit papers to *La Commission sur l'avenir politique et constitutionnel du Québec,* the challenge became one of what I could usefully contribute to a process that appears, from my vantage point, to be a societal celebration in full anticipation of a "birth of a nation."[1] I am obviously not a "Québécois." Moreover, although my family was part of the francophone "diaspora" — west in our case — and finally settled in the heart of Louis Riel territory (Batoche and Duck Lake, Saskatchewan) I do not include myself as part of "les francophones hors Québec." In terms of professional credentials, my training has been in economics and my research has, with some exceptions, been concentrated in the general area of the political economy of federal-provincial fiscal and economic relations. In the last decade or so, I have (for a non-Quebecer) written rather widely on the initiatives and achievements of Quebec society. If my colleagues both in Quebec and elsewhere in Canada are a guide, my writings on Quebec are generally viewed as pro-Quebec. Nonetheless, I clearly remain an outsider to the process of the Parliamentary Commission and I would classify myself as a Canadian first and only then an Ontarian or, preferably, a Saskatchewanian, if such a word exists. More to the point, my overall perspective is that if one incorporates the economic future into the political/cultural future of Quebec, then there exist internal restructurings of Canada that are preferable for Canada *and* for Quebec than a series of two or more independent nations on the upper half of the North American continent. I raise these points relating to my underlying perspective because there is, in my view, no such thing as "expert" (i.e., independent) commentary on an issue that is so caught up in emotion and in political/ economic risk, indeed uncertainty.

With these caveats in mind, the core of this submission is a radical proposal for the restructuring of Canada. I have entitled it the "Community of the Canadas." It is modelled after aspects of the European Community model, although it does not embody full sovereignty. The "Community" refers to the federal level, that is, Ottawa (or Brussels if the European Economic Community comparison is made) while the "Canadas" refer to the five designated "nations" comprising the community: Canada West, Canada East, Quebec, Ontario and the First Nations/Territories. This model is potentially very decentralizing, at least as far as Quebec is concerned. Moreover, it would give Quebec and other provinces control over culture and language in their areas of jurisdiction. It would replace the Senate with a Federal Council or Community Council where, for example, Quebec's representation on this Council could come from the National Assembly, if it so wished. In other words, it integrates "sovereignty" and "association" but wholly in the context of what is essentially a federal model (with a few confederal trappings). At the same time the model is completely flexible in terms of the rest-of-Canada (ROC). For example, the ROC status quo could prevail indefinitely. Thus, it maximizes the likelihood of acceptance by Canadians outside Quebec. However, I cannot say whether they, let alone Quebec, will find it acceptable.

My concept of a Community of the Canadas, may fall short in terms of the full sovereignty aspirations of many, perhaps a majority of, Quebecers. However, it does offer a political and economic environment within which the recent impressive achievements of Quebec on the social, cultural and economic front can continue to evolve and, indeed, flourish.

The first half of the paper is really background to my proposal. Briefly, the next section reviews the rather remarkable achievements of Quebec society over the last 30 years — achievements that are the envy of most if not all other provinces. The second background section reviews the implications for federal-provincial relations and in particular centralization versus decentralization emanating from selected changes in the global and domestic economies. In a word, the trend is towards greater decentralization.

As a bridge between the background material and the Community of the Canadas model, there is a section that focuses on what I believe to be the worst possible strategy for Quebec — namely an *early* unilateral declaration of independence (UDI) with the intent of then negotiating "re-association." This surely will, as its proponents claim, wake up English Canada. This may make sense on the political front. But, upon awakening, English-speaking Canadians will discover that the UDI has also threatened their economic future. In my view, re-association except under

GATT-type arrangements will become virtually impossible, which will in turn endanger both Quebec and Canada over the long term, not just during the transition to new arrangements. My perspective here is that it would be quite out of character for a society that has accomplished so much in the last few decades and that has placed so much emphasis on securing a successful economic future to opt for a solution or process that will likely embody a degree of irreversibility that has an excellent chance of unwinding both Quebec and Canada not only economically but on political/cultural grounds as well. For all our warts — Brockville, Sault Ste. Marie and the demise of Meech — we English Canadians believe in Canada and this, of necessity, means believing in Quebec. Although not music to the ears of Quebec sovereigntists, English Canada remains Quebec's best (only?) ally and contrary to what may appear in the Quebec press (*and* parts of the English Canada press) English Canadian elites are generally, perhaps wholly, sympathetic to Quebec aspirations within the context of an integrated Canada. An early UDI would destroy this.

This, then, leads me to my very radical proposal for a complete rethinking and reworking of Canada. I might add that underlying this proposal is the following two-pronged goal that, as an outsider, I have assumed to be appropriate for Quebec:

    i) "Québécois" must have the freedom to configure their society so that they can earn a North-American living standard operating in French;

    ii) These arrangements must be sustainable over time and they must be designed in such a manner that they are politically, culturally, and symbolically acceptable to all Quebecers.

While my Community of the Canadas may fall short in the eyes (and hearts) of Quebecers and other Canadians, it is motivated by these two principles in terms of Quebec as well as an equivalent set of principles for Canadians outside Quebec that address their own important and often long-standing concerns. In particular, it offers a degree of flexibility and manoeuvrability to recast their society or societies in their own likeness and image. This is critical because Quebec is not the only region or society that desires, indeed deserves, a "better deal" from Canada.

I now turn to the first of the background sections — the series of remarkable achievements by Quebec on the socio/political/economic front.

II. L'EPANOUISSEMENT DU QUEBEC

Over the last 30 years Quebec has undergone not one, but two, societal transformations — "la révolution tranquille" of the 1960s and what I have elsewhere (1989 and Chapter 1, *this volume*) referred to as "market nationalism" of the 1980s.[2] This is a remarkable achievement for any society,[3] particularly one that now views the constitutional framework under which these transformations took place as somehow threatening any future evolution. In order to provide some necessary background for the ensuing analysis of Quebec's constitutional options, I shall attempt (at the risk of not only oversimplification but also misrepresentation) to isolate from an economic perspective some key features of each of these societal transformations.

A. The Quiet Revolution

From the Quiet Revolution I would select three elements, all related. The first is the process of secularization, the high- profile aspect of which was to transfer all aspects of social and education policy from the church to the state (and epitomized by institutional changes like the creation of a provincial Ministry of Education). The second was the conception that further social and economic progress for Quebecers would require the active participation of the state — both as socio-economic legislator and as entrepreneur. Enter the period of active "state capitalism." From this, the third almost followed directly — the nationalization of Quebec Hydro, wrapped in the "maîtres chez nous" rhetoric of Lesage and Lévesque. Nationalizing Hydro accomplished a multitude of goals, not the least of which was the provision of a significant opportunity for French-speaking Quebecers to occupy the upper-management echelons of a major corporation. Quebec Hydro remains to this day absolutely critical to the development prospects for Quebec. Moreover, Lavalin and SNC, both world-class engineering firms, are examples of leading-edge enterprises spun off from Hydro's activities.

As part of the Quiet Revolution, the best and the brightest of the young Quebecers flocked to the civil service. One result was that Quebec came to possess the most professional provincial civil service, which arguably remains true to this day. Moreover, because of Quebec's opting-out policies, its civil service acquired expertise over a range of areas much broader than those of the other provinces. This became very evident in the discussions over Canada's public pension system where Quebec's input not only influenced the structure of the CPP but then the province opted for its own QPP, replete with the Caisse de dépôt. Finally an important adjunct of the Quiet Revolution was the Trudeau Liberals' policy of official bilingualism and particularly of a bilingual federal civil service. While I recognize fully the philosophical rift between a territorial and a pan-Canadian approach to bilingualism, it is nonetheless the case that in this time frame the official-languages policy played a critical role in expanding the boundaries within which Quebecers and indeed all Canadians could operate in French. To be sure, these policies did generate a backlash in some quarters of English Canada — Brockville and Sault Ste.

Marie are the most recent manifestations. But what tends to be overlooked is the other side of the coin, namely that thousands of English Canadians enrolled in French immersion programs. Quebecers should realize, even if they do not appreciate, that this represented a willing accommodation on the part of English Canadians to what they *perceived* to be their own best interests *and* the best interests of Quebec and Canada. Moreover, it laid the basis for the understanding and acceptance of Bill 101.

While obviously central in its own right, Bill 101 was really the link between the two transformations. Under the economic perspective adopted here, Bill 101 was not so much a cultural and linguistic measure as it was an economic one — French as the language of work. With the civil service no longer able to absorb the new wave of graduating Quebecers, Bill 101 ensured that they now had easier access to the upper echelons, and to the board rooms, of multiprovincial and multinational enterprises operating in Quebec. Business schools rather than law and public administration progressively began to attract young Québécois.

Then came the referendum. Support for separatism was probably already on the wane. But the victory of the "NO" forces had a massive cathartic impact on Quebecers. Virtually immediately, independence became a non-issue. So did further politicization of major policy issues. Culturally and linguistically confident, in firm control over the functions of state, and now in senior management positions in large enterprises, Quebecers took the logical next step in the process of gaining greater mastery over their economic destiny, namely seeking equity control of small and medium-sized enterprises and ensuring that selected key institutions facilitated this new venture. Enter the series of initiatives introduced by the Parti Québécois (PQ). State capitalism was giving way to peoples' capitalism.

B. Market Nationalism

The post-1980 message of Lévesque, Parizeau and company was clear — get the economics on side for its own sake and also in anticipation of a future referendum. To accomplish this it would in turn be essential to:
- build a much stronger corporate base;
- begin to put Quebec's fiscal house in order;
- develop a self-sustaining financial-institution network;
- decrease dependency on and economic ties to Ottawa and the rest of Canada (e.g., free trade);
- encourage self-reliance and an outward-looking mentality.

Not surprisingly, perhaps, this *was* the PQ agenda, post-referendum. Moreover, and consistent with the evolutionary thrust of this analysis, on the economics front it *remains* the agenda of the Bourassa Liberals.

The role of the state in Quebec has not so much been diminished as transformed. *L'État enterpreneur* has given way to *l'État catalyseur*. Thus, the essence of market nationalism was that the principal avenue by which Quebec would secure its long-term economic viability would be by a dynamic outward-looking private sector owned and controlled by Quebecers but aided and abetted by the state.

Further evidence that the Quiet Revolution's emphasis on the state and that market nationalism's emphasis on the private sector are part of the same evolutionary continuum is that many of Quebec's leading business-men and entrepreneurs today were in the public sector during the Quiet Revolution (or, more generally, prior to the market nationalism thrust). In part, this explains the incredible pace of change in Quebec. In many ways the homogeneity of interests in the province, whether cast along language or culture or economic lines, implies that Quebec society has "family" characteristics in the sense that a convergence of opinion leaders on an issue spreads quickly through the society, especially when the leaders are in effect not only saying "do as I say," but also "do as I do." As an important aside, with the Bélanger-Campeau Commission this quick convergence is occuring again, this time around "sovereignty."

This leads directly to (or rather explains) yet other significant features of the new Quebec — the commonality of interest between business and government in sharp contrast to the "two solitudes" in Ontario on the one hand and the continuity of policy from the post-referendum Lévesque regime to Bourassa's Liberals on the other. Contrast this last point to events at the national arena where most of the economic agenda of Trudeau's "second coming" has been overturned by the Mulroney Tories (Courchene, 1991e, and Chapter 2, *this volume*).

C. The Bourassa Liberals: Continuity in the Economic Sphere

As already indicated, Bourassa's "second coming" built further on this economic base. This is best illustrated by noting that one of the Liberals' first initiatives was to commission three blueprints for the economic future of Quebec. These were not ordinary task forces. They were headed by cabinet ministers or elected members with expertise in economic and financial affairs. The resulting trilogy of reports — Pierre Fortier on privatization, Paul Gobeil on the role of government and more generally on the delivery of socio-economic programs; and Reed Scowen on deregulation — represents, in my view, the most comprehensive market-oriented yet equity-conscious approach to socio-economic policy ever promulgated by any government in the western world. No other provincial government could have possibly produced such comprehen-sive blueprints, and certainly not Ontario. To be sure, much of the substance of these reports has not seen the legislative light of day. But the underlying framework still rings true.

In terms of more recent initiatives, I shall focus only on two areas. The first relates to the Canada-U.S. Free Trade Agreement (FTA). While it is probably wrong to suggest that Quebec gave Canada free trade, it is appropriate to note that had the Tories captured only 42 instead of 63 of the 75 Quebec seats (still a comfortable majority) Mulroney would not have had his 1988 majority and the FTA would likely have been stymied. Financial regulation is the second area. Not only has Quebec been innovating here for most of the 1980s, but the "Quebec model" is beginning to drive overall Canadian legislation. And when Canada is not following suit, there is at least a "hands off" approach to Quebec initiatives. These include privileging Quebec's indigenous financial institutions — allowing the caisses populaires to issue "equity" capital and allowing the mutuals to demutualize, to joint-venture and to acquire downstream holdings. More recently, Quebec has proposed the creation of "mammoth corporations" (to use Pierre Fortier's term) which would intermingle finance and commerce and which, among other activities, would attempt to ensure that selected commercial "stars" remain Quebec-based. On the Quebec legislative plate now are proposals for allowing mutuals to establish joint ventures with foreign financial institutions. These recent initiatives are completely foreign to the banking/financial tradition in the rest-of-Canada and the intermingling of finance and commerce is foreign to the entire anglo-saxon tradition. Yet, Quebec is well on the way to implementing these initiatives.

D. What Then is the Problem?

If Quebec can accomplish all of this under the current constitutional arrangements, why is there such concern that their cultural and economic future is jeopardized by remaining a full partner in the Canadian federation? To this question one might add a point not usually recognized by English Canadians, that over this period Quebec received *no special favours* on the constitutional front. But *other provinces did.* Specifically, in the context of the *Constitution Act, 1982,* Newfoundland asked for and received the right to hire preferentially for the offshore. And the west received special taxation powers for its resource sector.

Moreover, while there is obviously some concern in English Canada about Quebec's demands, there is also envy in terms of Quebec's remarkable accomplishments. Many provinces now have Quebec Stock Savings Plan (QSSP)-type provisions in place and several are trying to emulate the role of the Caisse de dépôt for their economies. More generally, they are searching for the degree of internal confidence and dynamism and entrepreneurial spirit that is flourishing in Quebec.

The question remains, however: Where and how is the constitution constraining Quebec? Alternatively, how would other arrangements be less constraining? In addressing this issue, it is convenient to fall back on a quotation from Ramsay Cook:

Nationalism...is about ethnic survival and growth. It is also about self-interest and power...Consequently, nationalism struggles are not only about *home rule* but also, perhaps even primarily, about *who should rule at home*. (1986, pp. 12-13, emphasis added).

My interpretation of the Quiet Revolution and market nationalism is that they were all about "who should rule at home." Post-Meech Lake, however, the issue has increasingly become "home rule" (i.e., sovereignty).

E. Symbolism

One answer to why the constitution is constraining relates to the powerful negative symbolism associated with the defeat of Meech. (Quebec said YES to Canada in 1980: Canada said NO to Quebec in 1990). With their new-found confidence in their home-grown enterpreneurial and business sector ("who can rule at home"), Quebecers appear increasingly willing to contemplate "home rule" as the appropriate response. If symbol is all that is at stake, I shall later argue that a response couched in terms of a declaration of "sovereignty" as a prelude to "re-association" may be an extremely risky strategy for Quebec (and for the country) because it could lead to irreversibilities. For example, it may preclude "re-association" other than through GATT, and, therefore, generate enormous transitional difficulties that could severely complicate further economic evolution.

Substance

A more important answer, at least from my vantage point, has to do with the *Constitution Act, 1982* and the manner in which it might ultimately reduce Quebec's powers to legislate across both cultural and economic fronts. In Andrew Petter's words:

The 1982 amendment undermined the constitution's stabilizing and unifying influence by formalizing and thereby privileging political values that were acceptable to elites in English Canada, but were inimical to elites in Quebec. The commitments made in 1982 to pan-Canadian identity over regional identity, to individual bilingualism over territorial bilingualism and to provincial equality over special status for Quebec have contributed to a deepening sense of anger and alienation among Quebec nationalists (including moderate nationalists), fueling demands for further constitutional reform. At the same time, the political values that were formalized in 1982 have attracted growing support from other Canadians, making it increasingly difficult to dislodge or counterbalance those values in order to satisfy the concerns of Quebec nationalists. This difficulty is heightened by an extremely rigid and procedurally complex amending formula. It is further heightened by the presence of groups whose interest in constitutional reform was recognized during the 1982 amendment process, and who now have an acknowledged stake in future constitutional amendment. Aboriginal groups, for example, continue to resent the failure of the 1982 amendments and subsequent constitutional negotiations to protect adequately their rights, and have promised to block changes that fail to rectify this injustice. Meanwhile women's and multicultural groups, both of whom won partial victories in 1982, have let it be known that they will not tolerate amendments that could weaken the Constitution's commitment to values with which they identify (1991, p. 48).

It was this combination of factors (helped substantially by Bourassa's use of the notwithstanding clause with Bill 178) that led to the demise of Meech. More problematical, these forces imply that future "Quebec rounds" may meet the same fate. In spite of the fact that there are also group rights embedded in the Charter and in spite of the fact that the Charter is selective in its application, it is my view that this confrontation between English Canada's new "distinctiveness" (i.e., Charter rights) and Quebec's traditional collective-rights approach is the foremost hurdle to our national integrity. Phrased differently, armed with the Charter the rest-of-Canada was able to defeat Quebec's "distinct society" clause. However, Quebec is now backed into a corner where it apparently *cannot counter* English Canada's "distinct-society" clause (the Charter).[4] Like the Meech Lake version of the "distinct society"[5] clause, the concerns about the Charter for Quebec may be more perceived than real. Nonetheless, if ultimately confronted with a full-blown Charter, replete with the removal of the notwithstanding clause, Quebec will really have no choice but to "go it alone." There may be a tragic irony to all of this. English Canadians are utilizing an American and Americanizing instrument (the Charter) to rend the nation which, in turn, will leave them at the mercy of the Americans!

This is much more than simply a Quebec issue: it is at the heart of our conception of a nation occupying the upper half of North America and wishing to avoid being swallowed up by the giant to the south. If Canada cannot accommodate Quebec's distinctiveness, then it cannot accommodate the First Nations' distinctiveness nor, in a few decades, the distinctiveness of the west coast, which will by then be Pacific Rim oriented and perhaps significantly Pacific Rim peopled.

This impasse has so concerned me that I have been led to argue (probably in error) that the ratification of the Charter by the federal government and all provinces except Quebec falls fully under section 94 of the *Constitution Act, 1867* and, therefore, does *not* apply to Quebec, since section 94 explicitly excludes Quebec. Specifically, this provision represents an amending formula for non-Quebec Canada to enable it to consolidate and unify its laws as they effect property and civil rights.[6]

The remainder of the paper is designed to search for other alternatives to bridge this impasse, beginning with a focus on the manner in which the emerging global environment will impinge on the operations of the Canadian federal system.

III. GLOBALIZATION AND THE CANADIAN FEDERATION

The purpose of this section is to argue that global forces will lead to a rethinking and restructuring of major aspects of our federation irrespective of the past or future of Quebec-Canada relations. Drawing very briefly from other work I have done (1990a), it seems to me that globalization and the telecomputations revolution will affect the role of national governments in at least four ways.[7] Two of these relate to a transfer "upward" of some of the traditional functions of national governments. The first is the growing importance of transnational corporations. Unlike the former multinational corporations, which entered countries subject to a host of "commitments," transnationals increasingly enter under "national treatment" conditions, i.e., treatment on par with national corporations. This has substantial implications. For example, one will no longer be able to speak meaningfully about a "national" production economy. Production will increasingly be international. One obvious consequence is that we must rethink and rework much of the welfare state, since national welfare states are in large measure geared to national production machines.

Second, it is the transnational corporation (i.e., the international private sector) not the international public sector that is driving globalization. What this means is that national governments will increasingly find that activities that used to be done at the national level will now have to be passed "upwards," partly as a countervail to the globalizing transnationals. The Bank for International Settlements (BIS) capital adequacy rules for financial institutions are a good example here. More than a dozen nations have committed themselves to abide by these international standards. Moreover, the European Community itself is probably part of this trend, particularly if it initiates EC-wide taxation in the area, say, of corporation income taxation. This trend towards international regulation, international standards and confederal or EC-type arrangements is bound to expand and multiply.

Two other forces are passing power "downwards" from nation states. First globalization and the information revolution are privileging citizens. There are many facets to this. For example, as recent as a decade ago, "transmitters" determined the information flow; increasingly "receptors" will. Indeed, the thesis of Kenichi Ohmae's current bestseller, *The Borderless World*, is that globalization is really about consumer sovereignty: "performance standards are now set in the global marketplace by those that buy the products, not those that make them or regulate them" (1990, dustjacket). Quebecers are all too aware of this trend in light of the restrictions placed by Vermont on the recent Hydro sale. The essential point is that consumers (both individually and as part of local, national or international groups of like-minded citizens) are exerting substantial power, which will surely complicate old-style governance for unitary and federal states alike.

A second, and more intriguing point is that globalization is spreading across the world through a network of "international" cities. These international cities (Montreal, Toronto and Vancouver for Canada) are the critical national nodes in the global communications and trading networks, i.e. the essential cultural and economic "connectors" (to use Jane Jacobs' terminology) outward from Montreal to Frankfurt and Geneva and inward to Quebec City and Sherbrooke. Over the last decade nothing much has changed in terms of the Ottawa-Paris relationship but much has changed in terms of the Montreal-Paris relationship. The dilemma here for Canadian federalism is obvious: these cities are "constitutionless." They are creatures of their respective provincial governments. But they will soon become much more influential. This poses rather unique problems because, for example, Saskatchewan's global city is not in the province and the Maritimes international city is (arguably) not even in the country. This again poses a constraint on the role and influence of national, even provincial, governments.

I shall limit myself to only one implication from all of this. In the face of a diminished role in the economic, regulatory and even cultural sphere for national governments, citizens will increasingly view "sovereignty" as the ability to have some influence on how they live and work and play. One can argue whether or not the level of government to deliver this is the international city or the provincial government or the local government, but under our federal system it is clearly *not* the national government. Indeed, will there be much left of "sovereignty" in the millenium other than distinct societies?

IV. DOMESTIC FORCES

It is difficult to escape the conclusion that the global forces are inherently decentralizing in terms of the internal workings of the federation. However, there are several domestic forces that are also pointing in the same direction. The first of these is fiscal-driven decentralization.

A. Fiscal-Driven Decentralization

Despite the fact that many non-Quebec Canadians tend to look to Ottawa to play a greater role in the economy, the reality of the last few years is that the federal deficit and debt burden is driving Canada into unprecedented decentralization. Leading the way here is the current two-year freeze in established programs' financing (EPF) after which the EPF growth will be the growth rate of the Gross National Product (GNP) minus 3 percent.[8] Since the financing of EPF is a combination of tax transfers and cash transfers, what this means is that the tax transfer component will progressively account for more of the total transfer. Indeed, estimates suggest that cash transfers to Quebec will fall to zero before the year 2000 and those for the rest of the provinces sometime before 2010.[9] Thus, the dozen or so billion dollars of federal transfers will eventually fall to zero. This can be viewed as decentralizing on three counts. First, if the provinces maintain service levels by increasing their taxes, the share of provincial to federal taxes increases. Second, if the provinces react by cutting back these programs or redesigning them, this is also decentralizing in the sense that these "national" programs will progressively be designed provincially. The third reason is closely related to the second: when the federal cash transfer falls to zero, how does or can Ottawa insist on any standards at all? Less dramatic, but nonetheless significant, are the selected freezes on the Canada Assistance Plan (for the "have" provinces) and the unemployment insurance (UI) strictures (which, for the poorer provinces, will transfer unfortunate citizens from "federally-financed" UI to jointly-financed welfare).

All of this focuses on "expenditure-shifting," as it were. On the revenue side, the GST invades the sales tax area traditionally viewed by the provinces as their home turf. In an intriguing way, there have been two polar responses to this. On the one hand, Quebec has signalled its intention to integrate its sales tax with the GST (and will collect it for Ottawa and presumably will, at Ottawa's expense, employ Quebecers rather than "feds"). Quebec will thus take advantage of the broader base to lower its sales tax rate. On the other hand, the western provinces at the Western Premiers meeting in Lloydminster, Saskatchewan, in July, 1990, have argued that the combination of "deficit-shifting" and the GST-driven revenue constraints may require that they develop, *à la* Quebec, their own, separate personal-income-tax system. Indeed, British Columbia has announced that it will issue a position paper shortly on a personal-income-tax system for B.C.[10] Both of these responses point in the direction of increased decentralization.

B. The FTA

The defining constitutional rhetoric in Canada and the United States — "peace, order and good government" for Canada and "life, liberty and the pursuit of happiness" for the U.S. — appear to be reflected in our respective citizen-state relationships. In effect, the emphasis in the U.S. is more on the "means" with little emphasis on whether or not the "ends" are appropriate. In Canada, the emphasis has been far more on "ends" with a willingness to use a wide variety of means to achieve these ends.

The FTA with its reliance on markets resonates more, as Simpson (1987) notes, with life, liberty and the pursuit of happiness than it does with peace, order and good government. Phrased differently, while the FTA need not constrain the "ends" towards which Canada and Canadians aim, it certainly constrains the "means" that can be used to achieve these ends. Specifically, given that the FTA embraces markets it is inherently decentralizing, since markets themselves are inherently decentralizing.

The FTA is decentralizing in yet another sense. The political economy of the east-west transfer system will come under increasing scrutiny in the context of FTA north-south integration. In particular, Ontario's magnanimity in terms of existing regional transfers contains a healthy dose of "Ontario first." As long as Canadian trade flowed largely east-west, with Ontario the north-south conduit to the U.S., the second (and future) round spending impacts of these regional transfers generally came to rest somewhere in Ontario. Under full north-south integration for all of Canada's regions, this may no longer be the case. Some of the erstwhile regional payments imbalances with the centre will, now, shift south with the result that the second-round impacts of regional transfers may no longer come to rest in Ontario but rather in North Carolina or California. At a political level, this will surely erode support for such transfers, particularly the ones that privilege "place" rather than people.

This may or may not be viewed as decentralizing, but what is clear is that our tradition of sheltering various regions of the country from market forces is going to become progressively more difficult both economically, politically and perhaps "legally" under the FTA.

C. The Charter

Countering the above centrifugal forces on the economic front is the role of the Canadian Charter of Rights and Freedoms in conditioning socio-political attitudes, particularly of English Canadians. While one can argue that the Charter, too, is decentralizing in that it bestows rights, via the courts, on individuals and designated groups (aboriginals, linguistic minorities, multicultural groups, gender equality) it is nonetheless the case that the "language of rights is a Canadian language not a provincial language" (Cairns, 1984): "the resultant rights and freedoms [are] country wide in scope, enforced by a national supreme court, and entrenched in a national constitution" (Cairns, 1979, p. 354). The Charter has caught on to such a degree that English-speaking Canadians are beginning to develop a new "non-territorial" conception of the federation, one that has little to do with traditional federal-provincial cleavages but rather with cleavages between these newly enshrined pan-Canadian interests on the one hand and vested interests or elites on the other.

What is emerging, then, is the juxtaposition of economics (and fiscally) driven decentralization and political or culturally driven centralization. As highlighted earlier, the cleavages are really much deeper. Quebecers cannot tolerate a conception of Canada where they become "citizens" by virtue of a set of rights adjudicated by a national Supreme Court and where any "collective rights" legislation must rely on the notwithstanding clause which is then open to criticism from the rest-of-Canada. This is inherently inimical to the conception of Quebec as a society. More to the point, it runs counter to the conception of Canada as embodied in the *Constitution Act, 1867* and as practised for over a century prior to 1982. English Canadians have to come to grips with the reality that a full blown "Charter Canada" means no Canada at all!

V. RESUME

The analysis to this point can be summarized rather succintly. First, Quebec has made major societal and economic strides over the last few decades. While the initiatives have obviously come from Quebec, it is probably fair to say that the rest-of-Canada has welcomed these initiatives and, where they have not, they have at least accommodated them. Moreover, all of this was accomplished under the existing constitutional arrangements. Why should the future evolution for Quebec and Quebecers on this score be different than the recent past? One answer to this is that the Charter is inimical to Quebecers' conception of themselves and their society. Thus, the second summary point is that for any future arrangements to be acceptable to Quebec, control over language and culture must reside with the province. Third, Quebecers moreso that other Canadians (or at least moreso than most other Canadians) would prefer a much more decentralized version of the federation. Fourth, both global and domestic forces are driving us in the direction of greater decentralization and a weakened role in traditional areas for the national government. My reading is that even if Meech had not appeared on the scene, Canada would be much more decentralized in the year 2000 than it was in 1980. Thus, the "powers" issue in any new arrangement is not (or at least *ought* not to be) as problematical as it would have been in, say, 1980. Finally, apart from the "fun" and "symbol" of having one's own country, there will be correspondingly much less value to traditional sovereignty in the year

2000 than there was in 1980. Sovereignty in a global era will increasingly be about distinct societies or, as noted earlier, about having influence on how citizens live and work and play.

The challenge facing not only Quebec but all of Canada is how to adapt to, or accommodate, all of these features. This is the purpose of the remainder of the paper.

VI. SOVEREIGNTY FIRST, THEN RE-ASSOCIATION

As I read the reports of the evidence before, and proceedings of, the Bélanger-Campeau Commission and as I interpret the many polls emanating from Quebec, the single most striking message that I draw from all of this is how different it is from 1980. Quebecers now know that, if they wish, they have the will (and likely the votes) to "go it alone." The issue still stirs up incredible emotion in Quebec, but none (or little) of the societal and even family confrontation that characterized 1980. In other words, Quebecers now have the confidence in themselves and in their society to recognize that *they, and not the rest of Canada, will determine key aspects of their future.* As this sense of control over their destiny begins to permeate throughout Quebec society, as well as throughout Canadian society, my view is that the overall tenor of the discussion in both Quebec and the rest-of-Canada will begin to move off the emotional plane and move on to a more strategic plane. Thus, I fully expect that Quebecers will begin to ask themselves the following: "We know that we have the will and ability to become a separate country, but is there a set of arrangements within Canada that is not only less risky but that might lead to an even greater flourishing of the Quebec language, culture and living standard?" I think that there is. Likewise, many, but obviously not all English Canadians (who are now, or at least the elites are, by and large totally shocked by what is occurring in Quebec) will begin to ask themselves: "Is there not a positive-sum game whereby we can accommodate Quebec and other regions and yet continue to reap the benefits of a society that remains distinct from that which exists south of the border?" I think that there is. However, given the momentum of what is transpiring in Quebec, this new "Canadian game" has to go well beyond tinkering and symbols. The proposal that follows, tentatively entitled "The Community of the Canadas," is, accordingly, very radical and is based largely on the European model, although the critically important areas of culture and language also draw on the Swiss experience.

Prior to addressing this model, however, I want to devote some attention to the process dimension which appears to be garnering support in Quebec, namely a quick declaration of "sovereignty" (partly on principle and partly to wake-up English Canada) and then negotiating the terms of "re-association."

Of all the strategies that Quebec and Quebecers might adopt the one most fraught with risk is an early unilateral declaration of independence as a prelude to negotiating association or re-association with the rest-of-Canada. This has nothing to do with the ability of Quebecers to manage change, since throughout I am assuming that they have both the determination and the capability to excel on this score. Rather, it has to do with the nature of the challenges they may be forced to confront. I shall focus on two general types of challenges, one political/ constitutional and one economic.

Quebec cannot really declare itself "sovereign." What it can do is, by a referendum, declare itself independent from Canada. Sovereignty comes when other nations recognize this declaration of independence. Suppose, however, that the Grand Council of the Cree holds a coincident referendum in which they declare themselves independent from Quebec or a separate nation within Quebec or a part of Canada (e.g., to restore northern Quebec to its pre-1912 status). What and who does Canada recognize? What will other nations do? Does the fact that the United Nations (UN) has a subcommittee on aboriginal peoples and that the Grand Council of the Cree has nongovernment observer status at the UN carry any weight? And so on. This particular scenario may be off base, but the general range of issues relating to boundaries and "nations" will surely surface in one form or another.

The challenges on the economic front come precisely because such a unilateral declaration of independence would wake English Canada up — and on awakening they would find both their political and economic future in doubt. This is hardly conducive to re-association, particularly from the vantage point of western Canada. Why would western Canada agree to reconstituting a commercial policy that subsidizes Quebec clothing and textile workers or more generally one that continues the degree of subsidization to the Atlantic region? And on and on. The point is that once the Canadian "fabric" is rended, it is unlikely that it can ever be put together again. There will, of course, be substantial incentives for the natural economic allies, Quebec and Ontario, to forge a deal between themselves. But this will be viewed by western Canada as a "coup" by the centre to reconstitute the country along Quebec-Ontario terms. In effect, this would be an "expulsion" of western Canada which would, in turn, feel (with some justification) that it can now exit without taking any of the federal debt.

Now that the issue of the federal debt has been broached, setting aside the international-capital-market implications of a Unilateral Declaration of Independence (UDI), it will take something like a decade for Quebec to float its share of the national debt (Côté, 1990). For this to come to pass, Quebec-Canada relations must proceed more smoothly than they are likely to in the face of a UDI as an opening salvo. My colleague Douglas Purvis refers to this as "the bonds that tie."

This does not mean that some version of a UDI can be avoided as the process unfolds or that some alternative referendum that stops short of a UDI would be inappropriate. Rather it argues for adequate prior negotiation in order that the attendant risks and uncertainties become more manageable for both sides. There remains Quebec's concern that English Canadians are "asleep at the helm," as it were. Needless to say, it is also a principal concern of many of us in non-Quebec Canada. But this will sort itself out rather dramatically once the story hits the cover pages of any or all of *Time, The Economist, The Wall Street Journal* or *The New York Times.* Moreover, the release of the Allaire Report has reverberated resoundingly across the country as well as in the corridors of power. The same will apply to the release of the findings of the Bélanger-Campeau Commission. We will not need a UDI to wake us up!

More importantly, my underlying approach to the Quebec-Canada impasse is that there is a preferable strategy, to which I now turn.

VIII. THE COMMUNITY OF THE CANADAS

Elsewhere (1990b, and Chapter 5, *this volume* and 1990e), I have argued for a reconstituted Canada that would embody asymmetry (special status) in practice but symmetry in principle. The mechanism for accomplishing this might be section 94: all provinces would receive more powers and non-Quebec Canada could then utilize section 94 to transfer these powers back to Ottawa. While this approach still has some potential, I think that the march of events have "passed it by," although the Allaire Report (1991) suggests this as an option for the rest-of-Canada. More is needed, not only with respect to powers, but as well to symbol.

Accordingly, the proposal that follows is motivated not by any firm belief that it is in any way the "ideal" model, but rather that it is essential that we begin to break away from the existing Canadian federal mold and place alternative approaches on the bargaining table. For presentation purposes, I shall focus first on the broad characteristics of the model. This will be followed by an elaboration of some of its more important (and, no doubt controversial) features. The final section will deal with aspects of process, i.e., can we get there from here?

A. The Community of the Canadas: Overview Powers

The "reworked" division of powers would consist of two broad provisions. The first of these would isolate a set of powers that would remain at the Community level, e.g., external affairs, commercial policy, the maintenance of the internal economic union and internal economic harmonization generally, weights and measures, monetary policy, aspects of fiscal policy, redistributional policies with respect to the Community nations, and so on. My list is no better than anyone else's here, but the message should be rather clear, namely that the Community government should be entrusted with powers that, by their very nature, relate to the Community rather than to member nations. This list would result in a reduction of existing exclusive federal powers, but it would be more generous to Ottawa than is the Allaire Report (1991).

All other existing federal powers (and for that matter *all* other powers) should be assigned *jointly* or *concurrently* to *both* levels of government *with provincial or community-member paramountcy*. David Milne (1991) conveniently refers to this as CPP (concurrency with provincial paramountcy). Concurrency means that both levels of government can legislate in these areas. Provincial paramountcy implies that where legislation of the two levels of government is conflicting, provincial legislation will prevail. Therefore, the key characteristic of the model in terms of powers is "decentralization if necessary, but not necessarily decentralization." What this means is that Quebec, for example, can access its new powers *immediately*. Others may wish to proceed more slowly or perhaps not at all. In this case they can keep these functions at the Community level.

Among the powers falling under CPP would be language and culture. Community institutions relating to exclusive community powers would remain bilingual. This is a version of the Swiss model where rights are generally national in scope except for language and culture, which are basically territorial. One should note that this is broadly in line with one of the key recommendations of the Pepin-Robarts Report (1979). My personal view is that while this will have important *symbolic* implications for all community members, it is not likely to alter much of the substance of language legislation in those areas where French or English represent substantial minorities.

B. Community Institutions

The structure of the Community level government would remain bicameral. The lower chamber, the House of Commons or House of Representatives, would continue to be popularly elected, along "Rep-by-Pop" lines. The upper chamber would be a Federal Council or Community Council, somewhat along the Beige Paper lines (Quebec Liberal Party, 1980). Specifically, there would be equal representation from the five Community nations — Canada East, Quebec, Ontario, Canada West and the First Nations/Territories. To be sure, others might opt for a different "community of nations." This particular configuration maintains, roughly, the existing voting power in the Senate, except that First Nations/Territories are given additional weight. Now to some details.

C. House of Commons.

The popularly elected assembly (House of Commons) would function pretty well as it does now with the important difference that it may become increasingly difficult to sustain the Westminster model (i.e., to sustain parliamentary government). This is discussed more fully below. The Commons would continue to be the primary legislative body, with the prime minister and the cabinet coming from its ranks. Not much change so far.

One area that will prove challenging, however, is whether all members (MPs) will have identical voting rights. Specifically, should MPs be able to vote on measures where their home "nation" has exercised paramountcy? At the time of my appearance before Bélanger-Campeau, my answer was "yes" and it remains "yes" despite the fact that this aspect of the paper has attracted substantial criticism. Hence, some elaboration is warranted.

The first point to make is that there is an important difference between the present model which embodies CPP and symmetric powers on the one hand and an asymmetric-powers (special-status) model where Quebec would have powers that other provinces do not have on the other. In this latter case, it is difficult to avoid asymmetric powers to MPs, i.e., constrained powers for Quebec MPs. Federal or Community legislation does not, by definition, apply to Quebec in these areas so that Quebec MPs should play no role in the legislative process.

CPP is quite different, however. The federal government can still legislate for the entire Community in these areas. In advance, it is not at all evident that provinces will find such legislation problematical to the degree that they will exercise paramountcy (i.e., pass alternative legislation). Moreover, since the possibility always exists that provinces which previously asserted paramountcy could opt back into federal legislation, it seems inappropriate for MPs of such provinces to be relegated to second-class status. That they may not wish to exercise their right to vote on such measures is quite another matter.

A second area of concern is that the federal government could fall (i.e., lose a confidence vote) on an issue coming under CPP simply because Quebec MPs, for example, decide to abstain. There are two ways to address this problem. The first is, admittedly, a bit of a cop out — confidence votes would be restricted to those areas in exclusive Community jurisdiction. In other words, a government could not fall on a vote relating to an area coming under CPP.

The second approach is more general, namely that we are likely going to have to rethink aspects of parliamentary government in any event. From the perspective of Spring, 1991, it appears that the next Parliament could have representatives from five, perhaps six, parties. (Tories, Liberals,

NDP, Reform, Bloc Québécois and the Confederation of Regions). The likelihood is not only a minority government, but one with shifting coalitions depending on the issue at hand. As a result, we are likely to move considerably towards the current practice in the British Parliament which moderates party discipline by spelling out which votes involve confidence and which do not.

D. The Community Council.
Each of the five designated nations or Community members would have equal representation on the Federal Council. How these representatives are selected is left to the discretion of the Community members. Some member nations, presumably including Quebec, may wish to appoint them, perhaps from sitting members in the National Assembly. This is "confederal" in the sense that Quebec will be represented on the Federal Council in its "own right," rather than by popularly elected members. Some may prefer elections. Some may opt for a combination of these two. Note that while representation on the Federal Council is on the basis of equality among the five Community members, it is not necessary that Canada West, for example, constitute itself into a single political unit. The provinces can remain as they are. In terms of Federal Council representation, however, the four existing western provinces will be treated as *one* member state (but not required to cast a "bloc" vote).

The reader will recognize that this Community Council structure does not square well with Alberta's, and more generally the west's, aspirations for provincial equality in the upper chamber. Admittedly, the full Triple-E Senate approach (equal, elected, effective) is not inconsistent with the proposed division of powers under the Community of the Canadas. However, the rationale for five-"nation" rather than ten-province equality rests on two criteria that differ from the criteria that underlie, say, the U.S. federation with its two Senators per state. First, whether the rest-of-Canada likes it or not, the constitutional rhetoric is shifting from "province" to "nation." This is not limited to the Canadian scene. The Catalins, the Scots, the Bretons, and other ethnic groups in other countries, are increasingly viewing themselves as "nations" and hoping to link themselves directly to Brussels. The rest-of-Canada may be only one or two "nations" rather than four. But it certainly is not nine (or ten with the First Nations). The second rationale is related to the first. If provinces other than Quebec (and Ontario) wish to exert paramountcy over a range of new powers, this is unlikely to make sense unless they do so in the context of "regional" groupings. More on this later.

The Federal Council will not, in general, be a legislative body in the sense of initiating measures. However, it would ratify all legislation from the lower chamber. Double majorities may be required for certain areas that relate to the patrimony of individual Community members. Even with greater decentralization, this may be important for Quebec and the First Nations/Territories and even for Canada West, for example, as it desires greater integration with the Pacific Rim.

The Federal Council will also have to ratify all appointments to major Community boards and/or secretariats. This is particularly the case with respect to two areas that are clearly malfunctioning at the present time. The first of these relates to macroeconomic policy. I agree with the many representations before Bélanger-Campeau that the "parliamentary" relationship between the Bank and the Minister of Finance should be severed; with the Bank becoming more independent and autonomous in its policy role, but at the same time more responsible to its (by then meaningful) board of directors. Ratification of the lower chamber's appointments to the Bank's board would obviously come under the purview of the Federal Council. The second area is the environment and here I have no easy solution. The ongoing problem in this area is that policy with respect to the environment is becoming more and more a not-very-disguised "disallowance clause." The country, under any model, cannot long maintain itself under a set of provisions whereby the nature of environmental assessment differs markedly across megaprojects. This will be a challenge under the Community model, but since it also is a challenge under the existing arrangements it should not be viewed as a special complicating factor in any transition.

The Federal Council will have the power of "disallowance" for any sub-Community legislation that serves to fragment the internal economic union of the Community. For example, changes in social policy in Canada West that require residency periods or otherwise inhibit the free flow of people across Community member states should be disallowed at the Federal Council level. (Note that since the Council has to ratify all lower chamber legislation, this also applies to any Community legislation).

Where a Community member has "patriated" a policy area to its own legislative level, it will not be allowed to veto Community legislation in this area designed to implement policy for other members, unless, of course, this legislation contravenes the internal common market of the Community.

Finally, should the Community wish to shed one of the last vestiges of our formal ties to Britain, the Federal Council could elect, preferably on a rotating one-year basis, a president of the Community as the "head of state," as it were. The functions would be similar to those of the Governor-General, whose office would be rendered obsolete.

E. The Community of the Canadas: Selected Issues
Abandoning Aspects of Party Government

The introduction of the Charter and the emphasis on "due process" has taken us some way towards a checks and balances system. The Community of the Canadas would take us yet further in this direction.

Most Canadians would presumably agree that parliamentary or responsible government has served us very well over our first century. For more than a decade now, however, one could mount a persuasive case that it is driving us apart. Briefly put, the policy "swings" have simply become too large for Canadians to handle. Examples abound — the anti-Americanism of the early 1980s (the Foreign Investment Review Agency, FIRA, and the "back-in" and Canadian content provisions of the National Energy Program, NEP) was completely overturned by the FTA; the "made-in-Canada" energy prices of the NEP era have been replaced with the market orientation of the FTA; the imposition of the *Constitution Act, 1982* and particularly the Charter on Quebec which eventually led to the Meech Lake debacle and still, in some way or another, requires "overturning"; and the institutional crisis where a government with a 14 percent rating in the polls can ram through a policy (GST) disliked by nearly 80 percent of the population.

Canadians are increasingly demanding "representative" government, not "responsible" government. This is reflected, in part, in the west's push towards a Triple-E Senate. It is difficult to conceive of ways in which a Triple-E Senate (or the Community Council) would coexist comfortably within a parliamentary democracy or a system of responsible government. On the other hand, there is "little point in establishing an elected Senate to introduce a significant element of intrastate federalism and then to make it almost meaningless by giving it a weak suspensive veto to reconcile it with responsible government" (Smiley and Watts, 1986, p. 130).

This shift away from parliamentary government is, in part, also reflected in the demise of national parties. Albertans have time and again seen their MPs side with national parties rather than vote constituents' interests. If one cannot change the institutions of government, then at least one can change parties and, in particular, opt for regional parties which, by definition, will (or should!) vote regional interests. While regional parties are in principle fully consistent with responsible government, the fact is that the origin of the Reform Party has its roots in attempting to offset the implications of responsible or party government.

The bottom line here is that the Community of the Canadas does *not* require that Canadians reject the parliamentary system. What is true, however, is that this model, like the introduction of a meaningful Triple-E Senate, would contribute to the pressures on our system of responsible government.

F. Centralization/Decentralization

The proposal embodies, in principle at least, a marked decentralization of powers. However, two important observations are warranted here.

First, there is little question about what Quebec will do — it will remain poised to exercise its paramountcy. (Note that it may not need to do so if Community legislation meets the province's needs). It is far less clear how the other provinces or "nations" will react. The rest-of-Canada (ROC), in whole or in part, could maintain the status quo. They could "rebalance" by drawing some powers down, and by passing others upward to the Community level. Or, they could follow Quebec and exercise paramountcy. For the provinces in Canada West, for example, accessing greater powers would probably mean doing so within the context of some increased economic and/or political integration. It does not make sense for Alberta to exercise paramountcy over manpower policy. It might make sense for Canada West to do so.

An integral component of the Community of the Canadas is a requirement that the ROC hold a constitutional conference prior to altering the status quo. The rationale for this is: a) to insure that any exercise of paramountcy takes place in an orderly and coordinated way, and b) to ascertain whether there is scope for common Community legislation that would obviate the need for provincial paramountcy.

Ultimately, whether parts of the ROC access these new powers will likely depend on the degree to which English-speaking Canada is more than one nation. If the nine non-Quebec provinces comprise a distinct society, the end result for the ROC will likely be greater harmonization and perhaps greater centralization. If, however, Canada West's emerging needs and challenges are very different from those of, say, Ontario then the result will presumably be some difference in the devolution of powers or between these two "nations."

Implicit in this proposal is a transfer of tax points where competences are devolved. This would be done in a manner that ensures that no net fiscal benefit attaches to decentralization. However, any transfer of tax points must recognize the debt-servicing needs of the Community as well as the necessity of ensuring that Ottawa retains control of cyclically sensitive tax bases sufficient to discharge its stabilization role.

This represents, as noted, a potential substantial decentralization. However, this must be set against the manner in which the world is evolving. By the millenium, it is likely that the Community will have "signed on" to all sorts of international agreements — environmental, financial institutions, trading arrangements, competition/merger policy agreements, numerous industry-specific arrangements (telecommunications, airlines, agriculture, aspects of resources, etc.), codes of civil rights, etc. The point of this is that decentralization in the year 2000 is no longer the same issue that it was in, say, 1980.

G. First Nations' Representation on the Federal Council

Among the more innovative (and surely controversial) features of the proposal is equal member-state representation for the First Nations/ Territories on the Federal Council. Effectively, this gives some power of veto over legislation at any level that erodes their enshrined rights. It does more than this, however. It recognizes that the First Nations have to be part of any reconstitution of the federation. Moreover, as argued earlier, they are likely also to play a significant role in any break-up of the federation.

My personal preference here would be to go much further — to allow the First Nations to incorporate their existing reserves into a formal territorial, but noncontiguous, province (see Courchene, 1990i and Chapter 4, *this volume*): a "fax-machine" province, as it were. In effect, Indian Affairs is now a "provincial government," operated out of Ottawa, since many of its responsibilities (social policy, roads, health, education) are really "provincial" responsibilities. This option would transfer Indian Affairs and its responsibilities to the First Nations themselves. But I have not included this aspect as an integral part of the Community of the Canadas.[11]

None of this has any formal implications for existing land claims (although Canadians would do well to note, as my colleague John McDougall has, that "land to the First Nations is what language is to the Québécois"). They are currently progressing along a separate track and would continue to do so.

H. Flexibility, Symmetry, etc.

The Community of the Canadas is explicitly designed to maximize flexibility and to minimize change for those provinces or Community members that prefer much or all of the status quo. Since most powers will be concurrent (albeit with provincial paramountcy), it is conceivable that the rest-of-Canada might want to have *more uniform* policies in certain areas than is now the case. For example, social policy or health policy for the ROC could be run at the Community level, if this is what the ROC wants. This represents a degree of flexibility in terms of centralization/ decentralization or "re-balancing" that the ROC currently does not have. Moreover, by the very nature of the proposal, these decisions do not have to be made immediately. The status quo for the ROC is a viable option while various Community members sort out their priorities.

A second area of flexibility relates to the "five nation" aspect of the Federal Council. The formal "sovereignty-association" or confederation is between these five Community members. But Canada East need not incorporate itself into a political unit called Canada East. The four Atlantic provinces can maintain their separate provincial identities, and their British Parliamentary traditions for that matter. They will be required to cooperate in sending members to the Federal Council. Even here, uniformity is not required. For example, the members could run in Canada East elections. Or Newfoundland could elect its allocated share of members while New Brunswick could, if it wished, nominate its members. And so on.

My personal hunch is, as already noted, that if individual provinces want to acquire greater powers they will find this option more realistic if they reconstitute themselves into larger units. But nothing in the proposal requires this.

In principle, symmetry prevails. All Community members have the same potential powers. Thus, this is *not* a "special status" model. If, however, non-Quebec Community members choose not to utilize these powers, the Community *will* have the appearance of being asymmetric in terms of provincial or Community member powers. Yet, at any time a Community member can exercise the right to full powers. Thus, any *de facto* asymmetry can arise only because this is what Community members desire.

I. De Jure Symmetry, De Facto Asymmetry

It is worth elaborating upon the aspects of the potential for symmetry in principle yet asymmetry in fact. The first point to make in this context is that asymmetry has always been an integral part of Canada and that a good deal of this can be traced directly in the *Constitution Act, 1867* (see Milne, 1991). Phrased differently, the groundswell of support for equal powers for all provinces is of recent origin and reflects, among other things, the "symmetry" of the amending formula required for Meech (i.e., all provinces treated equally, and in this case all having a veto). The second point is far more important in terms of the thrust of this paper, namely that Canada has also had considerable experience of *de facto* asymmetry.

Consider the following examples. In the mid-1950s, Quebec opted for its own personal income tax (PIT). While other provinces were and are free to follow Quebec's lead (and on several occasions Ontario postured in this direction), none has yet done so although, as noted above, British Columbia appears to be coming close to such a decision. Influenced in part by events in British Columbia, the recent federal budget has promised to investigate the possibility of giving provinces greater flexibility under the *existing* shared PIT. Specifically, the proposal under consideration is to give the provinces freedom over provincial tax rates and tax brackets provided that they apply this rate-and-bracket structure to the federally determined definition of taxable income. This would replace the existing system whereby provinces are limited to applying a single tax rate (e.g., 53 percent for Ontario) to the federal tax payable. My purpose is not to become involved in the intricacies of the shared PIT system. Rather it is to make the case that this resembles closely the essence of concurrency with provincial paramountcy that is the core of the Community of the Canadas model. Provinces can opt for a separate PIT. Yet Ottawa can also legislate or, in the case at hand, signal an intent to legislate, in order that the environment is less conducive for provinces to embark on their own PITs (or, to exercise paramountcy). A related example in terms of PIT has to do with Quebec's opting for a tax point transfer (of 16.5 percent tax points) rather than a cash transfer in the mid-1960s. This option was presumably open to all provinces. Yet no other province followed suit. A final example on the tax side has to do with corporate income taxation. Three provinces have their own corporate tax systems — Quebec, Ontario and Alberta.

The pension area is, in a sense, more relevant since concurrency with provincial paramountcy actually prevails here (under section 94A of the *Constitution Act, 1867*). The result was that Quebec mounted its QPP as a similar but separate program from the Canada Pension Plan. All other provinces had and still have the same option. None exercised this option. Moreover, *à propos* the earlier discussion of the voting rights of MPs, Quebec MPs do have a right to vote on Canada Pension Plan legislation.

Immigration is another relevant area. For years, the so-called Cullen-Couture agreement allowed Quebec to exercise its (constitutional) concurrent power in this area. More recently, this agreement has been "enshrined," or nearly so. Similar arrangements are available to all other provinces and some (e.g., British Columbia) have indicated that they are interested.

A final general example relates to aspects of the general social envelope. Quebec has taken over some responsibilities in the areas of manpower and employment, for example, that were offered to, but refused by, the other provinces. Several provinces have taken advantage of varying family allowances per child depending on the number of children in the family (see Milne, 1991).

All of these areas appear to fall under the general CPP (concurrency with provincial paramountcy) approach to powers. Yet except for one or two cases, only Quebec has exercised the right to access these powers. Thus, generalized decentralization was not the result. Indeed, the opposite was and is true. With Quebec on its own chosen path, the other nine provinces along with Ottawa were able to mount a much more harmonized approach to many of these areas, an approach that would *not* have been possible if Quebec had not opted out.

In terms of the core of this paper, the evidence from our recent past is that the concurrency-with-provincial-paramountcy aspect of the proposed model is of and by itself not likely to lead to generalized decentralization, particularly if Ottawa enacts framework legislation that allows some degree of provincial flexibility. All provinces could have followed Quebec's lead. Few did. This implies that the recent asymmetry in our federation reflects a conscious decision by the non-Quebec provinces *not* to exercise their powers. One cannot forecast the future from the past. But it is my view that if provinces other than Quebec were to access any newly available powers, it would be because their needs and challenges differ from those of other parts of the country. In this context, a passage from one of Robert Sheppard's recent columns (1991) is quite instructive:

> When the unsures and don't-knows are weeded out, 50 per cent of New Brunswick respondents [to a Baseline Market Research poll], 49 per cent of Nova Scotia respondents and 56 per cent of Newfoundland respondents favour the hard option of political union for all four Atlantic provinces, which is a taboo subject among the political set. Opposition to the notion was, not surprisingly, the most pronounced in PEI (only 36 per cent in favour of political union).

Were political union to come about, or even economic union replete with substantial rationalization of several policy areas, Canada East would likely seek greater powers under CPP.

J.   Redistributional Implications of the Community of the Canadas

While not always recognized, the principal reason why the Canadian federation is as decentralized as it is relates to the equalization program and, more generally, to interprovincial redistribution. It would have been impossible (or at least highly problematical) for the have-not provinces to agree to the postwar transfer of personal- and corporate-income-tax points unless these tax-point transfers were equalized. On the other hand, there is no question that redistribution is currently undergoing hard times in Canada — whether from the requirements of the FTA, the dictates of globalization, or the pressure arising from the federal debt and deficit overhang. The most likely scenario (largely independent of the constitutional crisis) is a complete reworking of the entire federal-provincial fiscal interface. Within this context, one possible outcome is the disappearance of explicit federal funding for the Canada Assistance Plan and the Established Programs which would be replaced by a transfer of equalized income tax points. In this sense, equalization would become the omnibus federal- provincial transfer scheme.

This would be an intriguing development. What held us together, east-west, in our formative years was an economic strategy — tariffs, other aspects of the National Policy and the transcontinental railway, but little in the way of explicit redistribution (except via the economic strategy that effectively transferred income from south to north). A century later, global and North American economic forces have led to the abandonment of this strategy. The new east-west "railroad" is social policy infrastructure and the archetypal social policy is the equalization system which ensures that Canadians, wherever they reside, have access to reasonably comparable public services at reasonably comparable tax rates. Intriguingly, in his 1952 article "The National Policy — Old and New," Vernon Fowke suggested as much — and well before Canada put in place its comprehensive social policy network.

What does this mean for the Community of the Canadas or vice versa? The first point to make is that the provinces' options under concurrency with provincial paramountcy should be "fiscally neutral," i.e., provinces should be in the same *net* positive fiscally whether or not they exercise paramountcy. The second is that Quebec, rather conveniently, is *not* a major recipient of *net* federal benefits. The Atlantic provinces as well as Saskatchewan and Manitoba are major net beneficiaries. What this implies is that the degree of redistribution should be independent of whether Quebec becomes more decentralized. Phrased differently, interprovincial redistribution would be largely determined by and within the ROC. My hunch, however, is that one of the reasons why the four Atlantic provinces (or at least the three Maritime provinces) are increasingly attracted to greater economic and political integration relates to the realization that these federal-provincial transfers are likely to grow more slowly in the future (under any regime) and that, therefore, this may require greater rationalization and coordination in their operations.

Thus, the Community of the Canadas is consistent with a wide variety of approaches in terms of redistribution. In particular, it is ideally suited to a shift from an economic to a social policy "railroad." Most likely, however, events on this front will be driven by factors other than the proposed redesign of the federation.

K. The Community of the Canadas: Process
Can we get there from here? The short and long answer is "not easily." It will take immense goodwill on all sides and substantial good luck. It may also require a full recognition of the consequences of failure, again on the part of all.

One thing is sure. All of this cannot be "constitutionalized" in a short period. This is the bad news. The good news is that it need not be. One of the lessons of the 1980s is that we attempted to "constitutionalize" far too many initiatives when other alternatives — ordinary legislation, tax-point transfers, reworking fiscal arrangements, bilateral agreements, uniform devolution of powers on Ottawa's part, etc. — could, and in the future, must, carry some of the freight, as it were.

Nonetheless, many aspects of the proposal require constitutional amendment. This would include, for example, the substitution of a

Federal Council for the Senate. In terms of powers, it would be necessary to designate those specifically assigned to the Community level and to the Federal Council. Beyond this, it is "simply" a matter of assigning all other powers jointly with provincial paramountcy. Members who wish to take advantage of provincial paramountcy would presumably sign bilateral arrangements under a provision similar to section 43 of the *Constitution Act, 1982*. This would go both ways. Should the rest-of-Canada desire that the Community government take over some existing provincial areas, they could use this same provision (or section 94) to pass authority upwards (accompanied by appropriate compensation). If a more formal division of powers is desired, this can be worked out over time; the above provisions should be sufficient in the interim.

I view all of the above as challenging but feasible. Perhaps the most daunting initiative is the assigning of culture and language to the Community members. This implies the end of pan-Canadian bilingualism and replaces it by a territorial variant, *à la* Switzerland. In other words, it probably requires an amendment to the Charter. (A more relaxed notwithstanding clause will *not* suffice here). The overall proposal could founder on this issue. But this is the very issue that is at the heart of the deliberations of Bélanger-Campeau (even though it is frequently couched in other terms). My only comment here is that there is no possibility of an integral Canada that does not allow Quebecers control over culture and language. As noted earlier, such a provision will not likely have much impact on the role of English in Quebec or French in New Brunswick and parts of Ontario. On the positive side, this proposal might well remove one of the most divisive symbols in both Quebec and non-Quebec Canada. Moreover, it would allow the rest-of-Canada, through a provision similar to section 94, to reconstitute the full charter, as it were, and even remove the notwithstanding clause.

VIII. CONCLUSION

Momentum is growing in Quebec for sovereignty. The "votes" appear to be there. The question not yet being addressed by Quebecers is whether or not there is an *preferable* alternative to sovereignty that would not only allow further evolution of their economy and society but would do so in a manner that ensures that unavoidable risks are kept to an easily manageable minimum. The question not yet addressed by English Canadians is the nature of their options in the event that Quebec opts for sovereignty. In my view, far too much time and effort has been devoted to the calamities that could befall Quebec should it go its own way, while almost no analysis recognizes that many of the same challenges will apply to the ROC.

The Community of the Canadas proposal is offered as one — not *the* — approach that not only overcomes the constraints imposed by the status quo but, more importantly, "wakes up" both sides to the potential gains that the other side can offer. For indeed both sides at base, face quite similar challenges, namely how all Canadians can ensure that their major achievements towards insuring their respective distinctiveness as inhabitants of the upper part of North America are preserved and enhanced within an increasingly integrated North American and global environment.

The model advanced here is clearly in the federal mold, albeit with some confederal tinges. For community nations that take up all the options, it effectively confers "sovereignty" over language and culture and it allows Quebec, for example, to be *directly* represented on the Federal Council. Whether this model will evolve towards a "bi-national" relationship over time or towards a "multi-national" relationship (if, say, Canada West and Ontario also take up their full potential powers) is, at this point, unclear. In either case, the model approaches that of the European Community and may eventually embody full sovereignty-association. The key point from my perspective (as reflected in the earlier section on recent Quebec achievements) is that there is ample room for new opportunities and new challenges within the framework of the Community of the Canadas to fully engage Quebecers for some considerable time *without* the added (and in my view rather dramatic) risks and irreversibilities that would attend a declaration of independence.

To be sure, consideration let alone recognition of this (or some similarly radical) proposal will require a substantial shift in popular allegiances among Quebecers, now that they perceive that sovereignty is at hand. Moreover, it will take an equally dramatic realignment of allegiances on the part of many English Canadians who, on the whole, feel rather comfortable with the status quo. Yet, without such recognition that there is a creative and mutually beneficial set of options between these polar solutions, all Canadians will inevitably become caught up in a highly intriguing, but fully predictable, "end game."

Endnotes

1. While what follows is faithful to the thrust of the paper submitted to Bélanger-Campeau in the fall of 1990, it has been updated in places to take account of more recent events and has been oriented more towards all of Canada, although the principal focus remains Quebec.

2. This section draws heavily from my Robarts' Lecture, *What Does Ontario Want?* (1989) and Chapter 1, *this volume*).

3. This may well be viewed as a biased remark. For example, what was the nature of our early history that it took two "transformations" for Quebec to pull itself up to its current level?

4. It is, of course, also true that many Quebecers have welcomed the Charter *and* many English Canadians regret its imposition. Nonetheless, in terms of elites, the above generalities would appear to ring true.

5. In terms of the definition of the "distinct society," before the House/Senate Joint Committee on the 1987 Constitutional Accord *La Federation des femmes du Quebec* offered the following definition (adopted from the Beige Paper):
    > Our laws, our legal system, our municipal and provincial institutions, our volunteer organizations, our media, our arts, our literature, our education system, our network of social and health-care services, our religious institutions, our savings and loan institutions as well as our language and culture.

    Cited in the *Report of the Special Joint Committee,* 1987:41.

6. Section 94 of the *Constitution Act, 1867* reads:
    > Notwithstanding anything in this Act, the Parliament of Canada may make Provision for the Uniformity of all or any of the Laws relative to Property and Civil Rights in Ontario, Nova Scotia, and New Brunswick, and of the Procedure of all or any of the Courts in Those Three Provinces, and from and after the passing of any Act in that Behalf the Power of the Parliament of Canada to make Laws in relation to any Matter comprised in any such Act shall, notwithstanding anything in this Act, be unrestricted; but any Act of the Parliament of Canada making Provision for such Uniformity shall not have any effect in any Province unless and until it is adopted and enacted as law by the legislation thereof.

    Frank Scott argues that the role of this provision was to allow the original non-Quebec provinces (and future non-Quebec provinces as well) to "centralize" if and when conditions became more favourable. (See LaSelva, 1983).

7. Sections III and IV are adopted from Courchene (1990b and Chapter 5, *this volume* and 1990e)

8. As a result of the February 1991 federal budget, this EPF freeze has been extended through to fiscal 1995-96.

9. The impact of the 1991 federal budget is that cash transfers will fall to zero sooner. The reason why Quebec reaches zero cash transfers sooner is that Quebec has long received extra personal-income-tax points in lieu of cash transfers for aspects of EPF. Thus, its cash transfers fall to zero before cash transfers for other provinces. Indeed, after all cash transfers fall to zero, Quebec will *still* be in receipt of these tax points. Clearly, this will become an emerging issue in fiscal federalism.

10. Again, recent events have altered aspects of this. Saskatchewan has decided to follow Quebec's lead and "join" the GST. Second, in the 1991 federal budget, Finance Minister Michael Wilson indicated his willingness to consider greater income-tax flexibility for the non-Quebec provinces. Specifically, Ottawa will consider allowing the provinces to apply their own rates and bracket structures to (the federally determined) taxable income. This may well stall the B.C. initiative towards an independent personal income tax system.

11. The First Nations/Territories will have difficulty exercising paramountcy unless they have provincial status.

4. A First-Nations Province

We Canadians and our governments are apparently having enormous difficulty coming to grips with the First Nations' conceptions of, let alone demands for, "sovereignty". This is surprising since a federal system, by its very nature, is explicitly designed to accommodate different levels of sovereignty. Thus, one obvious "Canadian" (but perhaps not the native) solution to aboriginal demands is to integrate the First Nations fully into the federal structure, that is to grant provincial status to the First Nations. What would this First Nations province (or dominion or confederacy or commonwealth) be like?

First, like the other provinces, the First Nations' province (henceforth FNP) would be territorially based, and would encompass the roughly 2,250 reserves. Unlike the other provinces, however, this land area would not be contiguous. But this should pose no particular problem in this progressively telecomputational age. The native population is near 3/4 of a million. About 500,000 have status and roughly 250,000 live on reserves. Thus, the potential population of FNP is not far off that of Newfoundland. The 600 or so bands have, as noted, over 2,000 reserves. The land area of these reserves (excluding land claims) is about half that of Nova Scotia. Phrased differently, in terms both of land and people, FNP would be at least twice as big as PEI.

In terms of governance structures, the FNP would presumably have some sort of legislative assembly. There would be considerable latitude here since the Constitution is largely silent on this issue. For example, the platform of Parti Québéçois under Pierre-Marc Johnson (and presumably under Parizeau as well) provides for a "presidential" system for Quebec, replete with a popularly elected prime minister (or president?). To my knowledge, no one has suggested that this would be ultra vires, except that some accommodation would have to be made for the Lieutenant Governor (which is mentioned in the Constitution). Thus, the First Nations could organize themselves either along "rep by pop" or "rep by reserve" or "rep by band" lines or more likely some combination of the first and third. Somewhat more cumbersome, but not particularly complicated would be the procedures for electing House of Commons members. Since constituencies follow provincial boundaries, First Nations MPs would run in multiple-reserve constituencies.

Henceforth, the FNP grand chief or first minister would automatically be at the constitutional and First Ministers' tables. Moreover, in the event of a reconstituted Senate, say along triple- E lines, FNP would have the same rights as would Alberta, for example. And if in any reconstituted Senate Quebec can insist on a "double majority" in order to protect aspects of its "distinct society", this same right would, with even more force and logic, be granted to FNP. Several longstanding concerns would thus be "solved".

FNP would, like the other provinces, have "sovereignty" over section 92 powers. In one fell swoop, this solves the "self- determination" issue. Toronto and Kingston and their governance structures are the business of the province of Ontario. Similarly, reserves and their governance would be creatures of FNP. Another perennial issue appropriately accommodated.

Criminal law would be Canadian, but FNP would have considerable powers under "property and civil rights" to introduce aspects of traditional native law and custom and even policing (Ontario has the OPP). With property and civil rights would come a very substantial range of provincial regulatory powers over a wide range of activities running the gamut from social policy to health and safety regulation to aspects of environmental protection, etc. Under section 93, education would fall under FNP and from section 109 FNP would control all lands, mines, minerals and royalties.

FNP would be constrained in terms of its ability to deal with other nations, but presumably would be allowed the same latitude here as that available to other provinces, which includes "goodwill or economic ambassadors" in addition to selected powers to sign certain types of international agreements.

The financial status of FNP would be patterned along existing provincial lines. FNP would be eligible for equalization payments as well as the full range of other transfers (e.g. for the established programs and the Canada Assistance Plan). Moreover, the couple of billions associated with Indian Affairs would be channelled to the FNP bureaucracy. (Ottawa does not have a department of Saskatchewan Affairs). Some special arrangements would have to be made for the delivery of social programs. Large reserves may be able to mount their own delivery systems. For those that cannot, the existing arrangements would have to be formalized, with FNP replacing Ottawa as the negotiator for the natives.

Income earned on reserves and earned off reserves by persons resident on reserves would be subject to federal income taxation. However, the 52% provincial tax on federal tax (using Ontario's rate as an example), would go to FNP. The GST would apply to FNP, but natives resident on reserves would be exempt from other provinces' retail sales taxes. If FNP imposed its own sales tax, these funds could go either to FNP or to the reserves themselves.

One could go on and on through the various provincial powers, but by now the general thrust should be clear.

Obviously, there are a myriad of difficult problems associated with this proposal. Foremost among these is the definition of a native. The logic of the above proposal is that a native is anyone residing in FNP. Would this mean that natives living off reserves would lose their aboriginal rights? Could both co-exist? More generally, this proposal is intended to be neutral with respect to the on-going land claims. They would proceed along their existing paths. Moreover, the proposal is intended to focus only on the natives in the existing other ten provinces. The above arguments hold with even more force in the North. Why bother settling land claims in the north when the alternative is to create one or more provinces where, by definition, these provinces would control their lands and resources.

Passage of this proposal would require consent of Ottawa and seven of the ten provinces with at least 50 per cent of the population, as well as the consent of the First Nations. No doubt this is a tall order. At the very least, however, the proposal places the issue of First Nations "sovereignty" within a framework that is familiar to Canadians. How much more than the powers of Quebec or Saskatchewan are the First Nations asking for? The answer I think is very little, if any. More to the point, why do they merit less?

Part II
Global Imperatives

5. Global Competitiveness
and the
Canadian Federation

"If I had my way, I'd pay a third of my taxes to an international fund dedicated to solving world problems, such as the environment and finance. A third to my community, where my children are educated and my family lives. And then a last third to my country, which each year does less and less for me in terms of security and well-being and instead subsidizes special interests" (Ohmae, 1990, p. 215).

I. INTRODUCTION

Even I am willing to concede that this quotation from the penultimate paragraph of Kenichi Ohmae's current bestseller *The Borderless World* is rather unorthodox as an entrée into an analysis of global competition and Canadian federalism. Yet it captures the essence of much that follows in the sense that globalization is systematically undermining the traditional role of national governments. Increasingly, functions normally associated with nation states are being passed "upward" to international regulatory agencies, to multilateral monitoring agencies, to free-trade arrangements and, for Europe, to a supra-national political structure. At the same time, globalization is also inherently decentralizing both in the consumer sovereignty sense (i.e., citizens everywhere are acquiring "rights" to access consumer goods and services regardless of country of origin) and in the sense of heightening citizens' awareness of their local communities where they live and work and play since, in this interdependent world, this is about all that remains under their control. To be sure, this is hardly a novel insight: McLuhan's "global village" anticipated as much a quarter-century ago. As a final and highly subjective introductory comment, were Ohmae steeped in the mentality of federalist Canada rather than his unitary-state Japan, the consumer-sovereignty thrust of *The Borderless World* would probably have led him to rethink entitling the "country" with as much as a third of his tax money.

Not surprisingly in light of the above, I shall embrace most aspects globalization and view as largely salutary its inevitable implications for the evolution of nation states. Section III will focus on four of these implications. Two of them relate to the impact of globalization in terms of privileging supra-national entities - transnational corporations (TNCs) on the one hand and transnational organization structures (which I label as the trend toward "global federalism") on the other. The remaining two implications deal with the transfer of power downward from nation states. The first of these is the "power to the people" aspect of globalization whether cast in Ohmae's terms of enhanced consumer sovereignty or in the more general terms that view citizens as one of the principal beneficiaries of the on-going information revolution. The second is the increasing importance of "international" cities as the national hubs for the globe-spanning networking of finance, information and services. Within Canada, then, globalization appears to be pointing in the direction of a significant devolution of powers.

With this as backdrop, section IV then focuses on a series of internal pressures that bear on the future of our federation. Two of these also point towards increased decentralization - the transfer of Ottawa's fiscal burden to the provinces and the FTA (which, for purposes of this paper, I deem to be an 'internal' pressure). Offsetting these centrifugal forces is the "Canadianizing" or integrating role that the Charter is playing at the socio-political level, at least for English-speaking Canadians. The section concludes by focussing on three other internal factors. One of these - initiatives directed toward freeing up internal markets -represents a curtailing of provincial powers or, more correctly, a curtailing of provincial measures designed to mount barriers to the free flow of goods, services and capital across the nation. The remaining two - a focus on decentralization and regionalism -represent necessary "detours" in terms of emphasizing key aspects underlying the nature of the Canadian federation.

The challenge, therefore, is to reconcile this globalization- triggered devolution of power on the economic and intergovernmental fronts with the emerging Charter-driven, Ottawa-centred conception of the country on the socio-political front. Section V attempts to address these issues. Specifically, how do we re-organize ourselves politically and constitutionally so that we can meet the global competitive challenge while preserving our national polity? This would be challenging enough in its own right, without having to layer in the post-Meech-Lake implications. Needless to say this section is highly subjective and is intended primarily to draw a few implications from the analysis rather than to provide an overall blueprint for "le fédéralisme renouvelé".

Implicit in this brief overview of the paper is a rather specific conception if not of globalization itself then at least of the implications of globalization, namely among other things a transfer of political and economic power both upwards and downwards from nation states. But globalization is both more and less than this. Accordingly, Section II will survey some of the varieties of globalization with a view toward motivating the particular conception adopted for the ensuing analysis. However, the section serves as more than a mere litany of approaches since aspects of the general thrust of the paper are advanced *inter alia* with the consideration of alternative versions of globalization.

II. VARIATIONS ON GLOBALIZATION

A. "Nothing is 'Overseas' Any Longer"(Ohmae, 1990, p. VIII)
At a basic level, globalization is easy to define. It is the process of the increasing internationalization of manufacturing and progressively of services as well. As Porter (1990, p. 14-15) notes, firms now compete with truly global strategies involving selling worldwide, sourcing components and materials worldwide, and locating activities in many nations to take advantage of low-cost factors. Thus, globalization in this sense decouples firms from the factor endowments of a single nation since raw materials, components, machinery and services are not only available globally but can be realigned geographically quickly and easily. Boundaries on a political map may be as clear as ever but boundaries on a competitive map have vanished (Ohmae, 1990, pp. 18-19). It is increasingly meaningless to speak in terms of an "American" car: indeed, favouring an "American" over a "Japanese" brand name may well *increase* Japanese value added! As Ohmae's phrase suggests, nothing is overseas any more or, if one prefers, everything is.

One can, following Ostry (1990), identify three phases of globalization. The first was dominated by an explosion in *trade* and witnessed the dismantling of tariff barriers in the successive GATT rounds. *Financial Integration* comprised the second phase coming on the heels of global imbalances, initially triggered by commodity shocks but now more associated with external payments imbalances and made possible by the on-going telecomputational revolution (Courchene, 1990a). The third and on-going phase relates to *foreign direct investment* where the prime agent of globalization is the multinational or transnational enterprise. This is to be contrasted with the first phase where the catalyst was multilateral government action (e.g. GATT). Thus, an important feature on this emerging globalization (and the "financial integration phase as well) is that it is "private-sector" driven - the TNCs, whether financial or commercial, are the only organizations that have so far been able to globalize themselves (Petrella, 1990).

This functional approach to globalization is assumed to be implicit in all remaining conceptions of globalization.

B. Globalization as Consumer Sovereignty

Probably not universally accepted, but certainly central to the ensuing analysis, is Ohmae's thesis that the dominant feature of business today is the emergence of consumer sovereignty: "performance standards are now set in the global marketplace by those that buy the products, not those who make them or regulate them" (1990, dustjacket). How else can one explain the Japanese dominance in the American market initially for autos but now for an enormous range of consumer goods? This is particularly so given that in the early years of Japanese inroads the U.S. was still recognized as the hegemon and these inroads were made at the expense of the hegemon's largest corporations. Thus, the key to winning in this new global environment is for companies to act as "insiders" within countries, catering to consumer preferences, and not by "exporting" to them (pp. 18-19).

One of the principal factors at play here relates to the democratization of information (an approach that will also be dealt with in more detail later under "globalization as the information/ knowledge revolution"). Governments' previous monopoly of knowledge and information about things happening around the world "enabled them to fool, mislead, or control the people, because only the governments possessed real facts in anything like real time" (p. 19). No longer. The burgeoning flow of information is eroding the ability of governments to pretend that their national economic interests are synonymous with those of the people (p. 185).

From this conception of global consumer sovereignty follows Ohmae's prescription for the role of government:

> The role of government in a borderless world, then, is to represent and protect the interests of its people, not of its companies or its industries. It should let in the light and then allow its people to make their own choices. Anything less is to put the class and career interests of government bureaucrats ahead of those people they are sworn to serve (p. 201).

A pro-active focus to the above re-active role will be elaborated later in the paper.

C. Globalization as the Information/Knowledge Revolution

Drucker's insightful *Foreign Affairs* article (1986), "The Changed World Economy", does not set out to define globalization, per se. Rather it documents three fundamental changes or uncouplings that have occurred in the very fabric of the global economy:

1. The primary-products economy has come 'uncoupled' from the industrial economy;
2. In the industrial economy itself, production has come uncoupled from employment;
3. Capital movements rather than trade in goods and services have become the engines and the driving force of the world economy. The two have not, perhaps, become uncoupled. But the link has become quite loose, and worse, quite unpredictable (p. 21).

Implicitly, if not explicitly, underlying Drucker's triad of uncouplings is the information/knowledge revolution.

Because these uncouplings are so relevant to the Canadian economy and to the future Canadian competitiveness some further elaboration is warranted. In terms of the first of these, the Club of Rome predictions have been completely overturned: the world is awash in raw materials and, except for prolongued or strategic wars, their prices are likely to remain low relative to the prices of manufactured products. Combined with this is the information/ knowledge induced shift in industrial products away from heavily material-intensive products and processes. In Drucker's view primary products are becoming of marginal importance to the economies of the developed world (p. 29).

This is of obvious importance to Canada. Moreso than any other G7 nation, Canada is integrated to the world economy through raw-material exports rather than through exports of manufactured goods (Drucker 1989, p. 50). Thus, the challenge confronting Canada is to make the transition from a resource-based culture to a human-capital-intensive culture (or in terms of our regional policies, for example, from boards and mortar to mortar boards!). This is proving to be a most difficult transition since our traditional fascination with resource megaprojects still remains high on the agendas of all first ministers. In this context, the FTA represents a once-in-a-lifetime opportunity. Thus far, however, our macro authorities have, via high interest rates and an overvalued Canadian dollar, stymied the potential FTA investment boom (and, therefore, the potential for increased integration to the U.S. and global economies via manufacturing exports) and converted it to a consumption binge, triggered by interest-rate- induced deficits. (These macro implications will be dealt with in Section V). More generally, resources will probably always play a more important role in Canada than in other developed nations. Increasingly, however, their continued importance will require high-value-added or knowledge-intensive applications.

In terms of the second of the uncouplings, Drucker argues that "a country, an industry or a company that puts the preservation of blue-collar manufacturing jobs ahead of being internationally competitive ... will soon have neither production nor steady jobs" and "the attempt to preserve industrial blue-collar jobs is actually a prescription for unemployment" (p. 32). Recent data indicate that it is not the American production machine that is being "de-industrialized", it is the American labour force (p. 30). One major implication of this uncoupling of manufacturing production from manufacturing employment is that the choice between an industrial policy that favours *production* (productivity) and one that favours *employment* is going to be a singularly contentious issue (p. 35). Canadians lived through this trade-off in the free trade debate. The economic arguments for free trade with the U.S. rest on productivity, market access and investment opportunities and the implications of these for longer term employment and standard-of-living prospects, but the debate itself quickly moved to short-term employment implications which may or may not be "favourable".

The final fundamental change is the emergence of the "symbol economy" (capital movements, exchange rates and credit flows) as the new flywheel of the world economy (p. 37). This too, I think, has its origins in the information revolution and particularly in the integration of the global financial markets. Indeed, elsewhere I have argued that the global financial system is best viewed as a sophisticated information, coordination and telecomputational network (1990h and *this volume*). Drucker goes on to note that Euromarket and foreign exchange trading is now about 40 times the dollar value of goods and services trade. However, traditional economic theory still views exchange rates as the product of comparative domestic productivity and inflation behaviour. Yet for much of the 1980s the symbol economy has been driving the real side. One need look no further than Canada's recent experience - high interest rates pulled in foreign capital, appreciated the Canadian dollar which in turn led to a shift in our current account balance from a $3 billion surplus in 1983 to a deficit of nearly $20 billion in 1989. As recently as the 1970s, a deterioration of this magnitude in the current account balance would have implied a sharp fall in the exchange rate to equilibrate the balance of payments. Not when the symbol economy is in the driver's seat: the high exchange rate (reflecting the operations of the symbol economy) is driving the current account balance. Thus, getting one's macro house in order (in particular, aligning aggregate national savings more in tune with aggregate national investment) has emerged as a major factor in the second half of the 1980s and promises to continue to play a critical role in the longer term prospects for nations (Courchene, 1990b).

Let me backtrack at this point and return to the notion that the global financial system is really a sophisticated information, coordination and telecomputational network. From this vantage point, it seems inevitable that the system will develop in the direction of globe-spanning payments and settlements networks. Indeed, two of the most controversial issues in Canadian finance (apart from the perennial issue of the ownership of trust companies) relate to this potential for networks or information systems to dominate institutions. The first is the granting of a Schedule II foreign bank charter to Amex. The large chartered banks are not worried about facing a few more foreign bank branches competing for Canadian deposits. But Amex is different. It may not ever open a retail branch. Rather, Amex wants to (and will) integrate in vast credit-card network into the Canadian payments system. The bankers have a rather strong case against Amex when they point out that the U.S. payments system has kept Amex out. So why should Canada be offering privileges to Amex that it cannot obtain in its home jurisdiction? The deeper concern, however, is that Amex brings a powerful new network to bear on Canadian finance and one that has the longer term potential for integration with its global credit-card system.

The second "network" concern relates to the BCE Inc. takeover of Montreal Trust. The issue here has to do with the potential competitive edge resulting from comingling telecommunications and finance. Home banking cannot be that far off and already Bell is testing the Alex system, which is Canada's version of France's Minitel. Again, the concern is with networks and communications systems, not with Montreal Trust as an institution.

As noted earlier, these three "uncouplings" do not constitute a definition for globalization. They are, however, part and parcel of the way that the global economy is evolving and they represent enormous challenges to Canadian competitiveness and more generally to our ability to adapt to the emerging global economy.

D. Globalization as "Mobility"

Focusing on an enhanced degree of mobility as the essence of globalization serves two roles in the context of this brief survey. First it acts as a summary of sorts for the above approaches since enhanced mobility, whether of goods, services, capital, information, etc., effectively underpins all of the earlier conceptions. Second, an emphasis on mobility or its counterpart, the potential for "bypass", provides a bridge to the political as distinct from the mainly economic perspectives highlighted earlier.

The first proposition here is that "ultra" mobility seriously constrains national decision makers. Consider the power to tax, for example.

Taxation falls on immobile factors, not mobile ones. If Canada attempts to levy taxes on capital that are higher than those applicable elsewhere, capital will simply leave (or not contemplate entry) until the real returns rise sufficiently to offset the higher tax. The resulting lower capital/labour and capital/land ratios imply that labour and land will ultimately bear the burden of the higher tax on capital. This is hardly new. All of us are familiar with the "Delawarization" of America in terms of corporate headquartering. However, the scope for seeking out tax havens is significantly magnified in the new borderless globe. One reason for the recent American expansion (in spite of its twin- deficit problems) relates to the stimulus arising from the Reagan "supply side" tax cut. It is no accident that Canada quickly followed suit. Thus, no nation is now sufficiently dominant globally to be able to act alone in extracting a larger tax share from capital.

Intriguingly, Albert Breton (1990) has argued recently that one of the reasons why a socialist like François Mitterrand and a conservative like Margaret Thatcher can both support Europe 1992 is that they come at it from very different perspectives. For Thatcher the appeal is (or was while she was Prime Minister) a straightforward economic one - the gains from trade resulting from market enhancement and liberalization. The attraction to Mitterand in supporting European economic integration is that the resulting political superstructure may finally be able to extract an appropriate share of taxation from capital. This is particularly the case if the Americans and Japanese (and their trading blocs) can be enticed to follow suit. Breton argues further that this desire to enhance tax revenues is sufficiently powerful that if increased cooperation does not do the trick then pressures to "federalize" will intensify. While this particular insight is novel, the underlying principle is not. Most federations concentrate revenue raising at the federal level and then make use of intergovernmental grants of various sorts to transfer some of these revenues back to the provinces/states. Factor mobility along with other concerns such as scale economies and distributional implications mean that the federal government typically has a comparative advantage in raising revenues in a federation. Enhanced international mobility simply moves this comparative advantage up one more level to the supra-national level.

This same principle applies to aspects of regulation. In terms, for example, of financial sector regulation, a recent *Economist* article (Ziegler, 1990) zeroed in on the essence of the issue: "Who, in the future, should regulate an Australian firm that trades Japanese futures on Chicago's Globex out of London?" There is no obvious answer at the present time. However, what is developing in response to this and similar concerns is the formulation of international standards. The International Organization of Securities Commissions has adopted a common framework for assessing the capital adequacy of firms engaged in the securities industry. Of more significance are the BIS (Bank for International Settlements) capital-adequacy standards for banks. Canada and some dozen other nations have already "signed on" to these standards. What this means is that one result of globalization as it relates to the financial sector is to "pass upward", as it were, aspects of regulating domestic financial institutions that operate globally.

The key message deriving from this focus on regulation and taxation is that as the world approaches economic integration, driven largely by the global "private sector", this is generating important changes in the nature of the global "public sector" or political integration. More on this later.

The second proposition is that as the degree of mobility or the potential for bypass increases, this is in many cases tantamount to "redrawing" the border between public sector and private sector activity. This is most evident in the telecommunications area. As long as the potential for bypass is minimal, it makes sense to conceive of Teleglobe, for example, as a natural monopoly and to keep it under government control. Now that bypass is increasingly possible, the rationale for government ownership essentially vanishes, so why not privatize it? Whether one wants to view this as the product of the information revolution (and, hence, included in the previous section) or of increased mobility or bypass is largely irrelevant. What is relevant is that government's ability to regulate across an increasing range of fronts is being effectively eroded.

E. Globalization as Non-Hegemony

It may well be sheer happenstance that the advent of globalization coincided with the decline of American hegemony. Nevertheless, there is a sense in which meaningful globalization may require the absence of a hegemon. What this effectively means is that there is a "global" market quite independent of any national market. Moreover, it implies that success in this new environment requires that both companies and countries put their competitive position in the world economy, not in any particular national economy, as the first priority of their policies. As Drucker (1986, p. 49) notes:

> From now on any country - but also any business, especially a large one - that wants to do well economically will have to accept that it is the world economy that leads and that domestic policies will succeed only if they strengthen, or at least not impair, the country's international competitive position.

Or even more to the point:

> Because of the emergence of the transnational company and of the symbol economy as the determinant force in the world

market, there is no more economic superpower. No matter how big, powerful and productive a country is, it competes every day for its world-market position ... It does not matter to the transnational company which country is in the lead. It does business in all of them and is at home in all of them. There is no superpower in industry, either; there are only competitors (Drucker, 1989, p. 58).

However, this represents a major structural change in the world economy - one where the underlying economic challenges can in the short term be accommodated much more easily than the underlying political challenges. Perhaps this should be phrased differently - the "global" private sector (TNCs) has been able to adopt to the emerging economic challenges much better than the "global" public sector has been able to adopt to the emerging political challenges. Thus, the rapidly integrating world economy is overlain with a "splintering world polity" (Drucker, 1987, p. 65).

One response to this is the rise of regional trading blocs and the pressures for a return to some form of protectionism. While there are many reasons for this, including the massive trade imbalances between the Americans and Japanese, Drucker suggests that the changing role of trade itself is playing a part. In particular, the shift from "complementary" trade in Adam Smith's era, then to "competitive" trade for the last century and now "adversarial" trade has now made reciprocity rather than free trade the new instrument of integration:

"The emergence of new non-Western trading countries - fore-most Japan - creates what I call *adversarial* trade. Complementary trade seeks to establish a partnership. Competitive trade aims at creating a customer. Adversarial trade aims at dominating an industry. Complementary trade is a courtship. Competitive trade is fighting a battle. Adversarial trade aims at winning the war by destroying the enemy's army and its capacity to fight".

[As a result], *reciprocity* is likely to become the vehicle for the integration of the world economy just as competitive trade was the vehicle for the integration of the international economy during the past 150 years. ...

[Reciprocity] is clearly going to be the main trade policy of the European Community, if only because it alone offers a compromise between the traditional protectionists in the EC (the French and the Italians) and the traditional free traders (the British and the Germans). It is fast becoming also the policy the United States is choosing for economic relations with Japan, Korea and Brazil (Drucker, 1989, p. 58-59).

The vision that emerges, then, is one of free-trade within regional trading blocs and reciprocity or reciprocal trade between these regional blocs. To this conception I would note the importance of the earlier reference to foreign direct investment or trade-related investment as the on-going phase of globalization. To the extent that this development proceeds (including the emphasis on the "right to establishment" and on "access") there may be a decline in the current friction associated with aspects of goods trade. This is so because under conditions of freer investment and the right to establishment, the "national origin" of a product or corporation will progressively have less to do with the national origin of the value-added embodied in the product. In an important sense, trade-related investment is a substitute, as well as a complement, for traditional trade. What then becomes "traded" is not goods and services, per se, but earnings and profits.

F. Globalization as International Governance Structures

This approach looks at globalization in terms of international organization or "regime" theory. Regimes or international governance structures (IGSs) are the formal and informal devices through which political and economic actors organize and manage their interdependencies. As Eden and Hampson (1990) note, typically this implies one or more of organizing negotiation processes, setting standards, performing allocation functions, monitoring compliance, reducing conflict and resolving disputes. These interdependencies can arise in firm-to-firm, firm-to-state and state-to-state relations. These regimes can be classified along the four general rationales suggested by Eden and Hampson, e.g. efficiency failures (public goods, externalities, transactions costs, non-competitive markets), macroeconomic instabilities, distribution conflicts, and security concerns. For each regime, then, one could assess the range of challenges for national policy makers and in particular focus on the problems or opportunities, as the case may be, arising because Canada is a federal nation.

However ideal this framework may be, it is not the route I shall pursue. Nonetheless, even these few sentences indicate caution must be exercised in grappling with the implications of globalization since the manner in which firms and nations interact internationally will likely vary quite dramatically across industries. To take only an extreme example, the policy challenges arising from an internationally cartellized sector like fossil energy differ markedly from those associated with a typically (except for the U.S.) domestically cartellized industry like telecommunications. And so on.

G. Globalization à la Porter

To conclude, but obviously not exhaust, these variants of globalization it is important to focus briefly on Michael Porter's *The Competitive Advantage of Nations* (1990). In a sense, Porter's thesis runs counter to much of the above thrust:

> As globalization of competition has intensified, some have begun to argue a diminished role for nations. Instead, internationalization and the removal of protection and other distortions to competition arguably make nations, if anything, more important. ... The view that globalization eliminates the importance of the home base rests on false premises (p. 30).

My role in this paper is not to argue that national governments no longer remain significant players, only that the nature of the role they can play is now highly circumscribed and certainly markedly different from that a decade or so ago. Indeed, the final substantive section is devoted largely to elaborating on this new role. Initial appearances notwithstanding, this is not inconsistent with the Porter view. When he elaborates on the importance of nations, it is in the following terms:

> National governments, for their part, must set the appropriate goal, productivity, which underpins economic prosperity. They must strive for its true determinants, such as incentive, effort, and competition, not the tempting but usually counterproductive choices such as subsidy, extensive collaboration, and 'temporary' protection that are often proposed (p. 30).

Indeed, the conclusion of his introductory chapter, "The Need For a New Paradigm" fits rather well as a prologue to the remainder of the paper:

> National differences in character and culture, far from being threatened by global competition, prove integral to success in it. Understanding the new and different role of nations in competition will be a task which occupies much of what follows (p. 30).

III: GLOBALIZATION AND THE TRADITIONAL NATION STATE

There are many ways to distill the essence of globalization and its implications. Somewhat arbitrarily, I have chosen to focus in somewhat greater detail on four aspects that I believe are particularly relevant to the evolution of the Canadian federation. Two of these serve to transfer "sovereignty" upward (i.e. the shift from multinational to transnational corporations and the emergence of supra-national organizations) and two transfer "sovereignty" downward (i.e. the enhanced role of individuals and the rise in importance of international cities). Most of the discussion will be very brief since, except for the focus on cities, these points have already been highlighted.

A. From MNCs to TNCs

Following Wylie (1989) I shall define multinational corporations (MNCs) as creatures of largely-closed, national markets and, therefore, frequently subject to host-country public policy initiatives such as requirements relating to domestic sourcing, R and D expenditures and sometimes ownership limits. What global integration, particularly of the FTA variety, favours is the emergence of the "transnational" corporations (TNCs) whose products and services can be delivered anywhere in the world without having to bend to local/national government pressures and dictates. In terms of the FTA, for example, this follows from the provisions relating to trade-related investment, the right of establishment and national treatment. National treatment maintains domestic policy sovereignty in that it allows national governments to regulate as they see fit with the key proviso that American firms must be treated exactly the same as Canadian firms. Thus, an American firm can do in Canada anything a Canadian firm can do.

Under Europe 1992, this is taken even further, particularly in financial services where institutions chartered in one country will be able to do business in any other member country on the basis of a "single community passport" as it were. What the host country can insist upon is that all institutions, wherever chartered, abide by certain conduct-of-business and consumer protection rules. Beyond this, however, the EC approach is at the opposite end of the spectrum from national treatment, i.e. an Italian chartered company will be able to do in France essentially what it can do in Italy.

As noted earlier, TNCs are the leading edge in terms of the recent phases of globalization - financial integration and trade- related investment. What this implies, also noted earlier, is that the process of globalization has been effectively "privatized", albeit with the support of national governments. That this should generate a movement in the direction of public sector countervail is hardly surprising and will be dealt with briefly in the following section.

However, it generates a quite separate problem for small open economies like Canada, namely, how important is domestic ownership? If TNCs have investment freedom, it is only a matter of time (and not much) before most of the so-called Canadian "heritage" firms will fall under foreign ownership. Among the developed nations it is largely those that are English speaking whose assets are up for grabs. The integration of finance and commerce in Japan and on the continent, and the resulting intricate web of cross-ownership linkages, implies that any takeover attempt of a major German firm, for example, will be foiled because it probably would also imply a takeover of one or more of the big three German banks - Deutsche, Dresdner or Commerzbank. Not so for countries like Canada that are in the Anglo-American, industrial-structure mode. I think that it is fair to say that economists and policy makers alike came to the conclusion that ownership was not particularly relevant in resource-based economies. The resource base is not mobile. Employment is likely to be Canadian. Moreover, the head office is likely to be located near the resource base. Finally, we know how to tax resource rents, even if we do not always do so. I am not sure that this applies as we move to a knowledge-based or human- capital-based economy. Will head-offices remain in Canada? How do we tax human-capital rents? In any event, globalization ensures that "protecting" these industries is not the way to go. What I have elsewhere proposed (Courchene, 1990h and this volume) and what the Senate (1990) has recommended is that we open up our regulatory process to allow (*not* require) our financial sector to buy into the commercial sector. Quebec is already committed to such a policy. The argument is rather straightforward. In this increasingly competitive world each country has to lever off its inherent strengths. For a country of some 25 million people, we have an incredibly efficient banking and financial system. Can we afford, competitively, not to allow the banks the freedom to manouevre on the commercial side of the economy and to create some home-grown TNCs? This is particularly the case given developments south of the border. It is true that the U.S. is keeping banks out of "commerce", but commerce is now encroaching on finance. The so-called corporate "in-house" banks (Ford, GMAC, G.E. Credit Corporation, IBM, AT and T, Sears, Amex etc.) are becoming major financial players. Indeed, Amex now has a Schedule II bank in Canada.

In any event, the message here is that globalization is privileging TNCs at the expense of national governments. It may well be that Ohmae (1990) is correct in arguing that TNCs will succeed only to the extent that their products are tailored to the preferences of domestic consumers (i.e. the loss of influence of the Canadian government is transferred to Canadian consumers), but this is, I think, a quite separate issue.

B. Global Federalism

The growing interdependence globally has meant that the ability of any one nation to act alone in an increasing number of areas is rapidly being eroded. Not surprisingly, therefore, the result has been a growing number of international agreements, alliances, and understandings across a wide variety of fronts - political, military, economic, environmental, sectoral, etc. Each of these constrains (in varying degrees) what a signator can do and in this sense represents a loss of autonomy.

One question that arises in this context, more related to rhetoric than to substance, is whether this loss of autonomy should be viewed as ceding aspects of sovereignty. Phrased differently, what does sovereignty mean in an increasingly independent world? The first point to make is that these agreements are typically reciprocal in that all signators are equally constrained. Second, and relatedly, a given country can now legislate with the knowledge that there are clear and generally well-defined rules in terms of how other nations will react. One might view this as an *increase* in effective sovereignty: for a small open country to retain complete freedom to legislate in an interdependent world, where there are no rules of the game in terms of how or when other nations may retaliate, hardly classifies as meaningful sovereignty. For example, Canadians are free, legislatively, to determine our own pollution standards. However, I am sure that most of us would gladly transfer some of this freedom to manoeuvre to an effective international body that was willing and able to implement binding norms on all signatories. Which of these advances our "sovereignty"?

Rhetoric aside, the global community is federalizing and we will be swept along. Allan Gotlieb (1990) predicts that Canada, the U.S. and Mexico will be part of a free trade zone before 2,000. One can already speak meaningfully in terms of a West Pacific bloc. Federations will spring up in Africa too. Perhaps more disconcerting to Canada is the point that these international political changes are eliminating many of the existing national units. As Gotlieb queries: is there any validity to maintaining our conception of being a "middle power" when there will soon be no more middle powers in Europe?

In more general terms, this transfer of power to TNCs and the countervailing trend toward international, rather than national, political ordering does significantly alter the role of the nation state. As Whyte [1990, p. 469] remarked recently [note that Whyte's use of the word "corporate" corresponds to the TNC role in the world]:

> ... it is the trend towards rooting the political culture in corporat-
> ism that is *the* facet of internationalization that has impinged most
> directly on Canada. This phenomenon, more than any other, has
> put in doubt the idea that the nation has a significant political role.
> Not only do national political and social objectives fit so poorly
> with the transnational objectives of production and profit, the
> instruments of national regulation are inept at constraining corpo-
> rate activity. The nation state has become irrelevant in two
> senses: what it traditionally has tried to achieve is now seen as
> confounding corporate progress (and, hence, in present thinking,
> social progress) and its methods mean that it has a very low
> capacity to restrain or reform.

While not everyone would be of the view that this "low capacity" of the nation state to "restrain" constitutes a problem, it is the case that the role of national governments in an interdependent world has to be rethought.

I now turn to the two selected features of globalization that transfer powers downward from the central or federal government.

C. Power to the People

Globalization is clearly empowering citizens. In my view, even more important than, although related to, Ohmae's consumer sovereignty aspect is the fact that individuals are the primary beneficiaries of the information or telecomputational revolution. A decade or so ago "transmitters" determined the information flow. Increasingly, the "receptors" are in the driver's seat. Consider telecommunications. With the increased possibility for bypass, soon to be enhanced dramatically by Motorola's plans for a comprehensive cellular network, the pressing national concern about "rate rebalancing" (i.e. removing the cross-subsidization from long-distance to local calls) is really last generation's debate. Janisch and Schultz (1989) correctly assert that, in this increasingly information/knowlege-intensive world, telecommunications "constitute a central business resource for developing, enhancing and maintaining competitive advantage" (p. 16). Ultimately, this has to mean enhanced competition, replete with user choice and control, so that telecommunications systems can be configured in conformance with an institution's needs in terms of addressing the global marketplace.

This is, of course, the central message to be gleaned from Janisch and Schultz (1989). However, I am less convinced that they have zeroed in on the correct "means" for addressing the problem:

"We have argued that one of the most pernicious features of contemporary Canadian telecommunications is the fragmentation or balkanization of what is a national, integrated system. ... The federal government must act on the recent Supreme Court decision to ensure that there is a single national telecommunications policy" (p. 33).

With respect, Canada does not necessarily need a *national* telecommunications policy. (Actually, Janisch and Schultz are in favour of some provincial role so that what follows may misrepresent their views. Thus, it is best to interpret the following as a general comment). Enforcing uniformity on the country based on a version of the status quo *would* constitute a "single national telecommunications policy"! But it is not a viable policy. Rather we need an *international* telecommunications policy. It seems to me that just as Quebec has moved more quickly than Ottawa in embracing global markets in its regulation of financial institutions, it is also the case that it would likely move to privilege its business community with telecommunciations freedom if it had control over the sector. All it takes is one province to open the door and the rest will be forced into line. In other words, I would hazard a guess that interests other than international competitiveness are likely to get *far more attention* at the CRTC level than they would if Quebec were running its own show.

This aside, the general point is that access to and the ability to process information on the part of citizens as well as their increasing role in terms of determining what information flows means that power correspondingly shifts in their direction as well. This has dramatic implications for all governments - federal, provincial and local. Thus, it is not necessarily decentralizing in the "federalism" sense of the term (i.e., the transfer of power from federal government to lower level governments). Rather, it represents a "democratization" of power, as it were.

D. The Internationalization of Cities

It may seem anomalous that, as society progressed from city states to nation states and now to supranational arrangements like a single Europe, globalization is having its principal impact on cities. Indeed, international cities are the institutional vehicles via which the globe is integrating.[1] As a result of globalization, nothing much has changed in terms of the Ottawa-Bonn (Berlin) relationship, except that Bonn will soon become Berlin. What globalization has altered, however, is the relationship between Toronto and Frankfurt. Moreover, Toronto will become more and more like Frankfurt and London and Tokyo and less and less like Kingston and Fredericton and Saskatoon.

The reason is fairly obvious. These international cities (Toronto, Montreal and Vancouver for Canada) are the critical national nodes in the global communications and trading networks. The information revolution and the accompanying explosion in services is occurring in these international cities and competition among them is intense.

At one level, this is surprising since the advent of the information society was supposed to diffuse economic activity. Not too long ago the vision of "electronic cottages" plugged into headquarters' mainframes was the received wisdom in terms of the future of work. Presumably this aspect of the information revolution will at some point come into play. For the immediate future, however, the economies of scope associated with the concentration of the information infrastructure means that these international cities have become not only growth poles but the essential "connectors" (to fall back on Jane Jacobs' terminology) outward to the Londons and Tokyos and inward to their regional hinterlands. As my colleague John McDougall puts it, McLuhan's conception of a global village may eventually come to pass, but for now the villagers' are the international cities.

The dilemma for Canadian federalism is obvious. In spite of their enhanced importance, cities are "constitutionless": they are creatures of their respective provinces. Yet as their role increases, one would expect them, among other things, to dispatch "ambassadors" to their sister international cities in other nations and to engage in a range of activities that used to be the preserve of nation states.

There is, however, another role that cities will increasingly play, namely they will progressively come to define the "community" referred in the introductory quotation from Ohmae. As the various implications of globalization begin to take hold, citizens will come to realize that among the most important "political" decisions over which they still have control is how they shall work and live and play. And for this, their focus is largely at the provincial or even local level. To have influence at this level, it is not necessary that one have an "international city" in one's midst. But without such an international city it is most unlikely that one could convert this notion of community into a notion of a "distinct society" (replete with visions of sovereignty association). Phrased differently, without the recent dynamism of Montreal (and, relatedly, the confidence of Montreal's business elite), there would be no "Bloc Quebecois".

As one looks across the country, apart from Toronto the only other city around which a "distinct" society could be formed is Vancouver. Its distinctiveness relates to a Pacific Rim orientation and in a few decades, perhaps, to a Pacific Rim population. The suggestion here is not that Canada West would want to opt out of Canada, only that its range of linguistic, cultural and economic interests would have little to do with those that drive the Canadian heartland.

Toronto could, of course, also assert its distinctiveness. But up until recently at least there was little point in doing so since Ottawa was essentially acting on Ontario's (Toronto's) behalf in this endeavour. Toronto's role was essentially to quietly collect rents (thanks to the National Policy) from the peripheries and publicly practice beneficence by agreeing to return some of these rents to the periphery in terms of equalization payments and in terms of grants to the "have-less" areas of Ontario. Except of course when Ontario's interests were perceived to be threatened, as in the case of rising energy prices. Here Ontario pulled out all the stops to ensure that Ottawa unloaded the NEP on the West (Courchene, 1989 and Chapter 1, this volume).

Matters are quite different in the post-Meech era since, in the presence of Quebec demands and more recently those of the West, *Ottawa's role* in the federation is challenged. Ontario and Toronto can probably be counted on to lobby on Ottawa's behalf. Pursuing these post-Meech issues will carry me too far afield. However, it is important to reiterate the underlying issue at play here. Cities are becoming increasingly powerful economic engines within the federation. Moreover, it is not obvious that the economic interests of these international cities coincide with the interests of their provincial governments. This is especially the case for provinces like Saskatchewan, where their "international city" is located in another province let alone for the Maritimes where their international cities (Boston/New York) are not even in the country!

To conclude this section on the impact of globalization on the nation state, sociologist Daniel Bell merits the last word: "The nation state is becoming too small for the big problems of life, and too big for the small problems of life" (1987). I shall return to this theme later. Now the focus shifts to the ways that various "internal" forces are driving the Canadian federation.

IV. INTERNAL PRESSURES ON THE CANADIAN FEDERATION

Coincident with the integration of the world economy, the Canadian federation is undergoing dramatic changes from within. In terms of the conduct of economic policy, two changes point decidedly in the direction of decentralization, by any definition of this term. The first of these relates to the impact of the FTA (recall that, arbitrarily, I decided to treat the FTA as an "internal" factor) and the second to the on-going process of decentralization triggered by the fiscal burden of the federal government. Countering these, to a degree, at least, is the role that the Charter is playing for many Canadians in terms of redefining the nature of Canadian federalism and with it the role of Ottawa. The remainder of the section deals briefly with three other features - the internal common market, decentralization and regionalism. I shall deal with each in turn.

A. The FTA and Canadian Federalism Competing Constitutional Rhetorics[1]

History, language/culture, geography and a sparse population have all played a role in developing among Canadians a more benign approach to government and a heightened concern for collective rights and welfare, in sharp contrast to the individualism that is the hallmark of the American Creed. Even the Canadian Charter of Rights and Freedoms (while arguably "Americanizing" because it transfers powers to individuals, via the courts, thereby introducing a checks-and-balances element into Canada's previous Parliament-is-supreme approach to governance) differs from its U.S. counterpart in that it enshrines aspects of collective rights - gender equality rights, aboriginal rights, linguistic minority rights, multicultural rights, etc. Nowhere are these national differences more clear than in the two countries' approaches to health insurance. Canada's publicly funded, publicly administered (although "privately" delivered) health-care system stands in sharp contrast to the more individualistic and market-oriented (largely privately funded, privately administered, privately delivered) U.S. approach.

The defining constitutional rhetorics - peace, order and good government" for Canada and "life, liberty and the pursuit of happiness" for the U.S. *are* reflected in our respective citizen- state relationships. In effect, the emphasis in the U.S. is more on the "means" with little emphasis on whether or not the "ends" are appropriate. In Canada, the emphasis has been far more on "ends" with a willingness to use virtually any means to achieve these ends.

In any event, the FTA with its emphasis on markets resonates more, as Simpson (1987) notes, with life, liberty and the pursuit of happiness than it does with peace, order and good government. Phrased differently, while the FTA need not constrain the "ends" toward which Canada and Canadians aim, it certainly constrains the "means" that can be used to achieve these ends. Specifically, given that the FTA embraces markets it is inherently decentralizing since markets themselves are inherently decentralizing. This does not mean, for example, that Canada cannot attempt to capture energy rents from the West if and when energy prices surge again (a not unrealistic scenario given the on-going Gulf crisis). What it does mean is that this would have to be accomplished via the tax-transfer system instead of the NEP price route. In my view, this is hardly a constraint, since the tax-transfer system was far and away the preferable route for "nationalizing" western energy rents the first time around, setting aside the issue of whether Ottawa ought to be in the game of alienating western energy rents.

1.   East West Transfers vs. North South Integration

Whether the economics of an east-west transfer system is sustainable under increasing north-south integration is an issue that will be dealt with in Part V. Here, the emphasis is on the political economy of these transfers. As Jacques Parizeau used to argue (and may still argue for all I know) Ontario's magnanimity in terms of regional transfers contained a healthy dose of "Ontario first". As long as Canadian trade flowed largely east-west, with Ontario the north-south conduit to the U.S., the second (and future) round spending impacts of these regional transfers generally came to rest somewhere in Ontario. Under full north- south integration for all of Canada's regions, this may no longer be the case. Some of the regional payments imblances with the centre will, now, shift south with the result that the second-round impacts of regional transfers may no longer come to rest in Ontario but rather in North Carolina or California. At a political level, this will surely erode support for these transfers, particularly those that privilege "place" rather than people.

This may or may not be viewed as decentralizing, but what is clear is that our tradition of sheltering various regions of the country from market forces is going to become progressively more different both economically, politically and perhaps, "legally" under the FTA. This leads directly to the third aspect of the FTA - north-south integration.

2. North-South Trade

Sir John A. was a brilliant nation builder. He knew exactly how to forge an east-west country over a vast territory where geography dictated north-south linkages. First, one mounts comprehensive tariff barriers (the National Policy) then one links east and west with a national transportation system. From an economic vantage point, the resulting east-west trade was highly distorted, i.e., much of it would not have flowed except for the tariff. If one then subsidizes east-west transportation the result is to increase what is already a distorted trade flow.

In any event, the FTA reverses this, initially by removing tariffs and later, perhaps, via a negotiated subsidy pact. The result will be an increasing degree of north-south integration along regional lines. (Note that this may not imply a significant drop in east-west trade since a) incomes will increase, b) Canadian firms should become more competitive with enhanced market access and c) overall trade should increase.) The fear expressed by many is that with each region looking more north-south this will mean that "allegiances" will shift along these lines too. Perhaps. But one should recall that until very recently Ontario-U.S. trade was larger than U.S.-Japanese trade. Yet, during the free trade debate Ontario assumed the role of defender of Canadian values, particularly as they related to social policies. Why should Saskatchewan shed its Canadian values if it too is allowed greater north-south trade?

However, one likely consequence is that the provinces or regions will now pay more attention to their competitive position vis-à-vis their cross-border regions. For example, presumably in anticipation of the FTA the 1988 Quebec budget presented tax comparison tables not only with Ontario, but also with New York, Michigan and Massachusetts. Relatedly, the provinces or economic regions will likely take greater umbrage at federal policies that, for whatever reason, place their economies at a disadvantage relative to the economies south of the border. My guess is that this will eventually lead to the provinces having more say in economic policy formation affecting their region. Similarly, the likelihood is that wage behaviour across the Canadian regions will become more diverse, perhaps even to the point of having wages for federal employees in the region be based more on regional than national scales.

B. Deficit-Triggered Decentralization

Unlike the above factors which point in the direction of a potential shift of power from Ottawa to the provinces, the debt/deficit burden at the federal level is already imposing an effective decentralization on the federation. This is most apparent in terms of the recent budget provisions relating to the established programs (health and post-secondary education). Ottawa has frozen cash transfers under established programs' financing (EPF) for two years (and the 1991 budget extended this to five years). Thereafter, the EPF ceiling will grow at the rate of GNP less 3%. Since EPF is structured so that these cash top-ups bring the value of the tax transfers up to the EPF ceiling for each province, capping and then slowing the growth of the ceiling means that the value of the growing tax-transfer component will eventually exceed the ceiling value. At this point, the billions of EPF dollars currently transferred to the provinces will fall to zero. Analysts expect that Quebec's cash transfers will hit zero before the millenium and those for the rest of the provinces before 2010.[2]

These "cuts" are clearly decentralizing. If the provinces maintain the health and post-secondary-education programs by increasing provincial taxes, this decentralization will take the form of a larger ratio of provincial to federal taxation, which is one form of decentralization. If the provinces respond by altering or cutting back on these programs, this is also decentralizing in the sense that these programs will come increasingly under provincial design (and erode aspects of "national" standards). Indeed, what control on design will or can Ottawa have once its cash contributions begin to taper off, let alone fall to zero. In this post-Meech and post-FTA era where "national" social programs represent much of the glue that binds Canadians together, these EPF developments may have profound political implications.

Alterations to EPF are, however, only part of the on-going fiscal-federalism battle. Payments under the Canada Assistance Plan have also been frozen at 5% growth for the three "have" provinces (Ontario, Alberta and B.C.). The UI system has also been reworked to link benefit weeks more closely to weeks worked. Potentially, this has major implications for certain provinces where erstwhile UI beneficiaries may now have to fall back on provincial welfare.

The provinces' fiscal concerns do not all lie in the transfer area. Pressures are mounting rapidly on the taxation front as well. For example, the initiative to claw back family allowances and old age security for higher-income taxpayers represents a substantial loss of income-tax revenue for the provinces. Under the existing provisions (and dealing only in very round numbers) a rich person would repay in taxes about half of his/her $4,000 OAS, of which one-third or roughly $667 would end up as provincial taxes. Under the claw-back feature, the province would lose this revenue (the surcharge goes to Ottawa and once the entire OAS has been taxed back it no longer is viewed as taxable income). At one level, it is difficult to argue against this on principle. After all, OAS payments come from federal coffers so why should the provinces get 1/3 of the existing tax back? At another level, however, this is viewed by the provinces as yet one more problem with the shared personal-income-tax (PIT) system: Ottawa can unilaterally alter the system and the provinces have no short-term recourse but to accept the resulting implications for their revenues.

For many provinces this concern with personal-income-tax (PIT) flexibility has been dramatically heightened by the proposed GST since they perceive this as an intrusion into their traditional taxing domain and, hence, as a constraint on their overall tax flexibility. In light of all of this, it should not come as a surprise that the Western Finance Ministers (1990), in connection with the Western Premiers Conference in Lloydminster in July, 1990, proposed the establishment of a separate Canada West personal- income-tax system. Several observers, including the Prime Minister, have linked this initiative to the post-Meech climate. The link may well be there but, as the above few paragraphs have attempted to demonstrate, provincial discontent over transfer and taxation issues has a history quite apart from Meech. And in their twenty-six page communique the Western finance Ministers (1990) made no mention of Meech.

For reasons elaborated elsewhere (Courchene and Stewart, 1990) my view is that the provinces of Canada West would settle for the freedom to apply their own rate and bracket structures to the (federally determined) definition of taxable income. (In its 1991 budget, Ottawa entertained this possibility.) If Ottawa balks at this, then a separate personal income tax along Quebec lines becomes more likely.

Thus, in addition to the *external* challenges to our federation arising from globalization, some *internal* challenges also point in the direction of circumscribing the policy freedom of the federal government. And by design none of this has dealt with the range of possible decentralization, let alone confederal, scenarios that may surface in the next round of Canada's continuing constitutional saga.

C. Non-Territorial Federalism

Countering the above centrifugal forces is a profound socio- political shift in the manner in which Canadians, particularly those in English-Speaking Canada (henceforth, EBQ, everybody but Quebec), are coming to view the federation. Underlying this attitudinal change is, of course, the Charter. As Cairns (1990) has noted the Charter "democratized" the Constitution by enshrining rights for individual Canadians and also for a range of groups of Canadians - aboriginals, visible minorities, linguistic minorities, multicultural groups, women (gender equality), etc. These rights transcend provinces, so much so that this new conception of Canadian federalism has little to do with traditional federal- provincial cleavages but rather with cleavages between these pan- Canadian newly "enshrined" interests on the one hand and vested interests or elites on the other. As one would expect, this focus on rights and equality is almost exclusively Ottawa-centred. Indeed, one of the major "process" concerns relating to the Meech Lake debacle was the fact that while the Charter democratized the constitution, the amending formula remained in the executive- federalism domain. The implications run much deeper, however. While EBQ recognizes and respects Quebec's distinctiveness in socio-cultural terms, the emphasis on equality stemming from the Charter is leading them increasingly in the direction of equality or *symmetry* across all provinces in terms of constitutional powers. Thus, while Quebec is now engaged in the process of evaluating alternative decentralized constitutional structures, it is difficult to get English-Speaking Canadians off their determined pilgrimage to rid the constitution of the notwithstanding clause.

This poses both challenges and opportunities for the future evolution of Canada. The challenge is straightforward: at the very time that Quebec is rejecting the status quo in favour of new powers which, at a minimum, would breathe life into their "distinct society", many other Canadians (rallying around the Charter) are developing a new conception of Canada. Moreover, this is a highly centralist conception and one that stems from "within" rather than the traditional conception that drew heavily on defining Canada as being "non-American".

On the surface this juxtaposition of economics-driven decentralization and political/cultural driven centralization would appear to be irreconcilable. Yet, there may well be a window of opportunity here since these conflicting forces basically amount to the age-old trade-off between efficiency/allocation on the one hand and distribution/equity on the other. This suggests that some decentralizing with respect to the former and some centralizing with respect to the latter, at least for the nine English-speaking provinces, may hold the key to not only unlocking Canada's constitutional log-jam but as well to positioning Canada well in terms of accommodating global economic change. Yet, how this might be accomplished is not obvious since part of the above argument ran in terms of on-going decentralization in the social policy arena. The purpose of the final substantive section of the paper is to advance some tentative suggestions along these lines.

Prior to proceeding to this prescriptive aspect of the paper, there are three other "internal" factors which merit brief attention.

D. Securing the Canadian Economic Union
Earlier this summer (i.e. 1990), the nine non-Quebec premiers (or their representatives in a couple of cases) agreed to a series of provisions relating to enhancing the Canadian economic union, i.e., to freeing up

cross-provincial trade in goods, services and factors of production. As I shall argue in the next paragraph, the substance of this agreement is not all that important since freer interprovincial trade is inevitable. However, the process and symbolic aspects are critically important. This represents one of the first answers to the post-Meech question: Who speaks for English-Speaking Canada? As Quebec develops its constitutional proposals, EBQ must develop processes and forums to respond to or counter them. While an assembly of EBQ first ministers may not be the entire answer (one of Meech's key lessons is the need for broad consultation across all Canadians), it is surely an integral part. Moreover, the process whereby these nine first ministers agreed to a proposal which was then to be forwarded to Quebec for its approval or disapproval is also one that will likely play a key role in the next few years. In particular, it speaks to Quebec's demand that in the future it wants to deal one on one with whoever represents EBQ.

In terms of why the substance of this agreement is not particularly important, at least three forces are going to tie the provinces' hands in this regard. The first is the influence of the FTA. Canada-U.S. free trade is going to make it much more difficult for the provinces to maintain interprovincial barriers. The provincial beer fiefdoms will soon crumble. Competition with the Americans will force Canadian food processors to by-pass Canadian marketing boards: the processors will either be granted competitive access to Canadian foodstocks or they will source their products from the U.S. (or move their capital south). The second reason relates to the role of the courts. Now that Canada-U.S. free trade is upon us it is inevitable (at least from my non-legal-training vantage point) that the courts will begin to breathe new life into clauses like section 91(2), the trade and commerce power, in order to ensure that freer trade is the rule internally. Indeed, I would expect that "provincial treatment" will become the standard: the provinces will find it progressively more difficult to lend special preferences to within-province firms. More generally, the recent ruling on the Communications case may be a bell-wether for future court challenges. The interested reader may wish to refer to Whyte (1990) who elaborates on some of these themes.

Finally, I think that Drucker's earlier-cited reference to "reciprocity" as the new integrating force in the global economy will play a major role in bringing the provinces into line. A recent *Financial Post* article (Morton, 1990), quoting an unnamed "senior" Canadian trade official, is highly illustrative:

> "A surprise move by the European Community to open up all levels of government procurement to the outside could mean hundreds of millions of dollars of trade for Canadian industries.
> ... The U.S. is considering following the European move and the

two might link together to shut out other countries such as Canada".

The punch line is straightforward: "Canada risks being shut out of two of the world's largest and newest markets if it doesn't bring down its own interprovincial procurement barriers".

With powerful forces like these tearing down internal trade barriers, the premiers may as well seek public kudos for enhancing free trade because the barriers will topple in any event. In the context of this general section one could, I suppose, argue that this is a centralization of sorts since it will be constraining on provincial governments. However, the more appropriate interpretation is probably that discriminatory policies will be eroded at both levels of governments and that consumers (or taxpayers) and markets will come out on top.

E. Regionalism

Much has always been made of the fact that Canada's geography implies that the natural linkages are north-south, not east-west. Morever, geography would also dictate this if each of the regions were replicas of Ontario. But they are not. The critical feature of Canada is not so much its geography as its *economic* geography (including population). Our geographical regions have vastly different economies. Inevitably, therefore, overall industrial (and exchange rate) policy involves not only industrial trade-offs but almost of necessity regional trade-offs as well. Thus, any preference for manufacturing over resources immediately becomes a regional issue as much as an industrial issue. This is markedly different in the U.S. where both industry and resources are distributed *far more equally* across the American regions. Thus, the argument for decentralization of powers in the Canadian context is not so much one of altering the federal-provincial balance per se. Rather it is an argument for a devolution of decision making to those distinctive regions or provinces whose future lies with ensuring that such decisions are appropriate to the long-term viability of their distinctive economic bases. In an integrating world economy, decentralization in the Canadian context should be viewed as being driven by *economic*, not political/constitution criteria. Phrased differently, this is not "giving away the store" in constitutional terms: it is ensuring that "absentee landlords" are not running the store.

F. A Necessary Detour on 'Decentralization'

From Prime Minister Trudeau's opening comments to the 1980 First Ministers' Conference on the Constitution:

> We ... know that a much higher proportion of public funds are spent in Canada by the provinces and municipalities ... than by the federal government and in this we are far and away the most decentralized ... of any country in the world (p. 4).

This is certainly true particularly if the comparison is with the U.S.: the Canadian provinces have much greater powers and control a greater proportion of spending than do the U.S. states.

However, this is a very narrow conception of decentralization: it focuses essentially on a comparative "federal structure" approach to decentralization. The fact is that in more basic terms, power is *much more decentralized* in the U.S. than it is in Canada. First and foremost, there is no "Ontario" in the U.S. that can command nearly 40% of the Commons votes, or no "central Canada" (Quebec and Ontario) that can easily command a majority should they so wish. Second, and as noted above, apart from a few resource- based states, the "regions" in the U.S. are quite similar to each other in their industrial composition, unlike the case in Canada. Third, economic power is much more widely dispersed in the U.S. With some notable exceptions, most of the dominant Canadian corporations are narrowly held, whereas in the U.S. they are widely held. It is still an intriguing parlour game to guesstimate how much of Canadian GNP is under control of, say, the top half-dozen Canadian "families". To address such an issue would never occur to Americans, although it is true that they are now becoming obsessed by Japanese inroads (which is minimal in comparison with the degree of U.S. ownership of Canadian enterprise). Finally, the Parliamentary system itself (or at least the way it is practised in Canada) centralizes power. One need look no further than the on- going GST debate where upwards of 80 per cent of Canadians oppose the tax but where a government with less than 20 per cent popular support will presumably be able, by stacking the Senate, to see the GST legislation through. We are in the ridiculous, or rather tragic, position where the constituency-based, popularly-elected chamber is, thanks to the numbers in the Tory ranks, effectively responsible to no one (except themselves) whereas the non-elected, non-constituency-based chamber is wrestling with whether they should reflect the will of the people on this issue. There is no doubt in my mind where *de facto*, as distinct from *de jure*, representative democracy lies.

Intriguingly, however, the bulk of the academic literature as well as popular opinion on this issue is directed toward rethinking the role of the Senate and, perhaps, converting it to a triple-E chamber. But the problem really lies with the Commons, not the Senate. The rise of the Reform Party in the West and to a lesser extent the Bloc Quebecois and the Confederation of Regions party in New Brunswick (and more generally the breakdown of national parties) are clear signals that Canadians are no longer willing to tolerate the excesses of power associated with our approach to Parliamentary government. This is not to say that this system served us poorly in the past. Policies like the bilingual legislation would never have surfaced if Commoners voted their constituency interests. In an information intensive era, however, this "rep by party" rather than true "rep by pop" is increasingly contributing to the fragmentation of our national polity.

Pursuing this line of inquiry would quickly take me well beyond the scope or intent of this paper (see Courchene, 1990d). However, there are two important derivative points that merit highlight. The first is that, contrary to popular belief, Canada remains a highly centralized country. Too centralized. International openness on the economic front and the Charter on the political front are, in my view, welcome forces that will serve to democratize power.

The second point is the more relevant one in terms of the thrust of the paper. The formal delineation of powers in the constitution may have little to do with the *de facto* degree of centralization or decentralization. For example, an *unchanged Constitution Act, 1867* allowed Canada to centralize dramatically during wartime and then move toward substantial decentralization in the post-war period. In other words, the driving force behind the waves of centralization or decentralization are not the written Constitutional words but rather the range of external pressures and societal preferences at any given point in time. Moreover, the enhanced degree of interdependence in a modern economy is such that one can no longer speak in terms of "watertight" power divisions. As Bastien (1981) notes:

> In the modern industrial state, government is involved in all areas. All its components are interdependent. A government's activities in the education field affect its activities in the area of employment; its activities in employment affect its social welfare programs, which in turn affect housing policy, and so on. ... This interdependence of government policies has serious consequences for a federal system: in effect, it means that the orders of government must cooperate if coherent action is to be taken. ... *Thus decentralization does not lead to a separation of powers, as in traditional federalism, but rather to cooperation in decision-making* (p. 47, emphasis added).

Phrased differently, workable federalism in the 1990s will have as much to do with *process* as with structure:

> "Federalism should not be seen only as a static pattern or design, characterized by a particular and precisely fixed division of powers between government levels. Federalism is also and perhaps primarily the *process* ... of adopting joint policies and making joint decisions on joint problems" (Friedrich, 1968, p. 7, underlining added).

This does not imply that selected amendments to the division of powers are not in order. What it does imply is that there should be a premium on the ability of the Constitution to accommodate changing societal needs and preferences. The *Constitution Act, 1867* was exemplary in this regard. Changes in the magnitude of and incentives within federal-provincial transfers (not formally enshrined until recently) were tantamount to changes in the formal divisions of power. Likewise, executive federalism has no roots in the *Constitution Act, 1867*, yet it has emerged as a key institution in the federal structure. Closer to the thrust of this paper, the existing constitution has allowed Quebec to undergo two "revolutions" over the last thirty years. And contrary to popular belief, it was the English Speaking provinces, not Quebec, that received constitutional "favours" over this period (e.g. the resource amendment for the energy-producing provinces, the right to discriminate against off-shore workers for Newfoundland and the notwithstanding clause to meet concerns of the Western premiers). The general point is that process is every bit as important as structure when it comes to constitution making. As a corollary, it is probably the case that many analysts (present company included) read far too much into the written constitutional word in terms of concepts like centralization and decentralization.

G. Recapitulation

Over the next few years, the role of Quebec within Canada and the internal structuring of EBQ itself will occupy constitutional centre-stage. What the above analysis has attempted to demonstrate, however, is that there are powerful other forces that will also be brought to bear on the future of Canadian federalism. Thus, with or without Meech, Canadian federalism is evolving. Obviously, a critical issue in this context is whether these forces for reform are pushing in similar or opposite directions. Although I have touched upon this only implicitly in the above analysis, elsewhere (1990c) I have argued that "distinct societies" will increasingly be what sovereignty is all about as we approach the millenium.

I now turn to few prescriptive observations in terms of the manner in which the implications of the above analysis ought to impinge on the operations of Canadian federalims.

V. GLOBAL FEDERALISM AND CANADIAN COMPETITIVENESS

A. Sustainable Economic Development

In a sense, the issue to be addressed is quite straightforward: How in this era of global integration and "global federalism" does Canada forge (or regain) both a competitive edge and an enduring national polity? The answer is far from straightforward, however.

I shall begin by taking the highroad, as it were, and propose, mimicking Brundtland (1987) and more specifically *Energy Options* (1988), the following general framework:

> Canadian policy should be designed and implemented in a man-
> ner that allows Canadians and their governments to manage and
> utilize Canada's resources in a manner such that future genera-
> tions of Canadians are bequeathed an endowment of capital -
> human, environmental and physical - that is hopefully superior to,
> but at least on par with, that which our generation inherited.

No disagreement thus far, I would guess, since this framework is consistent with the full range of philosophies for both governments, markets, and
citizens. For example, as stated the framework is even consistent with
"legislating" lifestyle changes on the part of citizens along "conserver
society" or "small is beautiful" lines. I will elaborate on this framework
in terms of the economists' triad of functions - allocation, stabilization and
distribution.

1. Allocation

In terms of the foregoing analysis, this "sustainable economic development" conception acquires a rather constrained (and admittedly subjective) interpretation. Specifically, it implies an acceptance that markets
will be allowed to drive most of the allocative function. There are limits
here, of course, particularly for long-lived investments. Governments
may have to step in when and where markets undervalue the future. But
as *Energy Options* (1988) pointed out some of the rationale for a high
discount on the future for long term investments stems from government-
generated uncertainty, so that government can be part of the problem as
well as part of the solution in terms of enhancing the efficiency of
intertemporal allocation. Governments still have the right, under the FTA,
to intervene in the allocative process. In doing so, however, the national
treatment aspect of the FTA ensures that such intervention will not
privilege local or national enterprise. This should ensure that genuinely
provincial or national objectives motivate such intervention.

A second implication relating to allocation that I derive from the
foregoing analysis is that the various regions should have more say in the
formation of policy relevant to their economic prospects. North-south
integration and the differences in the economic bases of the various
regions make this rather inevitable. This can occur either via process (i.e.
an enhanced regional voice in the formation of national policy) or via
some more formal restructuring of powers. With this globalization/
integration driven decentralization on the economic front, it is, I think,
inevitable that Canada has to rethink aspects of traditional policy. For
example, national pay scales will begin to give way to regionally based
scales: it does not make sense that federal employees in Metro Toronto
be on the same wage grid as federal employees in rural Saskatchewan. The
private sector has long recognized this. Now it is the public sector's turn.

Similarly, the nature of the social policy infrastructure will probably need to be tailored to the specific socio-economic needs of the various regions or provinces. Uniform design and delivery of day care does not make sense for the various "regions" of Ontario, let alone across provinces.

Relatedly, federal policy should, following the recommendations of the Macdonald Commission (1985), abandon "place prosperity":

Commissioners introduce a sharp distinction between federal and provincial functions in regional development. The federal government ... should not involve itself directly in regional job creation. Its responsibilities end with its commitment to overcome regional productivity gaps and labour market imperfections [and, I shall argue later equalizing opportunities for human capital development]. It has served regional equality if identical employments fetch roughly similar compensations, and if adjustment to change in labour markets proceeds equally efficiently in all regions. In addition, the federal government should bring to discussions of regional development a direct concern with building complementary and mutually beneficial links among provincial economies. In other words, it should set regional policy in a national framework.

Provincial governments and their electorates typically want more than this from economic policies. Specifically, they have absolute employment targets as well ... This emphasis on place prosperity is both understandable and desirable when it comes from a provincial government. *It should not, however, unduly concern the federal government.* Commissioners believe that community preservation, to the extent that people want it, is ultimately the responsibility of citizens and of their local and provincial governments. The federal government must not stand in the way of achieving that goal, in the sense that its economic and social policies must not consistently discriminate against particular groups, but neither need it devote resources directly to meet this goal. Provinces, however, must have access to such funds and be free to use them in this manner if they so desire (vol. III, ppp. 219-20, emphasis added).

This may seem harsh to some readers but Canada's experience in putting "place" before "people" is not a happy one.[3] To be sure, however, the phase-out period would have to be gradual.

Note, finally, that this shift in allocative responsibility toward the provinces represents a relative, not absolute, shift in powers. All of this is conditioned by the "global" shifts towards markets and citizens highlighted earlier in the paper.

This analysis raises a series of issues such as, what is the future of national programs? and what is the role of the federal government? These issues will be broached after a brief focus on stabilization.

2. Stabilization

Globalization, north-south integration, and Drucker's "symbol economy" all combine, in my view, to force a complete reappraisal of macro or stabilization policy. In particular, our macro managers have to reassess the role of the exchange rate: as north- south integration under the FTA proceeds the appropriate exchange rate policy will be one that favours fixity over flexibility. The argumentation supporting this is provided elsewhere (Courchene, 1990g, and *this volume*). Suffice it to note for present purposes that over the period from the initial FTA agreement in 1987 to the present, unit labour costs in Canada expressed in U.S. dollars have risen by nearly 25 per cent relative to comparable U.S. unit labour costs. Most of this is attributable to the rise in the Canadian dollar relative to the U.S. dollar. The FTA is thus becoming a nightmare for many Canadian employers and employees. What is particularly ironic is that this is the very period over which Governor Crow is targetting for "zero inflation", presumably to enhance our international competitiveness! Canada may not be willing to follow the European example in terms of moving to a single currency area with the Americans. But there is no question that we must abandon the notion that we can stabilize Canada in the 1990s with a conceptual framework designed to address the macro challenges of the 1970s rather than those of the 1990s.

3. Distribution (Social/Human-Capital Policy)

In the context of this paper, distribution is defined very broadly. Specifically it incorporates the range of policies and programs designed to maximize the opportunities for Canadians to enhance and employ their human capital. More to the point, this *is the role par excellence for national governments in the new global economic order.*

To understand why this will be a major challenge, one has to recall, à la Petrella (1990), that the so-called "welfare states" were really products of *national* industrial production economies. These welfare states were frequently not primarily people centred: apart from the already-noted role that "place prosperity" played in our national distributional system, the welfare or social policy incentives were tailored to the needs of the national production machine. However, globalization spells the end of "national" industrial economies *and* therefore, the supportive role played by the traditional conception of the welfare state. One relatively trivial, but nonetheless instructive, aspect of this has already been highlighted: the cross-subsidization of local calls by long- distance calls will have to fall by the wayside. If we wish to continue to subsidize local subscribers, it will have to be via direct subsidies since it is inevitable that competitive forces will insure that the erstwhile rents from long-distance tariffs will disappear.

The issue then becomes: What is the nature of the national "social contract" consistent with an international economy? In my view, it has to be to privilege people in terms of human-capital development and to do so from the vantage point of a *right of citizenship*, as it were, and not as a means for advancing some regional or sectoral goal.

Fortunately, this is also appropriate economic policy as we move into an increasingly knowledge-intensive or human-capital- intensive era. From this vantage point, social policy, as defined here, falls less and less in the realm of equity and more and more in the realm of efficiency. This amounts to nothing less than a paradigm shift. For example, in this context day care ceases to be viewed as a "transfer". Rather it represents an enhancement of the human capital prospects of the children and, as important, ensures that society does not undervalue and/or underemploy the female labour force or, from a different perspective, ensures that the human capital built up by women is not unwound as a result of childbearing. Elsewhere (1990a) I have elaborated briefly on some likely implications of this general approach, although the area is basically unresearched. The essential point is that social policy, particularly in its human-capital dimension, must come to be viewed as the centrepiece of a successful transition toward a new economic sustainability.

B. The Role of the Federal Government

What is the role of the federal government in all of this? Apart from its traditional functions and its newer role as a player in determining the future of the global commons (environment, sea- bed) and even the extra-global commons (space), this is not an easy question to answer if one is searching for areas of "exclusive" federal jurisdiction. However, as argued earlier, this is the wrong way to view the operations of modern federations. Thus, even though many of the social programs fall under provincial jurisdiction, Ottawa has a critical role to play in fostering an environment conducive to ensuring a human capital emphasis. Some of this relates to equalizing opportunities for all Canadians (s. 36 of the Constitution), some to ensuring transferability of benefits and programs across provinces, some to setting minimum standards, etc. In other words, Ottawa's responsibility is to forge "national" programs in the social policy domain and to ensure that the Canadian market is fully accessible for all citizens.

More generally, the emerging role for Ottawa has to do with securing and monitoring the internal economic union. This is where the "rebalancing" in the federation will come about - some traditional powers passed downward but *all* powers will subject to the free flow of goods, services, capital and labour. If the European Community is an example here, the scope of the economic union will include both the environment and aspects of the social contract. In a sense, this is the quid quo pro for any decentralization of traditional powers.

Beyond this, the federal government has an obvious leadership interest in the general area of education, particularly post- secondary education and training. In terms of the trade-offs across access, funding and quality for post-secondary education, the provinces have typically cut funding, ensured access and crossed their fingers that quality would somehow be maintained. Since human-capital formation and knowledge are at the cutting edge of international competitiveness, Ottawa has to step into this breach and emphasize (or fund) those aspects of higher education that underpin Canada's ability to penetrate foreign markets. Relatedly, through its role in training and more generally in funding post-secondary education, Ottawa can take the lead in forging a link between community colleges and universities, particularly in provinces like Ontario where they exist as two solitudes. More generally, a large aspect of the so-called disappearing middle class is the inadequate recognition in Canada of the role and status of "technologist". In a knowledge-intensive society, technologists will be synonymous with middle class. Yet Canadian tradition is to vest powers in self-regulatory professional associations which virtually ensure that technologists and para-professionals play virtually no role in our system. Again a clear role for federal leadership. And so on, not only for education but for other areas as well.

Thus, the critical federal role is to provide both leadership and a socio/ economic framework that ensures that policies at all government levels centre around maximizing the human capital potential of all Canadians. Not only is this the obvious policy approach for nation states in this changed global economy, but it is precisely the sort of policy framework that will cement the internal Canadian polity and, therefore, transcend any increased north-south integration.

In full recognition that this is probably an appropriate way to end an already lengthy paper, I want to address one final issue. Quebec will want control over many of these policies designed to enhance citizens' human capital. Yet the post-Meech-Lake mood in EBQ is running in terms of symmetric powers for all provinces on the one hand and for a larger role for the federal government on the other. Is this reconcilable?[4]

C. Asymmetric Federalism

It is axiomatic that Quebec's new constitutional proposals will insist on control over language and culture. Under a moderate set of demands, its list would include control over manpower and telecommunications. Under a more aggressive approach, control over science and technology and the environment, for example, might be part of the package. The choice facing EBQ is then two-pronged. First, to decide whether they want Quebec in or out, recognizing that in *neither* case will they be able to budge Quebec from controlling these areas. Assuming that the answer is "in", then the second question is how to reorganize EBQ, since it makes no sense either for the English-Speaking provinces or their citizens to have nine separate man-power/human capital policies, for example. Put differently, it is hard to imagine an outcome that does not embody "asymmetric federalism".

Asymmetry has long characterized our federation. Indeed, it is central to the *Constitution Act, 1867* in areas such as the legal system, language and education rights, etc. More recently, "opting out" by Quebec has been the principal avenue for increased asymmetry. In many ways, opting out has been an ingenious contribution to workable Canadian federalism. Consider personal income taxation. Quebec has "opted out" and set up its own, separate, personal income tax system. As a result, the remaining nine provinces have been able to combine with the federal government to design a highly coordinated (in terms of taxpayer compliance) and yet decentralized (in terms of transferring 1/3 of overall revenues to the provinces) system. Without opting out, we would presumably be some-where in-between these two systems, with all provinces and Ottawa forced off their preferencial outcome. In this sense, opting out, or asymmetric federalism, is a *solution*, not a problem.

However, asymmetry no longer appears fashionable as we count down to the appearance of Quebec's proposals. One alternative is "opting in", or as my colleague Ron Watts puts it, "section 94 federalism". Section 94 of the *Constitution Act, 1867* reads:

Uniformity of Laws in Ontario, Nova Scotia and New Brunswick

94. Notwithstanding anything in this Act, the Parliament of Canada may make Provision for the Uniformity of all or any of the Laws relative to Property and Civil Rights in Ontario, Nova Scotia, and New Brunswick, and of the Procedure or all or any of the Courts in Those Three Provinces, and from and after the passing of any Act in that Behalf the Power of the Parliament of Canada to make Laws in relation to any Matter comprised in any such Act shall, notwithstanding anything in this Act, be unre-stricted; but any Act of the Parliament of Canada making Provision for such Uniformity shall not have any effect in any Province unless and until it is adopted and enacted as law by the Legislature thereof.

LaSelva (1983, pp. 760-61) comments on the role of section 94 as follows (note that the internal references in the LaSelva quote are to Frank Scott (1977)):

> The Fathers of Confederation, he [Scott] suggested, desiring a legislative union, but being unable to attain one at that time, included section 94 so that in a more favourable political climate "as easy way should be left open for an even closer integration of the provinces" [p. 114]. All that would be required to transfer constitutional jurisdiction over property and civil rights, in whole or in part, to the federal Parliament would be that the respective provinces (Ontario, Nova Scotia and New Brunswick) adopt and enact federal legislation on that subject matter. Although it cannot be simply assumed that section 94 applies to provinces that have joined Confederation since 1867, Scott argued that it applies to all the now existing common law provinces. Only Quebec, he insisted, is excluded from its operation. Quebec is, in a sense, "less free than her sister provinces, who may employ section 94," [p. 122] for "no action under that section can include Quebec, even if Quebec wants to be included. Quebec is constitutionally incapable of giving up her legislative powers except by formal amendment" [p. 122].

What section 94 permits is symmetry in principle but asymmetry in fact. For example, suppose that the Quebec proposals requested control over telecommunications and manpower in addition to language and culture. These powers could then be assigned to all other provinces as well *(symmetry in principle)* who would then turn around and surrender, via section 94, selected aspects such that "national" approaches or programs would result *(asymmetry in fact)*. This approach is, I think, more than just the mirror image of opting out. It is a conscious act of constitution making on the part of EBQ where, by constitutional definition, Quebec is excluded. Moreover, it has its roots not in some novel design conjured up in response to Quebec's proposals, but rather in the original BNA Act itself. This is why I viewed as significant the symbol as distinct from the substance of the EBQ premiers' deal on internal markets: it parallels the section 94 process.

More generally, there is no magical division of powers that can or ever could satisfy Ottawa and all provinces. Process dimensions are essential to allow the formal structure (or division of powers) to accommodate changing needs and preferences. Not thus far utilized and largely forgotten, section 94 may yet prove valuable in this context and in the process may attest to the foresight of our Founding Fathers.

Endnotes

1. Much of this section is taken from Courchene (1988b).

2. The reason why Quebec's cash transfers fall to zero before those of the other provinces is that Quebec has long received some additional income-tax points in lieu of cash transfers for the funding of post-secondary education. Hence, the tax- transfer component of EPF financing for Quebec will break through the overall EPF ceiling much sooner for Quebec than for the other provinces.

3. Consider, for example, the impact of the operation of Canada's UI program (replete with the special regional and fishing provisions) on Newfoundland. Among the many serious problems that the Newfoundland Royal Commission on Employment and Unemployment (1986) associated with the operations are the following (in essentially point form):
    (i)   The system undermines the intrinsic value of work; ...
    (ii)   The system undermines good working habits and discipline; ...
    (iii) The system undermines the importance of education; ...
    (iv)   UI is a disincentive to work; ...
    (v)   UI undermines personal and community initiatives; ...
    (vi)   UI discourages self employment and small-scale enterprise; ...
    (vii) The UI make-work system encourages political patronage; ...
    (viii) UI make-work distorts the efforts of local development groups; ...
    (ix)   The system is vulnerable to manipulation (pp. 406-10).

4. What follows is a view of these issues that I have gone beyond in my more recent papers (e.g. 1991d). Nonetheless the ensuing analysis is consistent with the evolution of my thinking in this area.

6. Grappling with Mobility: The Role of the State as a Regulator of Financial Institutions

I. INTRODUCTION AND BACKGROUND

Financial deregulation or re-regulation is at the cutting edge of the ongoing computational and telecommunications revolutions. In large measure this is so because, at base, the global financial system is essentially a sophisticated information, coordination and telecomputational network. Thus, among the major new financial players one finds the likes of IBM, AT and T, Reuters and, in Canada, BCE Inc., with its recent purchase of Montreal Trust. As the *Economist* notes:

> Vast improvements in telecommunications links and computing power mean that, henceforward, financial deregulation and communications technology will have to be mentioned in the same big mouthful. In future, the battle to win business will be fought not just between financial centres, but also between globe-spanning trading networks (July 21, 1990, Survey, p. 8).

In effect, then, an evaluation of the role of the state as a financial regulator is essentially an analysis of how national regulators cope with international mobility. To be sure the degree of "mobility" in the financial sector is extreme. Sophisticated financial instrumentation is progressively blurring the line between various types of financial assets and even institutions and the degree of global integration is likewise blurring the distinction between transactions that are domestic and those that are international. Nonetheless, the nature of the underlying challenges currently facing the regulation of the financial sector will likely re-appear down the road a bit for many other sectors.

The purpose of this paper is to delve into the various aspects of this financial regulation challenge, largely although not exclusively as it applies to Canadian regulators. Part II surveys briefly the manner in which financial markets, international and domestic, have been evolving. Section A focuses on the period, not so long ago, where one could meaningfully distinguish between national and international markets. Section B documents the range of factors in the 1980s that led to global financial integration, how this interacted with the role of national regulatory regimes, and, in particular, how this led both to crumbling barriers and crumbling pillars. Section C speculates on what is in store for the 1990s. If the past is prologue, then finance in the 1990s will, as the above quotation suggests, have more to do with networks than with institutions: we will still require banking services but we may not require "banks".

Part III attempts to illustrate the implications of this evolving financial environment in terms of some specific Canadian regulatory challenges. The unshackling of the Canadian securities industry is the subject matter of section A. Section B probes the various regulatory landmines associates with the vertical (federal- provincial) sharing of jurisdictional authority. The equally thorny aspects of horizontal (cross-province) regulation and harmonization are dealt with in section C. In large measure, both sections B and C come face to face with a quintessential Canadian issue - two philosophies warring in the bosom of a single state.

A. The Financial-Commercial Interface

Prior to proceeding, it is important to recognize that the above conception of the range of challenges facing financial regulators is fairly circumscribed. For example, except for the later section relating to Quebec Inc., the ensuing analysis accepts what Zysman (1983) refers to as the "capital-markets-based" approach to finance which characterizes the English speaking world. This is in contrast with the "credit-market-based" system characteristic of, say, Germany and Japan. In addition to the fact that longer term financing of the corporate sector in market-based systems is accomplished largely through capital markets and in credit-based systems through loan markets, these two systems have very different implications both for the role of the state in the economy and for the underlying structure of the respective economies. In the capital-markets-based model, where prices are determined in competitive markets, economic adjustment is essentially company led. This is in stark contrast to the situation in state-dominated, credit-based systems (e.g. France and Japan) where

credit extended by institutions becomes a linchpin in the system
of industrial finance and government is drawn in to bolster the
system and to make administrative choices about allocation...The
borderline between public and private blurs not simply because
of political arrangements, but because of the very structure of
financial markets (Zysman, 1983, p. 72).

To be sure, the advent of global financial markets is eroding aspects
of this distinction between capital-based and credit-based systems. What
remains essentially intact, however, is the integration of banking and
commerce in these credit-based systems. For example, the big three West
German banks - Deutsche, Dresdner Bank and Commerzbank - have a
tight grip on the top-ranked German commercial companies: these big
three have two dozen seats on the supervisory boards of West Germany's
ten biggest firms. Combined with the law that allows the banks to vote on
behalf of other shareholders this means that these banks are frequently in
a position, if they wish, not only to dictate strategy but to boot out
incompetent management (*Economist,* August 4, 1990, p. 61-2). In
contrast, high-ranking commercial leaders in Canada dominate bank
boards.

This financial-commercial interface is even more complete in Japan
in the form of the Keiretsu, which are major industrial service groups
sometimes involving several hundred companies centred around a large
bank (Courtis, 1992). In terms, therefore, of the role of the state as
financial regulator, these two conceptions of financial structure (or the
relationship between finance and commerce) present quite different
challenges. As noted, however, most of the paper will proceed within the
framework of the capital-markets-based system.

B. The Regulatory Rationale

There is a second way in which the following analysis is constrained
- only limited attention will be devoted to *why* certain aspects of the
financial sector are regulated. The best example here is deposit insurance.
Canadian deposit insurance is set at $60,000 for each institution. If a
citizen has $300,000 of deposits spread equally across five institutions, the
entire $300,000 is insured. It is generally agreed that this first- dollar, full-
coverage (up to some maximum) approach is very problematical. No
incentives exist for depositors to ensure that the institutions they deal with
are financially sound. On the institution side, the incentives are even more
troublesome. If an institution runs into trouble (to the point where the
effective capital of the institution is reduced to zero, i.e. it is insolvent) the
deposit-insurance incentives encourage risky alternatives. Why not pay
higher interest rates to draw in additional funds and then invest them in a
risky portfolio? If the gamble fails, then neither the depositors (assuming

that they kept their deposits below $60,000) nor the shareholders (since the enterprise was insolvent anyway) are any worse off. The risk falls entirely on the insurer! If the gamble pays off, all is well, even for the insurer.

Not surprisingly, particularly in light of the S&L debacle south of the border, there is a renewed interest in reforming deposit insurance. Co-insurance (e.g. full insurance for the first $25,000 and then 80% insurance for the next $50,000 as recommended by the Senate in its 1985 report, *Deposit Insurance*), risk-related premiums for financial institutions, and provisions for the issuance of subordinated debt (so that the market itself assesses the risk inherent in an institution's asset portfolio) are representative of reform proposals. While any or all of these proposals would substantially alter the role of the state as a financial regulator (in particular, as insurer), there appears to be little interest at the policy level in Canada for such reform. Given that the S&L losses are expected to run somewhere between $2,000 and $4,000 per American, it is likely that the U.S. will address deposit-insurance reform before we do.

While, as noted, these sorts of issues (related to *why* governments regulate the financial sector) will not play a major role in the ensuing analysis, it is nonetheless appropriate that I reveal two underlying principles (others may refer to them as two underlying biases) that drive my approach to financial re- regulation or deregulation. The first of these is that in this era of rapid innovation in, and globalization of, the financial sector any initiative ought to be viewed as acceptable unless it can be demonstrated to be contrary to the public interest. The implication of this for regulatory policy is that the "burden of proof" with respect to the public interest should lie with those that *defend* the status quo, *not with the innovators*.

The second precept addresses globalization, namely that Canadian firms ought to be treated on par with foreign firms. Short of identical regulatory regimes, fully equal treatment is probably impossible. This is especially the case when it comes to negotiations relating to bilateral or multilateral reciprocal access. Inevitably, some Canadian firms will not be able to manoeuvre domestically to the same degree that identically-situated foreign firms can. "National treatment", the cornerstone of the FTA, will probably not even guarantee this. Therefore, the issue boils down to one of ensuring that any unavoidable degree of discrimination is viewed as acceptable to Canadians. My perspective with respect to this precept is that on more than one occasion in the recent past Ottawa has gone well beyond any reasonable level of general acceptability and, as such, this foreign preference has become the Achilles heel of the federal government's entire policy.

C. Jurisdictional Overlaps

A final bit of background relates to the jurisdictional overlap in Canada. From column 2 of Chart 1, the federal government regulates banking while the provinces regulate the securities industry. Loan and trust companies can be chartered/regulated either federally or provincially, although even federally chartered institutions must abide by certain aspects of provincial trust and loan regulations. Credit unions, not represented in the chart, are chartered and regulated provincially. The Canada Deposit Insurance Corporation (CDIC) insures all deposits of federally chartered institutions and all deposits of provincially chartered trusts held outside of Quebec. Quebec Deposit Insurance Corporations (QDIC) insures the Quebec-based deposits of Quebec-chartered institutions, including the caisses populaires. Deposits of credit unions in the rest of Canada are insured by the respective provinces.

Jurisdictional overlap has become more complicated still now that Canada has eliminated its version of Glass-Steagall (the prohibition against the mingling of commercial and investment banking). For example, Ottawa regulates the Bank of Nova Scotia, but defers to Ontario for much of the regulation for the Bank's securities subsidiary, Scotia McLeod.

Therefore, in terms of the title of this session and paper, the relevant "state" regulator will depend on the financial institution in question. This magnifies the regulatory challenge especially if the comparison is with unitary states like Japan or the U.K. In particular, it generates two sorts of harmonization concerns - "vertical harmonization" or the range of issues associated with federal-provincial regulatory overlaps and "horizontal harmonization" or the concerns associated with multiple regulation at the provincial level. Aspects of both vertical and horizontal harmonization will be dealt with below.

II. EVOLUTION AND REVOLUTION IN INTERNATIONAL FINANCE

A. Post-War to the Second Energy Shock: The Coexistence of National and International Markets

While the post-war period through to the early 1980s was characterized by a progressively enhanced degree of financial integration, it is nonetheless the case that one can, I think, speak meaningfully in terms of a coexistence of national and international (Eurodollar) financial markets until a decade ago. Two conceptually distinct (although related in practice) factors served to spearhead the development of an international marketplace. The first is what de Vries and Caprio (1986) refer to as the "internalization of finance", by which they mean the gradual post-war

CHART 1

Canadian Financial Institutions:
Jurisdictional and Ownership Regimes

	Regulatory Jurisdiction	Canadians	Foreigners	Americans after FTA [*]
Banks				
1. Schedule I banks	federal	10% max. shareholding for individuals	10% max. shareholding by individuals aggregate limit of 25%	same as for Canadians
2. Schedule II banks federal	federal	N/A		
foreign		N/A	wholly owned	same as for foreigners
domestic		can initially be wholly owned but must be widely held in ten years	N/A	N/A
Trusts				
new trusts	federal and/or provincial	no restrictions [**]	no restrictions in principle (but legislative moratorium)	same as for foreigners
existing trusts				
federal		no restrictions [***]	10/25	no restrictions [***]
provincial		no restrictions	10/25 [****]	10/25 [****]
Insurance	federal and/or			
(same as trusts) [+]	provincial			
Securities	provincial	no restrictions	no restrictions [++]	no restrictions [++]

[*]   Americans were treated as foreigners prior to the FTA.
[**] Can be subject to ministerial approval.
[***] May incorporate "big cannot buy big" provision.
[****] Provinces need not put controls on, but they are allowed to do so. Some provinces do.
[+]   Except that, for new foreign and American entry, there is greater flexibility (e.g. a foreigner can enter via a branch or subsidiary).
[++] Could be subject to foreign bank rules.

Source: Senate (1990, Table 1) with the addition of column 2.

development whereby financial institutions established branches or subsidiaries outside their home countries. Recent data indicate that there are over 700 foreign banks in the USA, roughly 550 in the UK and between 150 and 400 for Germany, Switzerland and France. As a result of the 1980 Bank Act, there are now upwards of 60 foreign (Schedule II) banks in Canada.

Roughly paralleling this was the emergence of the Euromarket - the offshore or extra-national market for U.S. dollar financial instruments but more recently for yen, marks and other currencies. The growth of the Euromarket was in large measure driven by a series of payments imbalances - in rough chronological order, Soviet-bloc money, U.S. deficits associated with Vietnam, the petro-dollar recycling of the 1970s and more recently the third world debt burden and the payments imbalances within the G7 (U.S. deficits and Japanese and German surpluses).

Both developments intensified pressures on national regulators - the former because the presence of foreign banks implied that the domestic regulatory authorities became apprized rather quickly of financial developments and innovations elsewhere in the international system and the latter because one of the characteristics of the Euromarket was its unregulated nature so that domestic institutions operating in the Euromarket had far greater freedom to manoeuvre abroad than they did at home. The position of the Royal Bank during this period was probably typical. Within Canada it was restricted to banking. Abroad, however, it could and in some regions did operate in the other three pillars. Intriguingly, the fact that U.S. banks emerged as the dominant Euromarket players can be traced in large measure to the very restrictive American laws and regulations (e.g. the McFadden Act prohibiting interstate banking, Glass-Steagall preventing the integration of commercial and investment banking, and provisions like Regulation Q that limited interest rates payable on deposits) that literally drove them offshore in order to acquire greater flexibility and, as a result, made London (rather than New York) the world's premier financial center.

Despite these pressures for either or both harmonization and deregulation, national regulators were generally able to adhere to their existing regulatory philosophies. In my view this can be traced to the fact that the world's major financial institutions, while competing head-on and on roughly equal terms in the Euromarket, were not really challenged in their home markets either by foreign firms or by enhanced cross-pillar competition in domestic markets. In terms of the latter, what this meant is that while there may have been little to distinguish the Euromarket operations of a securities firm like Salomon Brothers from a banker like Citicorp, their traditional *domestic* powers and market niches were largely unaffected.

Intriguingly, this coexistence of national and international markets still persisted in the aftermath of the first energy price shock, even though the resulting payments imbalances were of such a magnitude that international financial markets necessarily played a critical role in recycling these petro-dollars. The stabilizing feature here, from a domestic regulatory standpoint, was that the dramatic increase in international finance was essentially an increase in intermediated finance, i.e. in commercial rather than investment banking. This coincided with the dominance domestically of banks over securities dealers. Thus, the OPEC nations essentially purchased short-term bank deposits which, on the other side of the banks' balance sheets, led to a dramatic escalation in syndicated loans. Without question, this was the high-water mark of international banking.

Fortunately or unfortunately, however, the exuberance associated in placing syndicated loans led to inappropriate exposure to third-world borrowers and, in Canada at least, to the oil patch. When commodity prices tumbled in the early 1980s the world's great banks found themselves in dire straits. In tandem with several other critical developments which also served to downplay the role of banking, this led to the so-called revolution in global finance, one key feature of which was and is a shift toward investment banking. This *did* reverberate back on domestic financial markets and led to the crumbling of national regulatory barriers. The next section highlights briefly the range of factors that triggered this integration of finance across countries, across institutions and, thanks to sophisticated financial instrumentation (or "financial engineering") across aspects of time as well.

B. The 1980s: Global Financial Integration
In abbreviated form, and without assigning priority, the following were among the developments that served to usher in the era of global financial integration.

1. The Balance-of-Payments (Macro) Shocks
Of and by themselves, plunging oil and commodity prices would have created sufficient problems for the world's large banks. However, the resulting macro or balance-of-payments imbalances following close on the heels of the second energy shock, embodying massive payments deficits for the U.S. and equally massive aggregate surpluses for countries such as Japan and Germany, further complicated matters for the banks. It was not just the mere shift in the balance-of-payments surpluses that impacted on the banks. Rather, the portfolio preferences of these new surplus nations differed markedly from those of the OPEC nations — emphasis shifted away from short-term bank deposits and towards treasury bonds (i.e. away from bank intermediation and toward capital markets). Also contributing to this trend was the restructuring of corporate

balance sheets — reducing the excessive reliance on bank loans (incurred during the inflation and interest- rate cycle of the early 1980s) by recapitalizing balance sheets.

2. The Technology Revolution

Given that computational and telecommunications costs have been falling, per year, by a staggering 15% and 25% respectively for most of the post-war period (de Vries and Caprio, 1986), it is hardly surprising that these developments should coalesce to dramatically alter the nature of world financial markets since the financial services area is at the leading edge of the applications of the telecomputational revolution. The stagflation cycle of the first half of the 1980s with the resulting volatility in interest rates and exchange rates served as catalyst for both the speed and direction of this "financial engineering". By facilitating risk transfer ("bought deals" transfer price risk from the issuer to the broker, "financial futures" transfer risk temporally, "note issuance facilities" transfer credit risks and swaps transfer either or both of currency and interest rate risk) by enhancing liquidity (note issuance facilities and securitization) and by increasing the numbers of national currencies that comprise the global marketplace (swaps), technology driven instrumentation represented another factor that favoured investment banking relative to commercial banking.

Securitization (defined here as the pooling of various sorts of loans - car, home, credit-card - and issuing marketable securities collateralized by these pools) merits special attention. It led to a blurring of the distinction between financial instruments since, in the limit, there is very little difference between a securitized loan and a security or, more generally therefore, between commercial and investment banking. As Kapstein (1989, p. 325) has noted, national regulators, who had forged this distinction in many countries, were now uncertain how to respond to these changes.

This shift toward capital markets rather than bank credit as a source of funding was exacerbated because many of the high- quality borrowers were able to access capital on better terms than those available to the international banks. To a substantial degree this reflected, as noted earlier, the tarnished credit ratings of many of the world's largest banks. Why borrow through a financial intermediary (bank) when your credit rating is higher than that of the intermediary?

3. The Rise of the Corporate ("In-House") Banks

This combination of technology and globalization led to what must surely be the most significant alteration in the structure of both domestic and global financial markets, namely the rise of corporate banks as major financial players. Commercial giants like GE, Ford, Sears, BP, Borg-Warner and GM are now significant financial institutions. So are the telecomputational giants like AT and T and IBM. Consider Ford Motor Company's financial empire. Its First Nationwide Financial Corporation is now the second largest U.S. thrift company with U.S. $35 billion in assets and 330 branches in 15 U.S. states [CBA, 1990]. In Canada, Ford has very substantial leasing, consumer loan and insurance activities. Other U.S. commercial giants that have an important Canadian presence include GM, Sears, G.E. and most significant of all, American Express, which acquired Schedule II bank status a few months ago (more on Amex later).

What were the forces driving this development? At the international level it was the realization that, increasingly, finance is really in the information and networking game. These global commercial corporations already spanned all continents and their treasury departments were already "bankers" in terms of financing their far-flung commercial empire. Arguably, it is much easier for such corporations to acquire generalized international banking skills than it is for Royal Bank, for example, to acquire the globe-spanning network that GE, GM and Ford already have. Moreover, at least until the 1987 market crash, the returns to investment in the financial area were among the highest anywhere so that it was natural for these commercial giants to "diversify" into finance.

South of the border, the restrictive federal approach to banking (Glass-Steagall, McFadden) provided a very fertile ground for the likes of Ford, GM, Sears, etc., to end-run the financial regulatory system and become, in reality, "national" financial institutions, though typically not federally regulated. Moreover, the S&L crisis has effectively paralyzed Congress in terms of providing more manoeuvrability for federally chartered banks. However, a series of directives from the Federal Reserve System has, for selected banks, removed much of the sting of Glass-Steagall. And a few weeks ago at least one major U.S. bank entered the insurance sector.

In terms of the perspective of the present paper (indeed, running counter to the perspective), the U.S. regulators appear to be holding fast to the long-standing principle that banks cannot engage in commercial activities. What they have not been able to control (and what promises to overwhelm the national regulatory authorities unless some action is soon taken) is the move *by commerce into finance*. Indeed, Sears with its "Discover" card is now into the "plastic money" business and the U.S. is close to having two separate financial systems - one regulated and one non- regulated.

The integration of finance and commerce is proceeding in a quite different manner in Canada. CDIC-covered institutions are not allowed to have downstream commercial holdings. In this we follow the Americans or, for that matter, the English-speaking world. However, virtually all of the large trust companies are majority held (i.e., do not abide by the 10% ownership limitation applicable to banks) and most are part of large commercial conglomerates, e.g., Royal Trust (Brascan), Canada Trust (Imasco) and Montreal Trust (B.C.E. Inc.). This has led to a veritable "battle royale" at the federal level with the chartered banks pressing the case for 10% ownership (and, therefore, the severance of the link between trust companies and their commercial owners) and all of the provinces embracing a laissez-faire ownership policy for trusts. Since trusts can be chartered either federally or provincially, unilateral federal action (short of a Supreme Court challenge which, as in the recent communications case, I believe Ottawa would win) in terms of applying the 10% rule to trusts would simply lead to a charter flight from federal to provincial jurisdiction. Complicating all of this is that the trust companies have been growing much faster than the chartered banks. This is evident from Table 1, reproduced from a recent Canadian Bankers' Association document (1990). The more rapid growth of trusts reflects a spate of merger activity as well as the fact that the banks, over this period, were still reeling from their third-world and oil-patch losses. My personal view is now that the banks have refocussed their attention on the domestic market they will more than hold their own with respect to the large trusts. Anticipating the later analysis somewhat, Table 1 reveals the nature of the underlying dilemma: should Canada accept the bankers' vision of the appropriate nature of banking even though the trusts have exhibited growth rates two or three times those of the major banks?

The underlying issue goes well beyond ownership, however. The Desjardins Mouvement, with some $40 billion of assets, has long been involved in *downstream* commercial activities. Included among the scores of commercial activities under the wing of the Desjardins Mouvement are those in bakery and confectionary, machinery, steel, telecommunications, transportation, etc. As elaborated below, Quebec is in the process of extending this German or Japanese model to all aspects of its financial sector.

4. The Japanese Ascendancy

Prior to drawing conclusions and implications for domestic regulators from the foregoing analysis of the globalization of finance, it is instructive to focus on one further aspect of recent developments in international finance. A decade or two ago the list of the world's largest bankers read more or less like a who's who of North American banking. No more. There are no U.S. banks in the top 25, measured by value of deposits. The Japanese have taken over. All of the top 10 banks are Japanese. While

TABLE 1

Growth of Major Financial Institutions

Total Assets, including Assets[1] under Administration
(Billions of Dollars)

	1983	1987	1977	Average Annual Growth Rate
ROYAL TRUSTCO LIMITED				
Corporate Assets	10.6	24.5	28.5	
Estate, Trust and Administration	32.8	59.2	68.2	
Total Assets	43.4	83.8	96.7	17.5%
CT FINANCIAL SERVICES INC.				
Corporate Assets	10.2	25.5	29.2	
Estate, Trust, and Administration	36.5	60.6	67.4	
Total Assets	46.7	86.1	96.6	15.7%
MONTREAL TRUSTCO INC.				
Corporate Assets	2.0	7.7	10.2	
Estate, Trust, and Administration	17.3	28.0	33.6	
Total Assets	19.3	35.7	43.8	17.9%
NATIONAL VICTORIA & GREY TRUSTCO LIMITED				
Corporate Assets	3.3	10.9	12.2	
Estate, Trust, and Administration	11.6	26.9	27.4	
Total Assets	14.9	37.8	39.6	21.5%
GENERAL GUARANTY TRUST CO.				
Corporate Assets	*	9.9	13.6	
Estate, Trust, and Administration	*	8.6	9.7	
Total Assets	*	18.5	23.3	*
ROYAL BANK OF CANADA	84.7	102.2	110.1	5.5%
CIBC	68.1	88.4	94.7	6.9%
BANK OF MONTREAL	63.2	84.2	78.9	4.7%
BANK OF NOVA SCOTIA	54.8	71.4	74.7	6.5%
TORONTO-DOMINION BANK	42.5	54.5	59.3	6.95%
NATIONAL BANK OF CANADA	17.8	30.0	30.9	11.5%

*Comparative figures not available

Source: Company Annual Reports
(1) For both trust companies and banks, includes assets of mortgage loan subsidiaries

Source: Senate (1990, Table 2), adopted from the Canadian Bankers Association submission.

there has been much written about the U.S. decline as a commercial power, the American decline as a global financial power is altogether on another scale and not easily overcome given that the U.S. is now the world's largest debtor nation. My own prediction is that once the S&L debacle is settled, this loss of hegemony, let alone influence, will lead to a comprehensive overhaul of U.S. banking legislation and the creation of 5 or 10 U.S. "superbanks" that will be able to match the assets and influence of the Japanese institutions. While this is speculation of my part, it is sufficiently likely that Canadian regulators ought not to view the existing American model as reflective of the longer-term U.S. status quo.

5. Implications

Unlike the case in the pre-1980 period, national regulators found it much more difficult to ignore the implications of the financial integration of the 1980s. Some of this related to the increased ability of domestic economic agents to access directly the international financial markets. Of much more importance, however, were the changes in national markets arising from this integration. In particular, the international trend towards reliance on capital markets rather than credit markets, including the rise of securitization and the emphasis on "off-balance-sheet" items, also pervaded national markets. Again a focus on the position of banks is instructive. In the largely unregulated international markets, the world's major banks accommodated quite well to these trends, even to the point of becoming leaders in terms of introducing novel instruments. Where the banks ran into trouble was in their *home markets*. The shift from commercial to investment banking ran into all manner of domestic regulatory barriers, so much so that the banks found it much more difficult to "follow their customers" as the latter joined the general march toward direct finance. This is clearly the stuff of which "big bangs" are made - barriers crumbled in the U.K., Australia, continental Europe, Japan and effectively (although not legislatively) for the larger American banks. Canada's integration of commercial and investment banking will be highlighted later.

C. The 1990s and Beyond: Towards International Rather than Domestic Regulation

Ironically, while the range of challenges alluded to above will occupy national regulators well into the millennium, global financial integration promises to usher in further changes which will serve to undermine these national regulators. The July 21, 1990 *Economist*'s capital markets survey phrased the issue well:

> Just as deregulation in the 1980s meant a proliferation of competing financial firms, so the 1990s will see a proliferation of

competing trading systems. It will prove a nightmare for national regulators. Already they are struggling with the complexities of supervising the global trading of hundreds of different financial instruments. Who, in the future, should regulate an Australian firm that trades Japanese futures on Chicago's Globex out of London? (p. 8)

This prompts several observations.

The first is that the distinction between national and international markets will erode further because national markets will become increasingly international. The strength and growth of the extra-national or Euromarket was due to its largely liberal or unregulated nature in a sea of heavily regulated and compartmentalized national markets. Now that domestic regulatory walls are crumbling, national markets are repatriating operations that were typically conducted abroad. Again, from the *Economist:*

> Oddly, therefore, the result of global deregulation could be that markets return home to their domestic base from the liberal, international regimes to which they had initially emigrated. In Europe the continent's gain will be London's loss, particularly when Frankfurt's markets take a leading part in the financing of Eastern Europe. Some Euromarket houses - such as Credit Suisse First Boston, which dominated London's international markets in the early 1980s - are already putting less emphasis on their London operations and fattening up their branches on the continent. An international market will no longer be one "offshore"; it will be one at home that is plugged in internationally. (p. 8).

Second, and relatedly, the global marketplace is moving if not toward international regulation then at least toward international standards. The International Organization of Securities Commissions has adopted a common approach to assessing the capital adequacy of firms engaged in securities activities. However, by far the most significant development here is the Bank of International Settlements (BIS) capital-adequacy rules for banks. Canada and some dozen other countries have already agreed to abide by these international norms.

Third, there is an important initiative as part of Europe 1992 in the direction of prudential regulation by county of chartering rather than country of operation. To understand what is at stake here it is convenient to contrast the FTA with Europe 1992 as each applies to the regulation of financial institutions. Under the provisions of the FTA, American banks operating in Canada will essentially be subject to the same regulatory regime and will have the same powers as Canadian banks. Effectively, this conforms to the provisions of national treatment (although the term national treatment is not utilized in the FTA chapter dealing with financial services) which, in turn, enhances national regulatory sovereignty. In sharp contrast, the "home county rule" approach proposed for 1992 effectively enables financial institutions to trade in financial services anywhere in the community on the basis of a single "passport" from their *home* jurisdiction, subject only to host company operating rules. In somewhat more detail, three principles underlie the European model of financial regulation:

> The first is "mutual recognition" by member states of the authorization for a financial institution chartered in one state to do business in another member state. The second, and closely related, principle is that mutual recognition is subject to the harmonization of minimum standards, including minimum capital standards. Underlying this harmonization is, of course, substantial coordination, information sharing and the like among national regulators. These two principles pave the way for "home county rule" in which the regulator in the chartering nation is responsible for the supervisory oversight of the institution in its operations throughout the Community. The final principle is that the conduct-of-business rules or operating rules would be those of the host country, that is where the services are provided (Senate, 1990, p. 70).

A final speculative comment relates to the earlier conception of the global financial system as a sophisticated information, coordination and telecomputational network. It seems inevitable that the system will develop in the direction of globe-spanning payments and settlements networks. Indeed, two of the most controversial issues in Canadian finance relate to this potential for networks or information systems to dominate institutions. The first is the granting of a Schedule II foreign bank charter to Amex. The large chartered banks are not worried about facing a few more foreign bank branches competing for Canadian deposits. But Amex is different. It may not ever open a retail branch. Rather, Amex wants to (and will) integrate in vast credit-card network into the Canadian payments system. The bankers have a rather strong case against Amex when they point out that the U.S. payments system has kept Amex out. So why should Canada be offering privileges to Amex that it cannot obtain in its home jurisdiction? The deeper concern, however, is that Amex brings a powerful new network to bear on Canadian finance and one that has the longer term potential for integration with its global credit-card system.

The second "network" concern relates to the BCE Inc. takeover of Montreal Trust. The issue here has to do with the potential competitive edge resulting from comingling telecommunications and finance. Home banking cannot be that far off and already Bell is testing the Alex system, which is Canada's version of France's Minitel. Again, the concern is with networks and communications systems, not with Montreal Trust as an institution.

The underlying issue, therefore, is one of how to integrate the growing importance of these information/payments systems with the existing regulatory apparatus. It is not inevitable that these global networks will be built around national regulatory and/or payments systems. This will constrain the ability of national regulators to control banking/financial activity let alone the definition of what constitutes a bank. Access to these networks, not an imprimatur from a national regulatory authority, is likely to be the driving feature of finance in the near future. This is but another way of stating that banks and banking services are no longer synonymous.

With this as backdrop, the remainder of the paper focuses on a few case studies or challenges facing the regulators of the Canadian financial system. These are designed to highlight aspects of the above analysis as well as to focus on some specifically Canadian features that complicate the role of the "state" (however defined) as financial regulator.

III. SELECTED CANADIAN REGULATORY CHALLENGES

A. Unshackling the Canadian Securities Industry

Spurred on by the Merrill Lynch takeover of Royal Securities in the late 1960s, the Ontario Securities Commission (OSC) moved to keep the "Canadian" securities industry not only in Canadian hands but in industry hands. Registration with the OSC was required in order that securities firms could access the so-called "registered" (protected) market. However, registration also involved very strict ownership regulations - no single non-industry (non-insider) entity could hold more than 10% of the voting shares of a registered securities firm and foreigners in aggregate could not hold more than 25% of the voting shares. In contrast, Quebec formally deregulated its securities sector in the early 1980s (in practice it was "open" much before this) but this attracted no takers since the OSC stipulated that if a Quebec-based firm exceeded the 10% ownership rule it would no longer be eligible to trade on the Toronto Stock Exchange. Effectively, therefore, Ontario called the shots in terms of the operations of the Canadian securities industry.

While industry profits remained high (as expected in a highly protected market), Canadian firms accounted for a shrinking percentage of overall securities trading in Canada. Progressively, the securities sector became the weak link in Canadian finance. Our banks, insurance firms and trusts (if the comparison here is with U.S. S&L's) were clearly world class whereas by 1985 the capital of Merrill Lynch, for example, was several times that of the *entire* Canadian securities industry. Compounding this capital inadequacy was the fact that aspects of the on-going global shift towards investment banking were capital intensive (e.g. the "bought deal", which effectively meant that the broker assumed the role of principal rather than agent). Led by Gordon Capital, several registered securities firms began to press for greater manoeuvrability, particularly in relation to ownership and capital, in order to meet the foreign competition for Canadian business. This resulted in a prolonged set of OSC hearings in which the "core" of the Canadian securities industry argued for the status quo. Eventually, however, the OSC recommended (in mid-1986) that non-industry investors and Canadian financial institutions could own 30% of a Canadian securities firm. A month or so later it increased this to 49%.

At this juncture, two other developments came to bear on the Ontario regulators. The first was that the 1985 Green Paper (which initiated the still ongoing federal reform of the financial sector) recommended that federally chartered financial institutions ought to be able to acquire securities firms. In the fall of 1986 the word was out that the federal government was likely to endorse this recommendation. (As an important aside, while I do not question that Ottawa's motives here were driven by one or all of underlying principle, international competitiveness and maintaining Canadian control over the securities industry, it is also the case that a chartered bank takeover of the securities industry would over time lead to securities regulation falling increasingly under federal control). The second was the dam buster, however. In a surprise move, the Bank of Nova Scotia took advantage of a loophole in the Bank Act and established a wholly-owned, full-service securities firm (Scotia Securities Inc.) in Quebec. Not being able to trade on the TSE was hardly constraining for Scotia Securities since this option was not open to it in any event. Ontario's tentative moves toward deregulating its securities industry were abandoned virtually immediately in favour of full and comprehensive deregulation: in the fall of 1986, the OSC announced that as of July 1, 1987, restrictions on investment in securities dealers by domestic financial institutions would be completely removed. Entry or acquisition by foreign institutions would be delayed to July 1, 1988. Within one year, roughly 80% of the assets of the Canadian securities industry were owned by the Canadian chartered banks.

In a sense, all of the regulatory pieces fell neatly into place. First, the elimination of our version of Glass-Steagall was hardly a novel move, coming roughly a year after London's "Big Bang". Second, for reasons alluded to earlier, Ottawa was on side. Third, at the provincial (Quebec vs. Ontario) level, this was healthy competitive federalism at work: Ontario would have seen some of its securities firms migrate to Quebec unless it tore down its barriers. As the remaining episodes will illustrate, however, more recent regulatory challenges have proved far more problematical.

The lessons here are rather straightforward. When financial markets were essentially regional or at best national in nature, Ontario could use its effective domestic monopoly to define the system's structure. However, in an open economy, international-capital-markets framework, Ontario has no such power: the system will simply bypass Ontario. Phrased differently, the shackles that Ontario placed around its securities industry essentially pre- ordained that it would eventually become noncompetitive. One may take heart that, thanks to the banks, the industry remained largely in Canadian hands. Not so fortunate was the timing of the deregulation: essentially the OSC decision paved the way for American access to the Canadian securities sector in the middle of the FTA deliberations, thereby removing a valuable bargaining chip from the Canadian negotiators.

B. Vertical Harmonization Challenges

With some degree of misrepresentation, Canada has three national "banking" systems, one federally regulated (the banks), one under joint federal-provincial regulation (the trusts) and one under provincial control (the credit unions/caisses populaires). All of these institutions are members of (or have access to) the Canadian Payments Association, so that Canadians dealing with any of these institutions have access to the system of cash machines. Thus, from the customer vantage point, there is precious little to differentiate a bank from a trust from a credit union/caisse populaire.

In terms of the insurance industry, the most international of our financial institutions, regulatory authority is also shared between Ottawa and the provinces, although here the more relevant division is between Quebec-based firms on the one hand and the rest of the system on the other since virtually all of the larger non- Quebec firms are federally chartered.

As an opening observation, it would appear that exclusive jurisdiction facilitates the legislative process. The legislation for banks (federal) and securities (provincial) has been updated on a more or less continuous basis over the years. Contrast this to the trust and insurance pillars where the last major federal revisions were in 1913 and 1932 respectively. Note that this legislative paralysis has not extended to the provincial sphere in terms of legislating for trusts and insurance. In the case of the trusts this presumably arises because the provinces desire to privilege the trusts vis-à-vis the banks and because in designing trust legislation they merely take the bank powers as given - unlike Ottawa, they are not constrained to satisfy somehow the conflicting demands of banks and trusts.

1.   Asset and Liability Structures

This aside, the thrust of the present section is to focus on the challenges facing the "state" as financial institution regulator in light of the globalization trends outlined above. The first point to be made is that the advent of increasingly sophisticated financial instruments has blurred the distinction between these institutions in terms of the nature of their liabilities. Even the liabilities of insurance companies are now weighted more toward savings than insurance instruments. It is still true that dealing with an insurance company does not give one access to the payments system. This may change, however, now that nearly twenty insurance companies own trust companies.

With the increasing similarity in terms of liabilities, pressures mounted on regulators to grant roughly similar asset-side powers across institutions. In particular, several provinces have already replaced the traditional quantity constraints on various types of assets with the so-called "prudent portfolio approach". This appears to be the direction of federal proposals as well. If (or when) implemented, this will substantially reduce the differences across institutions. Insurance companies may still tilt their assets to longer term investments than will banks, but this will now have more to do with what is "prudent" given the term-to-maturity structure of their liabilities.

At this level, then, the developments are clearly in the direction of international trends. Quebec is even going as far as implementing BIS-type capital adequacy rules for trust companies and the insurance industry association, exasperated with the legislative paralysis, is establishing its own internal capital- adequacy rules in connection with the mounting of a depositor- protection scheme that offers coverage similar to that under CDIC.

2.   Integration Across the Pillars

A second area where globalization is impinging on the regulators relates to ownership integration across the pillars. Already two Quebec-based institutions - the Laurentian Group and the Mouvement Desjardins - effectively operate in all four pillars. Virtually all of the federal proposals (House of Commons, Senate, draft legislation) contemplate ownership integration across the pillars. Recently, however, the insurance industry has mounted a strong lobby to prevent the chartered banks from entering insurance. In part, the argument is based on the experience with the securities industry - as noted above, within roughly a year the banks' exercised their new powers by buying up the majority of the securities industry assets. My personal view is that this lobbying effort will fail. First, the large "stock" (non-mutual) insurance companies are already integrated within a diversified financial ownership structure, e.g. both

London Life and Royal Trust are part of the Trilon financial empire. Second, by definition the mutual companies cannot be taken over. Third, as also noted earlier, there are roughly twenty insurance companies that own trust companies. What is sauce for the goose ... .

Despite general acceptance at the conceptual level with respect to asset/liability powers and cross-pillar ownership integration, federal legislation toward these ends has been stymied. Why? The reason relates to the controversy surrounding the ownership of trust companies.

3. The Ownership Dimension

Chartered banks are required to be widely held and it has long been the banks' view that this ownership structure should apply to the trusts as well. For their part, the trusts want to remain majority held (although they are willing to have a 35% public float) and they want to be eligible to become "trust-banks". In return, they are willing to have the banks be owned anyway they like and even to engage in commercial activities. I shall not outline the arguments, pro and con, for widely held ownership. (The interested reader can consult the Senate Report (1990)). The essential point is that, at base, these are two completely conflicting philosophies of the financial/banking system. Were Canada a unitary state, I think that there is no question but that the bankers would have held sway. However, federal concern about provincial reaction (and in particular the federal Tories' concern about reaction from Quebec) led to near-complete legislative paralysis at the federal level. However, legislative paralysis is not neutral in its effect. Over the Tory reign the trust companies have become considerably more entrenched, including Royal Trust's initiatives in the U.S. S&L market. Embracing the 10% rule across the board for CDIC-insured institutions was relatively easy in 1980: it is much more difficult in 1990 since it means "rolling back" the ownership of virtually all of the large trusts.

It may well be that Prime Minister Mulroney's post-Meech-Lake rhetoric and Premier David Peterson's tough election-campaign rhetoric, both directed against Quebec' view of how the federation ought to evolve, will spell a new federal assertiveness across a wide spectrum of areas, including financial regulation. If this occurs, then we may still see the universal application of the 10% ownership rule for CDIC-insured institutions.

My personal view (admittedly a view not "widely held" in academic circles) is that a universal application of the 10% rule is not the way to go. I much prefer the approach of the recent Senate report (for which I was a scribe) to this issue. Basically, the Senate report argued that the essential competitive disadvantage faced by the banks related not to ownership but to powers. The challenge to the banks comes not only from the commercially-linked trusts but also from the U.S. in-house or corporate banks such as Sears, GMAC, Ford Credit, GE Credit Corporation, Amex etc., all of whom can free wheel in aspects of the financial sector (e.g. leasing) that represent forbidden territory to the banks. Accordingly, the Senate report decided to "unleash" the latent power of the banks and allow them to address their competition head-on. Chart 2 presents the Senate's novel approach. The chartered banks would be able to reconstitute themselves as a bank holding company by transferring the ownership of the bank to the bank-holding company which would then wholly own the bank. The holding company could then move into finance- associated areas (e.g. leasing, factoring, computational areas, travel insurance) or wholly commercial areas via a real-side downstream holding company. Note that this is *not* the German universal banking model since these real-side holdings would not be downstream from the bank and, therefore, *not financed by insured deposits*.

This Senate model was based upon the maintenance of the 10% rule for the bank holding company. Over time, this aspect would presumably be subject to rethinking.

My preference for this model is predicted on two precepts. The first is that the distinction between finance and commerce will become progressively blurred. In order that the Canadian financial system maintain its current world-class character, it must have the ability to meet its potential competition head-on, as it were. Note that the Senate model does not force the banks into this structure: it merely opens options to the banks. The second rationale derives from my view that in the increasingly competitive global economy, each country must play to its strengths in order to eke out aspects of comparative advantage. Despite the questioning nature of this paper, Canada has a tremendous financial/banking system and it would be a mistake not to lever off this strength to carve our way into greater international competitiveness.

What all of this means is that our financial regulatory authorities, federal and provincial, are being pulled, willy-nilly, into a much wider playing field - financial regulation will increasingly become embroiled in overall industrial policy. This, too, is the fate of the state as financial regulator in an increasingly integrated global financial environment. Thus, in response to global developments, what began as a federal-provincial and banks vs. trusts regulatory impasse over the regulation and ownership of deposit-taking institutions is progressively developing into a more fundamental impasse relating to the role of finance in overall industrial policy. There are no "right" answers to these impasses. There are only strategic responses. These strategies ought to take account not of where banking/finance is now but rather where it is likely to be in the year 2000. Within this perspective, I am reasonably confident of the appropri-

CHART 2

The Bank Holding Company Model: Alternative Structures

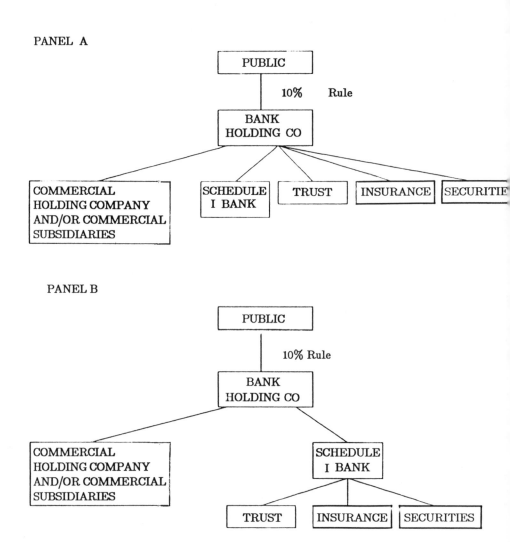

Notes: Panel A depicts all financial subsidiaries as coming directly under the holding company whereas Panel B has trusts, insurance and securities firms as subsidiaries of the bank itself. Under either version of this model there would be no asset-related transactions between the commercial and financial entities, only networking and fee-based services.

Source: Senate (1990, chart 1).

ateness of the forward-looking Senate report. Indeed, I would go further. If Canada broke down the finance/commerce barrier and we allowed for the chartering of trust-banks at the federal level, the federal-provincial jurisdictional overlap would vanish since all trusts would opt for federal regulation and trust-bank status. No province can offer this.

It is important not to misread the implications of this vertical jurisdictional overlap. While federal legislative process has been paralyzed, this does not mean that innovation has been paralyzed. It clearly has not. However, there is substantial uncertainty associated with innovation when the operational framework is in limbo. On the other hand, one could argue that this innovation is preferable to a situation where the authorities lock into place a very rigid framework (e.g. the 10% rule for all deposit-taking institutions). Phrased differently, thanks to the evolution of the system over the last decade we have considerably more information in 1990 than we had in 1980. Hopefully, this will imply that when federal legislation does come down it will benefit from this information.

C. "Horizontal" Harmonization Challenges

The spectre of Europe 1992 providing a unified *international* financial market for the European Community has enhanced concerns that our regulators have not been able to deliver a *national* market in Canadian financial services. In the recent hearings associated with the Senate study of the financial sector, this issue gained such prominence that the Senate opted to entitle its report *Canada 1992: Towards a National Market in Financial Services*. This section will, first, review the Senate approach to this harmonization issue and then focus on the underlying problem, namely the Quebec vision of the role of finance in the economy.

1. Canada 1992

Ontario is generally perceived as the culprit in terms of mounting barriers to the free flow of financial services across provinces. At issue is this province's so-called "Equals Approach" under its *Loan and Trust Corporations Act*. Under this provision, a trust company operating in Ontario is, for certain of its activities, subject to Ontario regulation and supervision in *all* its operations, even those in other provinces. This applies to federally chartered trusts as well as those chartered in other provinces. The stated purpose of the equals approach is to protect Ontario citizens from the costs of potential financial-institution failure arising from more lenient rules in the chartering jurisdiction. However, in practice the impact goes well beyond this. Because the Ontario market is so critical the net result is that Ontario's regulatory and supervisory standards effectively dominate the Canadian trust industry. In order to conduct business in Ontario, trusts must manage their business *outside*

Ontario according to Ontario law. In a sense, this exercise in extraterritorially is not all that different from Ontario's earlier attempt to hold the securities industry in line by refusing access to the TSE for firms that did not abide by the province's ownership provisions. The Senate report comments as follows:

> Canadians have had a long tradition of vigorously opposing U.S. legislation that applies extraterritorially in Canada. Surely we cannot countenance this sort of legislation *within* our boundaries. One of the Committee's challenges is to accommodate concerns like Ontario's without fragmenting the national market for financial services (1990, p. 27).

Drawing from the "home-country-rule" model for Europe 1992 as well as the Royal Trust model (1989), the Senate's proposal for a national financial market is built around the following tenets:

- a federal-provincial consensus or accord on key regulatory standards and principles;
- the acceptance of the "designated jurisdiction" concept;
- the acceptance of host-province conduct-of-business rules and consumer protection laws.

The Senate report elaborates as follows:

> Now that the BIS capital adequacy rules apply to banks in roughly a dozen countries and, within Canada, several jurisdictions are already moving in this direction, the time has surely come for all primary regulators to reach consensus on some minimum acceptable standards and principles. The Committee recommends that jurisdictions in which the policy or regulatory authorities insist on enacting more lenient rules with respect to capital or regulatory oversight shall not be eligible for CDIC coverage for their chartered institutions.
>
> Responsibility for regulating prudential aspects (capital, self-dealing, etc.) and for framing basic business and investment powers will rest with the chartering jurisdiction. This is the "designated jurisdiction" concept. Provinces will designate the chartering jurisdiction to have this responsibility. The general approach to this regulatory oversight will be governed by the federal-provincial accord on regulation.
>
> Provinces will be able to implement their own conduct-of-business rules and consumer protection laws. However, "provincial treatment" must prevail in the application of these conduct of business rules: institutions chartered federally or in other provinces must be accorded the same privileges as host-chartered

institutions. For example, it is likely that some provinces will prevent insurance networking on the premises of deposit-taking institutions. But for provinces that do allow such networking, this privilege must be extended to all institutions, irrespective of where they are chartered. ...

In establishing the basic precepts of the system there is bound to be a natural tension between the designated jurisdiction and the host-province conduct-of-business rules. As the recommendations indicate, the Committee believes that authority over prudential rules, corporate governance monitoring, allowable investments and basic business powers must reside with the designated jurisdiction (chartering province). Host provinces can regulate business conduct conditions such as disclosure and consumer protection provisions, as long as these do not impact extra-territorially. The model does not necessarily imply that a Quebec-chartered financial institution can do in Ontario everything it can do in Quebec, and vice versa. Thus, differing host-province business conduct rules convert the model into a "provincial-treatment" model, that is, a Quebec- chartered firm can do in Ontario everything that an Ontario firm can do. Note that the Quebec-chartered firm operating in Ontario would have the same operating rights as an Ontario firm irrespective of the Quebec firm's business powers or how it is structured. CIDC coverage for the Quebec firm in its Ontario operations is the only relevant criterion for the Ontario regulators: if the institution has CDIC coverage, it has all the operating rights and privileges of an Ontario firm (1990, pp. 71-2).

Short of stripping away provincial powers with respect to trust and loan companies, this approach would appear to be the most appropriate route in terms of freeing up the domestic financial market. Already New Brunswick and British Columbia have enacted legislation incorporating the "designated jurisdiction" concept.

However, there is in my view something far more fundamental underlying Ontario's "equals approach", namely the province's attempt at containing the financial sector philosophy emerging in Quebec. Indeed, this "Quebec Inc." philosophy is also at the core of some of the vertical harmonization challenges addressed in the previous section. The final substantive part of this paper focuses on aspects of the Quebec model.

2. Quebec Inc.

Beginning in the early 1980s Quebec began to deregulate its financial sector, initially opening up its securities sector and later allowing owner-ship integration across the pillars. These initiatives were hardly novel:

they were merely imitating the status quo in international markets. However, Quebec was the deregulatory leader in Canada and this served to favour its own institutions. The second stage of the deregulation was to privilege Quebec's indigenous institutions - the mutuals and the caisses populaires. By allowing downstream holding companies for mutuals and later encouraging demutualization and by allowing special "share" issues for the caisses, these institutions were able to attract new capital to take advantage of their new powers. More to the point, these initiatives were not particularly novel by international standards.

Far more controversial is Quebec's intention to generate "mammoth corporations" (Fortier, 1989) that comingle financial and real corporations. The rationale is in part to ensure that some of the commercial "stars" remain in Quebec hands and in part to enhance the viability of the overall Quebec economy. When the rest of Canada is debating whether the commercial sector ought to be able to own the financial sector, Quebec has already viewed this as yesterday's issue and is now pressing for financial sector ownership of commerce. While this is a variant of the German/Japanese model (and more recently the French model), it is at odds with financial policy in virtually every other English-speaking nation. Quebec Inc. clearly unnerves the rest of Canada and particularly Ontario since there is little likelihood that any such mammoth corporations would respect provincial boundaries.

But Quebec is not finished with financial innovation. This summer Madame Louise Robic, the Quebec Minister responsible for financial institutions tabled legislation that would do away with the 10-25 rule for foreign ownership of existing Quebec firms in the insurance sector. (See Table 1 for the current provisions relating to foreign ownership). To be sure there was (and still is) something quite anomalous about our treatment of foreign ownership in the financial sector. Foreign financial institutions could come in as wholly-owned entities via the Schedule II foreign bank route or they could buy 10% of existing firms, but nothing in between in terms of joint venturing, for example. This is exactly what Quebec is addressing in allowing a 30% stake by a non-resident, and even higher with Ministerial approval. While the legislation was no doubt triggered by the association between Groupe Victoire (part of Bank Suez) and Laurentian, it nonetheless opens the door for more general joint venturing.

This move seems to me to be both natural and inevitable. Like other recent initiatives, however, it runs counter to existing practice and thinking both in Ottawa and in the other provinces or at least in Ontario.

More to the point, the totality of the Quebec evolution severely complicates the pursuit of a national financial market. If the Senate "designated jurisdiction" model were adopted and if Quebec's recent initiatives served to privilege their own institutions, Ontario would be faced with either a) having its Ontario chartered institutions suffer a fall in market share or b) following the Quebec lead.

Phrased in this manner, the underlying issue is not really one of internal barriers but rather one of radically different Quebec/ Ontario philosophies relating to finance and its appropriate role in the economy. What compounds all of this, post-Meech Lake, is that control over its financial sector is surely one of the enduring tenets of the "distinct society". In sum, this is no longer a regulatory issue, but rather a policy issue. As the 1986 Senate report noted (p. 66), "for regulators to coordinate, legislators must harmonize".

It requires very little in the way of crystal-gazing to assert that this issue will play front and centre as Canadians rethink their federation. I cannot see Quebec willing to make compromises in terms of asserting autonomy over the development of its financial sector. Nor can I see the Anglo-American conception of finance in English Canada readily embracing the Quebec Inc. model. My personal solution would be for the federal government to effectively usurp provincial authority by adopting a wide-open policy and regulatory framework, including the bank-holding-company concept. Immediately, there would cease to be any advantages to provincial chartering for trust and insurance companies and our internal financial markets would automatically become national.

The combination of legislative delay at the federal level, the continuing evolution of the international financial system and, more generally, the impact of the information/telecomputational revolution on blurring the distinction between finance and commerce favours, I think, an eventual federal policy solution in this very open direction.

Endnote

* Parts of this paper draw upon my earlier writings (1986 and 1990). It is a pleasure to acknowledge my long-time mentor in the financial area, Gérald A. Lacoste, former Chairman of the Quebec Securities Commission and now a partner with Martineau Walker in Montreal. However, responsibility for what follows rests with me.

7. Zero Means Almost Nothing: Towards a Preferable Inflation and Macro Stance

I. INTRODUCTION

Canadian macro policy (fiscal, monetary and exchange rate) is in shambles.[1] If the policy authorities maintain their current positions, not only is the economy in for a hard landing, but likely a highly *inflationary* one as well. The Conference Board of Canada has already declared that the 550 basis point premium on Canadian short-term interest rates (vis-à-vis U.S. short rates) and the accompanying overvaluation of the Canadian dollar have saddled the country with its first-ever "made-in-Canada" recession. Thus, there is little doubt about the likelihood of the "hard landing" aspect of this scenario. But will not this so-called zero- inflation or price-stability policy at least wrestle inflation to the ground? This is increasingly less likely. While our inflation prospects are not unaffected by the price implications stemming from the Gulf Crisis and the GST, the underlying problem has to do with the dramatic escalation of the degree to which the Canadian economy now depends on inflows of foreign capital. A collapse in global confidence with respect to our prospects could send the (already-overvalued) dollar plunging and, with it, a rise in domestic inflation. The purpose of this paper is to elaborate on these themes and in particular to argue that existing macro policy is leading not only to the "hollowing out" of Canadian manufacturing but, if it persists, to the possible "Latin Americanizing" of the upper half of North America.

To anticipate the conclusion somewhat, the underlying proposition is that our macro managers have locked Canada in the late 1980s and early

1990s into a policy paradigm designed ideally to combat the macro dysfunction of the 1970s, namely runaway nominal magnitudes. However, Canada's current macro dysfunction relates to what Peter Drucker (1986) refers to as the "symbol economy" - exchange rates, capital flows and aggregate savings imbalances - and in particular to our shortfall in aggregate domestic savings. A high-interest-rate policy substantially aggravates this symbol-economy problem and the corresponding overvaluation of the dollar misreads the economic dictates that derive from the Canada-U.S. Free Trade Agreement (henceforth referred to as the FTA).

This paper has three sections. The first (Part II) presents the analytical underpinnings of the case against the current policy mix. Part III attempts to sort out the implications of the on- going macro stance. Part IV focuses on alternative re-entry scenarios. In the conclusion, I present my preferred policy alternative.

II. ANALYTICAL UNDERPINNINGS

A. The Erosion of the Interest-Rate Impact
The thrust of what follows is, as noted, that our macro authorities have misread and are continuing to misread the implications of globalization as it relates to both financial and real markets. The first point in this context is that the efficacy of monetary policy, in terms of its interest-rate impact has been eroded since the 1970s. Part of this relates to the fact that the new and creative financial instruments and technologies (financial futures, currency and interest rate swaps) mean that sophisticated private sector agents can increasingly "by-pass" domestic monetary restraint.[2] Hence, the monetary bite falls increasingly on those agents that are not international or not large enough or not sophisticated enough to access these instruments. This is not quite the same as saying that monetary policy is increasingly regressive, but this term will do until a better one comes along.

Thus, those agents that are already highly levered (e.g. farmers and mortgage holders) are obviously in the front lines of any inflation fight. Grant Devine's concerns are understandable in this context, since the current monetary policy represents a triple whammy, as it were, for the Saskatchewan farmers. First, resource prices, including those in agriculture, have fallen relative to manufacturing prices in the 1980s. Second, the interest-rate- driven, exchange-rate overshooting, roughly 25 per cent since 1986 in terms of the U.S. dollar, has aggravated the impact of resource prices on the Atlantic and Western economies. Third, the interest- rate hikes bear most heavily on farmers and fishermen not only because they have fared least well in the post-1982 expansion but also because they are already heavily levered.

Most problematic of all, given that roughly 55 per cent of our near $400 billion federal debt is short term in nature (T-bills and CSB's), is that a one per cent rise in interest rates leads to a near-$4 billion steady-state increase in annual debt servicing, one half of which surfaces within, say, 6 months. If fiscal policy remains passive, i.e., if it allows deficits to rise by this amount, then on this count alone monetary policy is inherently "expansionary". In this context it is instructive to note that the current $30 billion federal deficit is composed of a "debt- servicing deficit" of $40 billion and an "operational surplus" of $10 billion. Were our interest rates at U.S. levels, debt servicing would be close to one-half the current level and the overall deficit correspondingly reduced. Moreover, this debt-servicing probably aggravates the regional aspects referred to earlier since bondholders are presumably disproportionately located in the centre, not the periphery, of the country.

Chart 1 depicts short-term nominal and real interest rates for five countries as of June 1990. The Canadian nominal rate, while well above the U.S. rate, is less than that in the U.K. However, in terms of *real* (after-inflation) rates, our rate is well above that in the other four countries. What Chart 1 does not reveal (because it is a snapshot as of June, 1990) is that this historically-high Canada-U.S. differential has persisted for a few years now, essentially since Governor John Crow launched his zero-inflation policy. The theme of this section is that the existence of the federal debt overhang (particularly its short-term nature) and the increasing globalization of financial markets imply that interest-rate impacts of monetary policy are less effective than was the case in the 1970's. However, there are obvious discontinuities in this relationship - once real rates reach the 8 per cent level (Chart 1), it is difficult for anybody to escape their impact.

B. The Interest-Rate/Exchange-Rate Nexus

The second general point is that a high-interest policy does not operate in a vacuum. Specifically, it leads to an overvaluation of the Canadian dollar. The greater the degree of overvaluation, the larger the interest-rate premiums required by international investors. The OECD estimates that the purchasing power parity for the Canadian dollar vis-à-vis a basket of currencies is roughly 80 cents U.S. (At the time of writing, the dollar is fluctuating in the 85-87 cent range). Vis-à-vis the U.S. dollar alone, the overvaluation is higher, perhaps as much as 10-15 cents. Generating an overvalued currency is an effective anti- inflationary policy if the under-lying inflation pressures are coming from the export or import-competing sectors of the economy. But surely this is not the case. If there is one area in the economy that is under pressure to hold down wage and price

CHART 1

Short-Term Interest Rates

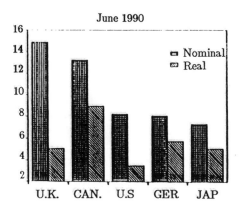

June 1990

CHART 2

Manufacturing Unit Labour Costs
In U.S. Dollar Terms

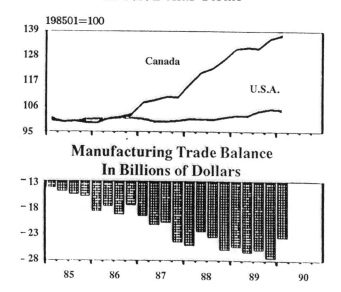

198501=100

Manufacturing Trade Balance
In Billions of Dollars

Source: Chandler (1990).

increases it has to be those sectors that are open to U.S. competition under the FTA. With the latest inflation figures (October, 1990) running just above 4 per cent the Bank is having difficulty convincing Canadians that inflation is the real problem. Moreover, it is generally recognized that the higher CPI increase over most of 1989 had to do with the increase in regulated prices and, in particular, increases in indirect taxes. Wage increases are running higher than inflation, but the leaders here are public and quasi-public (e.g., Ontario Hydro) settlements not private- sector settlements. Finally, one must sympathize with the Governor when it comes to the likely impact of the GST on inflation and wages. But this speaks to another theme of this paper, namely the incredible lack of coordination between the monetary and fiscal authorities. Why should Canadians pay for the inability of Crow and Wilson to coordinate their respective policies?

These considerations aside, the interest-rate-induced overvaluation of the Canadian dollar is clobbering Canadian industry as it attempts to integrate north-south. Essentially, Bank of Canada policy is transferring production and employment to the U.S. in precisely the time frame when Canada's industry has a once-in-a-generation (perhaps lifetime) opportunity with the FTA to take advantage of an expansion in our "domestic" market. This is very evident from Chart 2. The upper panel of the Chart compares manufacturing unit labour costs (ULC) for Canada and the U.S., where both are expressed in U.S. dollars. ULC for the U.S. have remained roughly unchanged over 1985-90 - the U.S. wage increases have been matched by U.S. productivity gains. However, Canadian unit labour costs have increased by nearly 40 per cent over this period. Some of this increase arises because wages are growing faster (and productivity gains growing slower) than in the U.S. But the lion's share of the Canadian ULC increase arises from the appreciation of the dollar and this, in turn, is due primarily to the Bank's higher-interest-rate policy.

The lower panel of Chart 2 reveals the impact on our manufacturing trade balance. Presumably one of the Bank's goals in pursuing its zero-inflation stance is to enhance the competitiveness of the Canadian economy. Yet, from early 1987 (when Governor Crow took the helm), Canadian unit labour costs have deteriorated by over 30 per cent vis-à-vis the Americans. It is hard to ignore the conclusion that macro policy and in particular Bank of Canada policy is converting the FTA opportunity into a veritable nightmare.

C. The Twin-Deficit Problem
The third point relates to what I have earlier referred to as the current "macro dysfunction", namely the behaviour of aggregate savings imbalances. The basic national income accounting identity can be expressed in

the so-called twin-deficit form, namely that the government (fiscal) deficit is identically equal to net private sector savings plus foreign savings (the current-account deficit). Alternatively, if private sector net savings are not large enough to cover the government deficit, then we will run a balance-of- payments deficit on current account, i.e. resort to foreign savings. While the Tories have not made much of a dent in the dollar value of the federal deficit, they have brought it down considerably as a per cent of GNP. However, net private savings have fallen much more as a per cent of GNP.[3] Hence, our current account deficit has risen dramatically.

There are alternative economic explanations of what is driving these results. What follows is my interpretation, not necessarily *the* interpretation, whatever that might be. Despite seven years of economic expansion, aggregate net domestic savings (fiscal deficit minus private net savings) have become increasingly negative. The fiscal deficit endures in the $30 billion range as private net savings falls. The high Canadian interest rates draw in the needed foreign capital which, in turn, appreciates the Canadian dollar. This leads to a balance of payments deficit on current account. From a *surplus* of $3 billion in 1983, the current account balance has mushroomed to a *deficit* of roughly $20 billion in 1989. This is exchange-rate crowding out with a vengeance - the domestic savings shortfall, driven in part by the interest-rate-induced fiscal deficit, is converted via high interest rates into a current account deficit. This is exactly what the Americans went through in 1983-85 and even beyond, namely their domestic "living-beyond- their-means" resulted in a rise in interest rates which a) brought in the needed foreign capital to finance Reagan's "military Keynesianism" (a combination of tax cuts and military spending), b) drove up their exchange rate, c) decimated their tradeables sector and d) ironically, increased their dependence on the existing deficit levels. The irony here is that the large deficits led to the "hollowing out" of the U.S. economy, partly by transferring production offshore. Now large deficits are needed to offset this loss of "production" in aggregate demand.

We are doing the same thing to Canada and Canadians, albeit a half-decade later. Some aspects of U.S. policy are no doubt worth importing. But why would we choose to mimic this particular policy?

As of the end of 1989 our "twin deficits" (fiscal and current account) were, as a per cent of GNP, roughly 1½ times those in the U.S. However, whereas this twin-deficit concern has long dominated U.S.-policy debates, it is essentially foreign to the Canadian debate. This is surprising because:

- the U.S. fiscal deficit is far more tractable than is the Canadian counterpart. Even setting aside the potential U.S. "peace dividend" (which may well be dissipated in the Gulf) a 5 per cent GST would

more than cover the U.S. deficit. Covering ours would require a 10
per cent GST *above* the proposed 7 per cent GST;

- Canada's net foreign indebtedness - somewhere around $250 bil-
  lion - is, as a per cent of GNP, well above the American indebtedness. More to the point, if one applies current value accounting to
  the U.S. indebtedness, Canada's external indebtedness is, in absolute dollars, likely the highest in the world although the U.S. will
  soon surpass us on this score. Another way of looking at this is to
  note that our external debt to GNP ratio - about 35% - exceeds that
  of Brazil which runs at about 30% (Nicholson, 1990).
- Unlike the Americans, we tend, on the margin, to borrow in "foreign
  pay", not "domestic pay". In terms of the U.S. deficit, one can
  legitimately ask, whose problem is it anyway? since a collapse in the
  U.S. dollar would impose costs on those that hold the debt. Phrased
  differently, the Americans can inflate their way out of their indebtedness (should they so wish). We can't.

Here is where the economics of all this comes into play. Living beyond
our means (a current account deficit) is hardly a problem if these foreign
savings add to our productive capacity and, hence, our ability to repay the
debt. However, the thrust of this paper is that if the current calibration of
the symbol-economy instruments remain unchanged, our ability to repay
our external debt will deteriorate significantly.

A final perspective merits highlight. In a sense, Canada and the U.S.
had the international capital market to themselves for most of the 1980s.
Not so now. The West German current account surplus will now be
deployed to rebuild "East Germany". More generally, Eastern Europe and
the Soviet Union will also attract foreign capital. What this means is that
these new demands for capital will raise global real interest rates. Thus,
whereas Canada has viewed its high real interest rates as an instrument for
combatting inflation, the likelihood is that they will now have to remain
high in order to draw in foreign savings. As an important aside, with this
high degree of international dependence, the last thing Canada needs is the
bout of on-going turmoil over the constitutional future of the country.

D. The FTA and the Exchange Rate

My fourth point is probably more speculative. Most of my market-
oriented colleagues who were in favor of the FTA argued that exchange
rate flexibility was the *sine qua non* of Canada-U.S. integration. If, for
some unexpected reason, free trade results in a downturn in Canadian
economic activity, the exchange rate would come to our aid (in this case,
depreciate). However, as outlined earlier, exchange rates are increasingly
driven, over the short term at least, by macro (monetary or savings) criteria

and not by real-side activity, so that this safety valve may be of little value as we integrate with the U.S. Indeed, the underlying irony is that we are using our exchange rate to *unwind* the potential benefits of the FTA!

In any case, this conception of the role of exchange rates is in my view seriously flawed. To be sure, when upward pressure on the exchange rate arises because the U.S. is inflating, the first best policy response is, and still will be, to allow the Canadian dollar to appreciate in order to shield Canada from U.S. inflation. In the current frame, this is an unlikely scenario (although the events in the Gulf have ratcheted up U.S. inflation). The traditional approach to the exchange rate has been that it is the ideal mechanism for handling global relative price shocks that impinge differently across regions. Assuming that this is a positive relative price shock (e.g. an increase in resource prices or an increase in manufacturing prices), the typical Canadian response has been to allow the exchange rate (via appreciation) to take off some of this pressure.

However, as the Canadian regions integrate north-south under the FTA, this approach will be much more difficult to sell both politically and economically. For example, from a position where the Canadian west adjusts its wages and prices to compete with the cross-border American communities, consider a world-price increase in raw materials. The typical Canadian response has been, as noted, to take some of this terms-of-trade-increase pressure off via an exchange-rate appreciation. However, under the FTA everything from the proverbial guns to butter will now be flowing north-south. What this means is that the appreciation will increase Canadian prices vis-à-vis those of *similarly situated* agents south of the border. Thus, not only the Canadian west is out of equilibrium, so is the rest of Canada.

The ability of the exchange rate to play this role of arbitrer of regional fortunes is severely circumscribed when trade flows north-south rather than east-west. This is because the "optimal currency areas" become the north-south cross-border regions, not the national economy. If exchange rate flexibility is optimal under real-side integration, why have the European countries opted for the European currency snake or corridor, let alone plans for a single currency? In my view, therefore, real-side integration will, particularly for a small, regionally-diverse, country integrating with a larger one, require *more*, not less, exchange-rate fixity. Otherwise, exchange rate uncertainty for the smaller country will erode much of the benefits of integration.

E. Provincial Stabilization Policy

If the Canada-U.S. exchange rate will, in the future, be driven toward fixity than flexibility, this then raises the question of how Canada ought to deal with the impacts of these terms-of-trade shifts. Part of the answer is straightforward - we have to abandon the notion of national wage setting and patterning. In a regionally diverse economy subject to global shocks, uniform national wage rates do not make economic sense. If we do not utilize exchange rates to offset terms-of-trade shifts, some of this will happen naturally. For example, appreciating the exchange rate in response to an oil price increase effectively results in underpricing of energy in Ontario, and allows Ontario labour to capture some of the rents transferred from, say, Alberta to the rest of the country. If, on the other hand, the exchange rate is not allowed to move, Ontario industry is confronted with the appropriate (world) constellation of relative prices. More to the point, as Toronto joins the class of the world's great cities, it is becoming more and more like London or Frankfort and less and less like Kingston. Why should federal employees in Kingston, let alone rural Saskatchewan, be on the same wage scale as those in Toronto?

The other part of the answer constitutes my fifth point. Given that the macro dysfunction relates to aggregate savings imbalances, we have to resurrect the role of fiscal policy as a key instrument in overall stabilization policy. And within this framework, there is an important role to be played by provincial fiscal policies. Specifically, provinces whose income is positively affected by a global price shock should be encouraged to "cool" their own economies, via fiscal measures. This was the idea behind Alberta's Heritage Fund. This is also the European approach to greater exchange-rate fixity: surplus nations are expected to temper their booms via fiscal measures.

In recent years, Ontario had several excellent opportunities to take some heat out of its economy. Unlike Alberta, which attempted to "bank" its resource-driven fiscal dividend, Ontario decided to spend it. The result was that over the last six years or so the incredible Ontario boom was fueled even further by a 10 per cent annual rate of increase in government spending. Thus, rather than tempering the boom, Ontario simply passed the job on to the macro authorities. Can there be any doubt that interest rates are higher today than they would have been if Ontario had acted in a more fiscally responsible manner? This is also part of Grant Devine's argument - Saskatchewan farmers are now being asked to help fight an inflation that was initially "made in Ontario".

It is probably inappropriate to place any blame on Ontario. The real problem here is that neither John Crow nor Michael Wilson suggested that it might be a good idea.[4] This, too, is part of the paradigm warp associated with the current policy mix. However, I would be remiss if I did not point out that the 5% cap on the Canada Assistance Plan transfers to B.C. Alberta and B.C. in the recent federal budget represents a version of provincial stabilization policy, *but implemented by Ottawa.*

III. THE IMPLICATIONS OF THE CURRENT POLICY MIX

Focussing, first, on the impact of current policy on economic activity, it appears evident that the high-interest-rate/ overvalued-exchange-rate policy is tilting expenditures toward consumption and away from investment. Clearly, the holders of short-term deposits or floating-rate bonds are winners (especially with real rates at 8 per cent) which accounts for the consumption tilt. Equally clear, the record-high real cost of capital is substantially dampening our prospects for penetrating the U.S. market. (The fact that investment has not been absolutely levelled by these interest rates reflects the powerful stimulus flowing from the FTA).

Another way to look at this is to note that we are turning "inward", as it were. Domestic activity (nontradeables) is gaining at the expense of the tradeables sector. Phrased somewhat differently, the macro mix is tilting production away from (tradeable) manufactures toward (non-tradeable) services. This is likely to create a long term problem both in terms of the ability to capture the potential gains from the FTA and, consequently, in terms of *increasing* our dependence on the existing level of the federal deficit. Note in this context that investment decisions are difficult to reverse. Choosing a U.S. rather than a Canadian location or transferring production south will cast a long shadow on Canada's potential, well after Crow and Wilson leave centre stage.

Both of these pose long-term inflation concerns since we are, in effect, drawing on foreign savings (building up international indebtednes) to finance this shift away from investment and toward consumption. Where is the productive capacity to repay this rapid increase in foreign indebtedness?

The other set of implications relates to the massive wealth and income transfers incorporated in the current macro mix. Some of these are well-known - the policy favours coupon-clippers at the expense (even devastation) of farmers. Some of these are more implicit than explicit. High interest rates and the resulting debt servicing are crowding out social programs - day care has already been scrapped and health and post-secondary education are being severely squeezed. Not only is the older generation (bondholders) the principal beneficiary but the current costs (as well as the eventual debt repayment) are being saddled on the young. This is particularly problematical since investment in our youth is the key to making a successful transition from a resource-based economy to a knowledge-based economy. Yet, if anything, we are involved in a process of "consuming our children" (to borrow from a phrase a recent *Atlantic Magazine* feature), rather than investing in them.

All of these substantial trade-offs, economic and social, might be acceptable if the current macro mix was sure to eradicate inflation. Yet, it is not obvious that it will succeed. The purpose of the following section is to focus on the range of possibilities for a successful re-entry, as it were. The remainder of the present section details the limit- or worst-case scenario in terms of inflation.

Underlying this limit scenario is the possibility (heightened by the Gulf Crisis) that Canada is headed into a policy-induced stagflation (*stag*nation and in*flation*). This is an incredibly bleak scenario since it would blow the deficit sky high - the inflation (or high-interest) aspect would increase government debt servicing while the recession would clobber revenues and trigger income-support-related transfers. Both serve to escalate the deficit. An "ordinary" recession (low economic activity and low interest rates) would have falling debt-servicing offsetting falling tax revenues and the increased recession-induced transfers. Not so for stagflation. Thus, the possibility exists that the entire Tory deficit-reduction agenda will be overwhelmed. We will be back in 1984, except with a much higher deficit and three-fold level for the debt. At this point, the dollar will surely run into trouble since the the global community will re-assess Canada's prospects. Moreover, the tendency will be to monetize the debt and deficit. In microcosm, this is the Latin America syndrome.

To be sure, this is the limit scenario. Nonetheless, it needs to be aired because it is a possibility today, even though it was inconceivable a few years ago. This leads naturally into the next section - alternative re-entry scenarios. Specifically, need we fall into the limit scenario?

IV. ALTERNATIVE RE-ENTRY SCENARIOS

1. Zero Inflation
Under what conditions will the current macro mix "work"? This is not a well-defined question because the goals of the current stance are not well defined. As the first alternative, I will focus on the prospects for zero inflation.

In order for zero inflation to come about at the existing exchange rate, Canada's inflation rate must first fall below U.S. inflation by the degree of overvaluation of the Canadian dollar. Of and by itself, this is an incredibly tall order in terms of what it implies for the pace of wages and prices in Canada relative to the U.S. At this point, 85-87 cents will be, roughly, the equilibrium exchange rate. Assuming, then, that the U.S. inflation rate runs at 4%, zero inflation in Canada means that our currency will appreciate 4% per year vis-à-vis the U.S. dollar. If productivity grows in both countries at, say, 1%, this means that Canadian nominal wages will increase by 1% per year while U.S. nominal wages will grow by 5% (inflation plus productivity).

This is effectively unachievable (at least in my view) and, more importantly, it is foolhardy. (It becomes more possible if the U.S. also opts for zero inflation). Phrased somewhat differently, zero inflation is not a credible policy. Canada has not achieved zero inflation for any reasonable time period in the post-war period. The international capital markets have obviously not bought into zero inflation since, if they did, the forward dollar would be at a *premium*, not a discount. The government has not bought in either, since most or all its policies are set with a 3% inflation goal in mind (i.e. zero indexing up to 3% inflation, full indexation beyond this). What this means is that the government "loses" if inflation is less than 3%. Thus, even Wilson's legislative parameters operate against zero inflation. For more detail, see Johnson (1990).

To this one could add a completely separate set of concerns, namely that there will be very substantial real-side (unemployment) costs to attempting to hold wage-rate increases to the rate of productivity growth (see Fortin, 1989). For all these reasons, aggressively pursuing zero inflation as a goal *will* likely trigger the limit scenario outlined above and, therefore, will hold the promise for a potential sharp escalation of inflation as a response. Phrased differently, there are substantial costs for Canada to attempt to become the "hard" currency in a soft-currency area!

2. Controlling Inflation

A more modest goal is to argue that the current interest rate/exchange rate policy is essential for lowering inflation and, with it, nominal interest rates. This is the mainstream economics approach and one that most business analysts as well as C.D. Howe Institute, for example, appear to have endorsed, although more recently the Institute has argued that monetary policy has recently become too tight.

However, this is the approach that Part II of this paper was directed against. In addition to the points made above, the short-term obstacles also include the GST concern and the unmeasurable, but nonetheless considerable, country-risk, interest-rate premium associated with the Meech Lake uncertainty. Since these are common to all approaches to combatting inflation in this time frame, one might argue that they ought to be ignored. As I will argue later, however, this is not evident.

There are two other issues associated with this alternative. The first is that there is no guarantee that if inflation stabilizes, interest rates will then fall relative to U.S. rates. This depends on whether Governor Crow will be satisfied with controlling inflation or whether he really intends to drive it toward zero. In turn this introduces an incredible degree of uncertainty into the conduct of monetary policy, one that will surely exact a toll in terms of investment.

The second is that the Canadian dollar is currently overvalued and eventually must fall. This will generate a once-and-for-all increase in prices, something in the neighborhood of 1% on the CPI for each 2-3 cent fall in the dollar. To be sure, the level to which the dollar will fall will depend on how well we do on both the external debt and the inflation front in the interim. The key point is that we are eventually going to have to take this price hit.

These issues introduce a further degree of both concern and uncertainty into fighting inflation. Suppose the rate of inflation steadies at, say, 4%. Will our monetary authorities then decrease interest rates, tolerate a fall in the dollar to purchasing power parity, and accept the resulting one shot increase in domestic prices? Unlikely. There is no "good" time to take this price hit. The underlying point is that this "mainstream" approach to combatting inflation promises high real interest rates for a long while. However, it will "work" eventually, if it can avoid dragging us into the "limit scenario", aired above. Indeed, with luck, we might get this unwinding of inflation, interest rates and exchange rates in a way that the depreciation will go largely unnoticed in terms of its inflation impact. But this appears to me to be unlikely, given the on-going public sector wage demands. What appears to be happening in the markets now (October 1990) is that the dollar is falling *without* a corresponding fall in interest rates. This is good news in terms of FTA, but it is bad news from the Bank's vantage point.

3. Wage and Price Controls

Recently, the CMA proposed that Canada consider the imposition of wage and price controls in the public sector, or more generally a public sector wage policy (and leadership). This was greeted with ridicule by most commentators, including our macro authorities. However, my guess is that the CMA has gone through the above analysis as well and realized that Canada's manufacturers' will be saddled with above-U.S. real-interest rates and an overvalued exchange rate for a period long enough to severely complicate Canada-U.S. integration. Moreover, the CMA is no doubt aware of the stagflation potential, which would undermine Canada's fiscal position and make an "inflation" solution (deficit monetization) more likely. What is completely befuddling is why the CMA did not make these points more clear when presenting its wage-and-price control proposal. As a result, it left itself open to overly critical responses from the mainstream, including Finance and the Bank. Yet, the basic thrust is surely correct: we do need a public sector wage policy since this is where the wage pressure is now focusing.

4. Exchange Rate Pegging

In the background piece (1990) where I argued the FTA would drive the system toward greater exchange rate fixity, I stopped short of opting for a fixed exchange rate with the U.S. dollar. In part, my reasoning at the time (January, 1990f) was that the February federal budget would likely redress the macro-mix balance, i.e., shift the macro mix sharply toward fiscal restraint. However, the budget took only very modest short-term steps in this direction. Moreover, the interest-rate projections underlying the medium-term deficit forecasts were, in my view, overly optimistic even without the recent run-up in Canadian interest rates and the increase in the Canada-U.S. rate differential. What this means is that the deficit reduction program is again way off track.

The arguments for flexible exchange rates have to be premised on at least two key propositions: first, that we have more confidence in our macro managers than those in the U.S. and second, that the exchange rate movements reflect fluctuations in economic activity and not "symbol economy" factors or portfolio shifts. Unfortunately, both of these propositions, particularly the latter, lack substance in the present environment.

Hence, I have now come to the view that a move to exchange- rate fixity with the U.S. dollar may well be the most appropriate macro strategy over the medium term. I will elaborate this in the conclusion. Prior to this, it is instructive to focus on the macro impact of the on-going constitutional crisis.

5. The Meech Lake Factor

Canada is already very exposed in terms of its foreign indebtedness. It is a measure the world's confidence in our economy that we can still draw in substantial foreign capital even with our substantial twin deficits and our external and domestic indebtedness. Presumably, this has already exacted a "country risk" premium on our borrowing costs, although this premium is difficult to measure.

Obviously, any post-Meech-Lake constitutional problems will complicate international "confidence" in Canadian economic prospects. Since this would be common to all possible macro stances it could be argued that it should be disregarded in assessing which macro stance is the most appropriate. I do not think that this is correct. By design, the Bank policy is to run with high interest rates and an overvalued dollar. If the dollar is overvalued (i.e. if there *already* exists a substantial forward discount in the market), then a confidence crisis hits with *all the more impact* since the Bank is then put in the unenviable (but policy choice) position of attempting to defend what is already an *overvalued* currency. This substantially exacerbates an already inappropriate policy stance and the Bank can react only by ratcheting interest rates up yet another few notches.

While I recognize that this is a political crisis and, therefore, would wreak some havoc with any policy mix, the fact remains that its impact on the exchange rate is similar to that of the existing policy stance. Specifically, it is driven by factors - symbol economy, portfolio management, political crisis - that have nothing to do with why Canada might consciously opt for exchange rate flexibility, namely that the exchange rate should react in ways to compensate movements in economic activity. Thus, the Meech Lake political crisis too (at least within limits) suggests that fixed rather than flexible rates are appropriate over the medium term.

V. CONCLUSIONS

Whereas the macro challenge of the 1970's was essentially one of runaway nominal magnitudes which in turn required a monetary (nominal) solution, the challenges of the current period are essentially threefold:

1) the enduring chestnut of inflation control;
2) the aggregate savings imbalance and in particular the domestic savings shortfall which has led to the development of our "twin deficits"; and
3) the likelihood that the appropriate exchange rate policy in the FTA environment is one that requires greater fixity than is generally recognized.

The thrust of the above analysis is not only that aggressive monetary (high interest) policy cannot solve all these challenges. Rather, it is that by single-mindedly pursuing restraint the Bank of Canada is not likely to be able to resolve *any* of them in a satisfactory let alone sustainable manner.

My first conclusion is not particularly useful, but the point must be made. Our major policy error was not to put on the fiscal brakes much earlier. This would have addressed the domestic savings shortfall directly, would have obviated much of the need to draw on foreign savings, and would have permitted the *same* overall aggregate demand restraint with a lesser reliance on monetary policy (high interest rates). As a result, our overall debt, both foreign and domestic, would be substantially less. Moreover, fiscal retrenchment made eminent economic sense in its own right (apart from the broader inflation implications), given the very substantial post-1983 boom.

Even as late as 1988, increased fiscal discipline would have made a substantial difference. Mulroney was right: free trade was a powerful stimulus. Had Finance moved quickly to cool the economy, the macro mix would have been far more balanced and more appropriate. Instead, the task fell to John Crow to make the first move. The resulting rise in interest rates led to a dramatic increase in debt servicing which in turn seriously constrained fiscal policy. In an abstract sense, there was some poetic justice here. For most of the mid-1980s, inappropriate fiscal policy seriously compromised monetary policy. More recently monetary policy has returned the favour with a vengeance.

As noted, from the vantage point of 1990, this is not particularly useful. However, the lesson needs to be retained for the next time around.

My second, and much more relevant, conclusion is that the Government ought to fix the Canadian dollar at, say, 80 cents and be prepared to defend it around a narrow band. The several rationales for this include the following:

- An 80 cent dollar means that Canadian producers can now take advantage of the FTA at more appropriate exchange rates, both in terms of level and certainty.
- Over the longer term, this means that Canada is buying into the U.S. inflation rate. This is the correct policy for the FTA, in my view, unless the U.S. begins to inflate. (There are some short-term concerns which will be dealt with below).
- Almost by definition, fixing the exchange rate brings fiscal policy fully into the stabilization picture because fixing the rate is a government, not a Bank, decision and the government must, therefore, defend the rate.
- It is no coincidence that the massive domestic savings imbalances (shortfalls for the U.S. and surpluses for Japan and Germany) occurred only *after* these countries opted for flexible rates. Phrased differently, fixed exchange rates exerted a powerful discipline on the exercise of fiscal policy, a discipline which essentially vanished under floating rates. As the Bank for International Settlements (1986) noted the combination of flexible exchange rates and a high degree of international capital mobility means that "governments can choose to delay implementing needed policy adjustments for longer periods than might otherwise be possible" (p. 249).
- Under the existing macro mix we are, almost by default, handing control over inflation to Governor Crow. Even apart from the above analysis, this is foolish. In a period of adjustment, coping with inflation pressures also involves ensuring that the country is not riddled with structures and regulations that inhibit moving toward lower inflation and economic recovery (e.g., provincial trade barriers, marketing boards, subsidies, excessive regulation, the timing of policy measures such as pay equity, cola clauses, bargaining processes in industries where employees are "tenured"). By the nature of its mandate, the Bank has difficulty speaking publicly about these inflation impediments (although Governor Bouey was certainly vocal). If Finance were forced to carry more of the inflation-fighting weight, as it would under a fixed-rate regime, zeroing in this range of impediments would become an obvious ancillary activity.
- Given that there is a need for more coordination of overall fiscal policy (federal and provincial) as part of overall exchange rate management

(particularly in response to terms-of-trade shifts), the likelihood of coordination is enhanced if Finance is responsible for the exchange rate.

- Finally, on the analytical level, fiscal policy is a more effective stabilization instrument under fixed rates than under flexible rates. Given that I have argued for an enhanced role for fiscal policy, a fixed exchange rate is the vehicle for making fiscal discipline more effective.

What does all of this imply for Bank of Canada policy and, in particular, interest rates? First of all, monetary policy will henceforth be calibrated in order to *defend* the 80 cent dollar, not to "pick" the appropriate exchange rate via interest-rate manipulation. Among other things, this avoids a Finance-Bank confrontation. Fixing the exchange rate effectively and appropriately neuters the Bank of Canada, but not monetary policy. There is a cost to this of course: Finance Minister Wilson formally accepts responsibility for the exchange rate and explicitly requires the Bank to conduct its policy with this exchange rate goal uppermost.

Will this mean lower interest rates? The answer is "yes" on three counts. First, the exchange-rate would now be at a "sustainable" level so that one would anticipate a significant decline in the "forward discount" on the dollar. This would mean rates could and would fall. Second, the exchange-rate impact on output and or enhancing exports over imports when combined with the impact on the fiscal deficit of reduced debt servicing would imply an increase in output relative domestic absorption. (As an important aside, the incentives in the fiscal plan should be geared to enhancing savings on the part of Canadians). In more familiar terms, aggregate domestic savings would rise which means that we would not need to attract as much foreign capital and, therefore, would not need to calibrate our interest rates with this in mind. This aspect is probably more important than might appear at first blush. For most of the post-1983 era Canada and the U.S. basically had the international capital markets to themselves. In the 1990s we will have to share this with Eastern Europe, among others, so that even attracting the existing level of foreign capital will be more expensive, real-interest-wise. The third reason is more speculative: I believe that this more balanced approach to fighting inflation, i.e. addressing all three of the earlier enunciated policy challenges, will be more successful and certainly more sustainable than the current policy mix. Thus interest rates will fall on this count too.

There are at least two sorts of challenges or risks associated with this approach. The first is where to peg the dollar. A value less than 80 cents would help on the export front but it would also a) embody more initial price increase and b) tend to be viewed as a "beggar my neighbour" policy vis-à-vis the operations of the FTA. Eighty cents has the advantage that it reflects, roughly, the existing forward discount and that it was in the range of exchange rates when the FTA was being negotiated.

The second challenge is somewhat more worrisome. How will we handle the once-and-for-all price hike associated with the depreciation from 85-87 cents to 80 cents? One answer is that since we probably have to take this hit anyway, let's take it now. The other (and related) is that Ottawa may want to impose some wage-restraints on its own sector and agencies and even to invite the provinces to follow suit. As argued earlier, I see no wage escalation in the tradeables sector - they are already reeling under FTA competition. At this point, a reference to the U.S. economics literature is valuable. Because there has been a spirited debate over the implications of the "twin deficits" and more generally the "consumption binge" made possible by drawing on foreign savings, there is also a recognition that restoring some semblance of sustainability will require some compensating consumption cost. This notion is essentially foreign to Canadians largely because we have been mired in an increasingly outmoded inflation-fighting paradigm and, hence, have ignored the trilogy of macro challenges brought on by increased integration, financial and real. This is particularly true of those privileged aspects of the labour force, largely public and quasi-public sector, that are protected by various tenure clauses. Not only have they been relatively untouched by the dramatic private-sector restructuring of the 1980s, but they feel entitled to COLA-plus contracts. If the provinces allow wage increases in this range, then Finance Minister Michael Wilson surely has ample evidence that federal-provincial transfers need still further paring. Appropriate fiscal policy, not high interest rates, is the way to get at this issue.

One final comment. Exchange-rate fixity need not be a permanent policy. If and when exchange rate flexibility is again likely to be driven by levels of economic activity rather than the "symbol economy", then a case could be made for untying the exchange rate link. This would require a restoration of our aggregate savings shortfall and a lengthening of the maturity of our domestic debt. Not until then, however.

This, then, is my preferred approach to calibrating macro policy. It is the right stance for addressing FTA integration. It is the right stance for correcting our aggregate-savings and twin- deficit problems. And it is the sustainable way to address inflation.

Endnotes

*   An earlier version was presented to the House of Commons Standing
     Committee on Finance (June 7, 1990). I would like to thank an
     anonymous referee for valuable comments.

1.   The Meech Lake and post Meech Lake constitutional crises have
     complicated the conduct of macro policy. However, the above
     statement holds even in the absence of the Meech Lake crisis.
     Some attention will be devoted to these political implications later
     in the paper.
2.   The Bank of Canada has finally begun to recognize this - see
     McNish (1990).

3.   Private sector net savings is defined as gross savings less gross
     investment. Since investment falls in a recession, particularly a
     recession as severe as that in the early 1980s, it is natural that as
     investment recovers, private sector net savings will fall. However,
     over the 1984-1990 period, gross savings fall as well: Canadians
     are saving less than they used to.

4.   In the longer paper (Courchene, 1990f), I offer an analytical
     rationale for provincial stabilization policy. Fiscal policy works
     best under fixed-exchange rate regimes, not flexible rate regimes.
     Basically, it is the provinces that operate under fixed rates (vis-à-
     vis each other).

Part III
1992: Canada in Play

8. CANADA 1992:

Political Denouement
or
Economic Renaissance?

I. INTRODUCTION

With the failure of Meech, Quebec threw down the gauntlet in the form of a two-pronged challenge to the rest of Canada (ROC). The first of these centred around Quebec's demands in terms of its "political space". The issues here are well-known - essentially greater powers, particularly in the area of "demolinguistics" (language, culture, immigration, as well as aspects of UI, training, R and D, etc.). The institutional arrangements that might deliver these new powers to Quebec are many and varied - special status, generalized decentralization, a confederal system, sovereignty with association (an economic and monetary union between ROC and Quebec). Apart from some inexplicable forays into pan-Canadian restructuring (such as the call for Senate abolition by the Allaire Report), the fact is that Quebec really does not care how ROC organizes or re-organizes itself to deliver these powers. Quebec's fallback position is quite simple - non-delivery will trigger independence. This is the "constitutional/political crisis" aspect of the Quebec challenge. And it is the aspect that ROC is responding to, or more correctly perhaps, not responding to.

However, co-existing with this emotionally loaded political- space component of the Quebec challenge is what I shall call the "economic-space imperative". Simply put, Canada no longer works economically. Significantly, the Allaire Report focussed much more attention on the economic than on the political challenge - duplication, entanglement, the inability to control deficits at the federal level, the interaction between the Bank and Finance with disastrous consequences for interest rates and the exchange rate, etc. While these two components are, as I shall later argue and as the Allaire Report argues, inextricably intertwined, they remain at the practical level as two solitudes, particularly in ROC where only the political/constitution aspect of our societal debate has taken hold. (Arguably, the Reform Party can be viewed as addressing the economic challenges). But even in Quebec, despite the cogency of the Allaire Report on the economic front, the debate has also focussed largely on these political/constitutional considerations, perhaps because Quebecers feel that it is only in this area that they have any leverage.

The nature of the linkage between these two prongs is rather straight-forward and has been best expressed by Liberal M.P. Paul Martin Jr. Paraphrasing Martin, Quebec's economic and entrepreneurial dynamism during the 1980s led Quebecers, rightly or wrongly, to harbour the perception that Quebec is a "winner". Quebecers would not contemplate independence if they were associated with a country that was also a winner on the economic front. But, again rightly or wrongly, the perception in Quebec is that, as already noted, federalism no longer works economically. The implication is clear: make Canada a winner economically and one can accomplish both goals - national unity and economic prosperity.

The thrust of this paper is that Quebec's political/ constitutional considerations cannot be fully understood let, alone dealt with, until all Canadians come to grips with the underlying economic imperative. Moreover, I believe that the nature of our ongoing societal debate will begin to shift away from these constitutional issues and focus increasingly on Canada's inability to keep abreast in this globalizing economic order. The good news here is that the debate will cease to be solely a Quebec-ROC confrontation. Progressively the dialogue will encompass *all* of Canada. The bad news is that this promises to be every bit as complex and emotionally charged as the current political/ constitutional debate, since it will inevitably involve a rethinking and a reworking, socio-economi-cally, of our nation for the millennium and beyond and will, among other things, pit the provinces against Ottawa and, at the provincial level, the "have nots" against the "haves".

Included among the catalysts that will trigger this shift in focus are a series of sober and sobering second thoughts relating to what the rending of the Canadian legal fabric really means in terms of economics and politics for both Quebec and ROC. However, some new factors are rapidly coming to the fore. One is the breakdown of fiscal federalism as reflected by the initiatives in the last two federal budgets. But by far the most dramatic development is Ontario's recent budget. Effectively, Ontario is also saying that, from its perspective, federalism no longer works economically. Yet from the perspective of Quebec and the other provinces, not to mention Ottawa, the more frequent question is whether Ontario's budget stance is compromising the country's ability to win on the economic front.

In somewhat more detail, and in lieu of a more formal introduction, the paper addresses the following set of rather controversial assertions:

- Quebec has overplayed its hand on the political/constitutional front. The costs of outright independence are very high and, potentially, devastating. Moreover, a full-blown economic and monetary union with the rest of Canada is likely a non-starter politically (for the rest of Canada) and economically (for Quebec because it would achieve only a Pyrrhic victory - its effective powers could be considerably less than under the status quo).

- Quebec will still demand some additional powers (e.g. language and culture) but will increasingly be willing to trade off aspects of its earlier set of demands for significant progress on the "making-Canada-a-winner" front.

- ROC is caught in a time warp. Its principal response thus far has been to dig in its heels and, even more fantastic, to embrace the "bon voyage" movement in the belief that a Canada without Quebec is not only costless for ROC but has the additional advantage that ROC could then be redesigned in its own likeness and image.

- While the sovereignty movement in Quebec has (in my view, at least) peaked, the "bon voyage" movement in ROC is still in its ascendancy. However, it will also peak soon when two realities are driven home. The first is that the costs of a Quebec exit are also very high for ROC *and also include* the possibility of the political rending of ROC. The second is that we Canadians have been incredibly adept in terms of working within our constitutional framework. Combined with the existing set of instruments as well as some new ones (e.g. section 43 and concurrency with provincial paramountcy) the reality is that there is ample flexibility for ROC to redesign itself in its own likeness and image, as it were, with Quebec *inside* the federation.

- To this point, the entire challenge is positioned within a Meech and Post-Meech context. However, there are a series of non-Meech factors (domestic and global) that will probably have at least as profound an impact on the Canada of tomorrow.

- One of these forces is the process of globalization which is effectively redesigning the role of nation states everywhere. Powers are being transferred both upwards and downwards from nation states.
- A second and related force, the FTA, essentially carries the same message. However, as an important additional factor it focusses attention on the dilemma inherent in maintaining an east-west social policy infrastructure in the face of increasing north-south integration.
- In turn, this highlights the fact that increasingly what binds us, east-west, is not an economic-policy railway but rather a social-policy and value-system railway. Yet this social policy infrastructure is now in shambles as a result of the last two federal budgets. The challenge facing Canadians (and indeed citizens of all western nations) is to rethink the welfare state in the context of globalization. In my view this will inevitably mean an increased emphasis on "people", at the expense of "place".
- However, there is an entirely new actor that is now coming to dominate the scene - Ontario. As I suggested in my Robarts Lecture (1989 - and Chapter 1, this volume), Ontario is embarking on its own Quiet Revolution. One aspect of this is that the forecast $35 billion Ontario deficit over the next four years will almost of necessity trigger a rethinking of the underpinnings of Canada's approach to macro stabilization.
- As important in terms of the on-going societal debate is that Ontario is becoming Canada's social policy leader, with the result that the comparative social policy envelopes for Ontario and most of the rest of the provinces will begin to diverge substantially.
- It is probably the case that the on-going thrust of the social-policy framework emanating from Queen's Park is unsustainable. Pressures will mount (perhaps à la Mitterrand) for a turnabout in order to protect its economic base. But this is the "low-wage, low-tax, low transfer" philosophy, which Ontario associates with "competitiveness". Ontario will attempt to seek alternative avenues.
- Thus, my assertion is that Queen's Park will shift away from its mostly social-policy role and begin to embark on an aggressive economic policy role within the federation. It may be inappropriate to label this "Ontario Inc.", but short of some dramatic federal turnabout, Queen's Park under the NDP will progressively model itself along the lines of Sweden or Germany with the result that Ontario, not Quebec, may become the catalyst for a more decentralized Canada on the economic front. In this it will have the support of the governments, but perhaps not the people of, BC and Alberta.
- This will reverberate rather dramatically on the six non- Quebec have-not provinces and, I think, on Ottawa as well. The cleavage will shift

from the current Quebec/ROC axis towards an *internal* ROC axis or a pan- Canadian axis since Quebec will side with the have provinces now that the transfer system is relatively neutral in terms of its impact on Quebec.

• Accommodating Quebec's demands when the economic and political imperatives are in play is a quite different game than the one now being played where only the political/constitutional issues are in play. In particular, aspects of Quebec's aspirations will resonate well with those in other parts of Canada. Moreover, the have-not provinces will come to realize that the deal with Quebec in Canada is preferable to what will result from a Canada without Quebec, especially since Ontario's pursuit of self-interest will be pressed to a much greater degree were Quebec to exit.

• Ottawa's role may remain strong, but it will be a quite different role. Offsetting some loss of power in terms of its traditional role will be a rebalancing involving Ottawa as a greater player in securing the economic union. Ottawa will continue its role as redistributor but this will also evolve. Except for equalization, the trend will be to shift distribution initiatives toward individual Canadians and away from provinces.

None of this guarantees the political integrity of the upper half of North America. Unforeseen events or initiatives, conscious or unconscious, may yet rend our nation. For example, recent federal thinking (taking over post-secondary education) and, as yet, musings (taking over the securities industry) do not auger well. Nonetheless, the underlying perspective arising from a twinning of the political/constitutional and economic components of our societal challenge is markedly different from that which dominates thinking in Canada today. Specifically, the "Quebec crisis" represents an opportunity for Canada to become a "winner" in the global context. If Canadians are not up to this challenge, then Canada will not likely survive intact. But neither will ROC!

The remainder of this paper attempts (no doubt unsuccessfully at times) to make the case that these are more than mere assertions. I should note at the outset that the "space" devoted to buttressing these various assertions does not necessarily relate to their importance to the overall thrust of the paper. Rather, it reflects more whether I am drawing on my earlier research or whether I am attempting to chart new territory. I shall begin with an analysis of why, unless pushed by ROC, Quebec will probably not exit.

II. Quebec Won't Go[1]

The appeal of sovereignty literally steamrollered in the minds and hearts of Quebecers when ROC in its "1990 Referendum" said no to

Quebec. This is hardly surprising in terms of the political dimension. The reason why the economic side did not come into play as a counterweight reflects in part the perceived reality of Quebec's entrepreneurial ascendency during the 1980's and, in part, the fact that the elites convinced Quebecers that an economic and monetary union with Ontario and, more generally, ROC was easily doable and clearly in ROC's interest. (As an important aside, one of the reasons why the international markets have largely ignored the "Canadian crisis" is that Quebec leaders *never* talk about a separate Quebec currency, even though this may be inevitable, as I shall argue later). In any event, the message was that Quebecers were free to vote their hearts and minds because ROC would respond only with its pocketbook uppermost.

This strategy has clearly backfired. Stunned by the Allaire and Bélanger-Campeau Reports (not to mention Bill 178), and angered, if not humiliated, by the realization that for more than twenty years now only Quebec issues (driven by Quebec Prime Ministers!) get to dominate the policy agenda, ROC Canadians are finally taking matters in their own hands. Influenced by the Charter and, relatedly, by the emerging view of the equality of the provinces, ROC Canadians appear intent on rethinking and remaking Canada in their own likeness and image and then challenging Quebec: Are you in or out? In my view, if this scenario materializes Quebec will have nowhere to go but out. Quebecers have not yet recognized this emerging reality, but in an important sense it represents by far the most challenging "crisis" to face Quebecers because it is a total rejection of the "compact theory" of confederation or, equivalently, of the "two-founding-nations" conception of Canada.

There is a tragic irony in all of this. Multicultural Ontario is turning against Quebec without full recognition of the fact that one of the principal reasons why multiculturalism flourishes (as distinct from the U.S. "melting pot") is *because* Canada was a "two-founding-nations" compact! The Reform-COR axis is even more inimical to aspects of Quebec's aspirations, although it may be the case that Reform would be comfortable with "territorial bilingualism", à la Switzerland - French in Quebec, English elsewhere. Buttressing this rising ROC sentiment (albeit in conflict internally) is an implicit, if not explicit, realization that trading-wise Quebec needs Canada more than Canada needs Quebec (Courchene, 1991a, Table 1). Unfortunately, however, this has been converted into a view that the costs of a Quebec exit for ROC are minimal.

Admittedly, this is a peculiar way to introduce a section entitled "Quebec Won't Go". In due course, I will address the wisdom of the ROC mentality. For present purposes, the overriding implication is that ROC will be in no mood to respond to Quebec only with its pocketbook. Indeed, the threat of a Quebec exit has intriguingly created within ROC the perception that we too are a "distinct society". That this is more fiction than fact will only be revealed if and when Quebec secedes. What is assured by all of this is that any break-up will be acrimonious, indeed punitive, including for example full ROC support for aboriginal (Cree) aspirations with respect to the territorial integrity of an independent Quebec.

Setting these highly-charged issues aside, a Quebec-ROC economic and monetary union is unlikely to be in the cards. To see this (following Courchene 1991d), one only has to recognize what a unilateral declaration of independence followed by a proposal for an economic and monetary union would entail. The first order of business would be to "reconstitute" a common external economic policy. This will be incredibly complex since embedded in our common tariff and commercial policies are literally decades of delicate regional and sectoral trade-offs. Why would B.C. agree to a "reconstituted" commercial policy that subsidizes Quebec textile workers and dairy farmers to the existing extent? Clearly, it would not. This is not merely a Quebec/ROC issue: why would B.C. cater to Ontario in terms of the Autopact, if this means Toyotas cost more to British Columbians. Alternatively, what would they demand in return from Ontario?

The second problem is debt sharing. Clearly, ROC will never accept an 18.5 per cent Quebec share as suggested by Bélanger- Campeau. This neglects entirely the workings of the tax-transfer system (e.g. equalization) and interprovincial redistribution systems (e.g. UI) which are perceived, correctly, to have worked massively in Quebec's favour over the years. ROC will settle, initially at least, for nothing less than population share. Nonetheless, Quebec has some leverage here since Canada's debt will be ROC's (not Quebec's) liability given that we desire "Canada" to continue to exist. Thus, debt-sharing will come down to a set of "side-payments" from Quebec to ROC. Any reneging here on the part of Quebec will in the first instance affect ROC's credit rating, *not* Quebec's. Even if the break-up is acrimonious, it is in the interests of both parties to tread delicately in this area. For more detail see Courchene (1991d) or Boothe and Harris (1991).

The third problem that Quebec will encounter if it declares its independence and then seeks a monetary and economic union with ROC will be to re-establish its trade links with the U.S. Quebec will face at least three challenges in terms of negotiating a FTA with the Americans. If Quebec is lucky, and is able to deal only with the U.S. Administration in terms of a Quebec-US FTA, then these problems may not arise immediately, but rather in the context of the operations of this new FTA. If Quebec is unlucky, and Congress gets involved from the outset, then Quebec is in for a very rough ride indeed.

Briefly the three areas where Quebec is vulnerable are 1) the role of "Quebec Inc."; 2) the role of Hydro Quebec, both as a significant subsidizer in terms of firms like Norsk Hydro (magnesium) and a discriminatory exporter in terms of the sale price of hydro to the U.S. northeast relative to the domestic price, and somewhat relatedly 3) the timing of any U.S.-Quebec FTA, since the ecological and environmental implications of the Canada- U.S.-Mexico talks will have critical implications for James Bay II.

Suppose, however, that all this is somehow sorted out (if only initially) and Quebec does sign a Quebec-U.S. FTA that is similar to the existing FTA. Has anything changed? The answer is emphatically "yes". Currently, Quebec gets an incredible "free ride" as a province, a free ride that it loses fully if it signs as a "country". For one thing, Chapter 17 (Financial Institutions) applies only at the federal level. As a province, Quebec is free to integrate financial-institution ownership and other aspects of financial policy into the general "Quebec Inc." rubric. Not so if it is a signator to the FTA. For another, the "government procurement" chapter applies only at the national, not provincial, level. Hence, if Quebec is a signator, open procurement policies will apply to the activities of L'Assemblée nationale (and, I assert, to Québec Hydro as well) while Queen's Park, for example, will continue to be exempt here (and in the financial institution area as well) by virtue of the fact that it is a provincial government, not a signator to the FTA). These represent major concessions on Quebec's part because they incorporate among other things the likelihood that Americans and Ontarians will be free to bid on all Quebec government contracts whereas both Quebecers and the Americans can be shut out from Ontario government operations.

Once these building blocks are put in place, the stage is set for mounting a full-fledged economic union between Quebec and ROC. Two features of such an economic union need to be highlighted. The first is that economic unions run through federal systems are far more "flexible" because the monitoring process is inherently political. On the other hand, economic unions of the Europe 1992 variety are highly inflexible because they are of necessity monitored via an overarching administrative/legal superstructure. The second is that if an economic, rather than a political, union is the name of the game, the result will, of necessity, be a very thorough-going economic union. ROC would presumably insist on this. Therefore, the resulting Quebec-ROC economic union would at the same time be both thorough (including, for example, the environment as is the case in Europe) and inflexible, the result of which would be that Quebec would be stripped of much of what led to its 1980s dynamism. Another way of looking at this is to recognize that the European single market will be a combination of the Treaty of Rome plus some 300 "integration directives". Clearly, a Pyrrhic victory and equally clearly, at least from my perspective, not worth the underlying societal risk associated with declaring independence in the first place.

Had I more space, I would now extend this analysis to include the implications of a monetary union, which would add further to the constraints on the fiscal side for both Quebec and ROC. However, the verdict would not differ - unless the "divorce" was on an incredibly friendly terms ROC would not submit to a confederal monitoring mechanism where Quebec had an equal say over ROC policy and, for its part, Quebec would not submit to an economic and monetary union where its powers on the economics side would be restrained, relative to the status quo (see Courchene, 1991d).

However, if an economic and monetary union is not in the cards, what is the likely relationship between an independent Quebec and ROC. The answer has to be, in part, FTAs with the U.S. and ROC. In a sense, this part is easy, although the outcome may not be in Quebec's favour. More difficult is the currency issue. Intriguingly, Quebec has recently put forward, via Bélanger- Campeau, the position that it will simply "use" the Canadian currency rather than seek a full-fledged monetary union on the one hand, or establish its own currency on the other. Thus, Quebec may end up with an "effective" monetary union without an economic union. This is clearly in Quebec's interest because it can lock into the Bank of Canada's "price stability" credibility. What is unclear is whether this is likely to be in ROC's interest. Because Quebec would represent such a large component of the overall Canadian dollar currency area, any major problems arising from Quebec's policies (particularly with respect to its international transactions) might carry over to ROC and compromise Bank of Canada policy, with no role for ROC or the Bank to influence Quebec's policies. On the other hand, any attempt on the part of ROC to frustrate Quebec's use of the Canadian dollar might simply push Quebec to lock onto the U.S. currency which, given the increasing north-south flow of economic activity, will in any event likely be the appropriate "currency area" for Quebec (and the rest of Canada!) in the not-too-distant future. The issue in this case is whether the resulting truncated Canadian dollar area will be viable - ROC may also have to lock onto the U.S. dollar.

My personal view is that Quebec will rather quickly come to the view that a separate Quebec currency is inevitable. However, as I have noted elsewhere (1991d), there are ways in which this can be done that will not only minimize price stability concerns but as well give Quebec a competitive advantage vis-à-vis both ROC and the U.S. Specifically, suppose that Quebec initiated an *internal* devaluation, e.g. all wages fall by 10% (or, alternatively, via the supposed societal cohesion of Quebec society, suppose that over a relatively short period of time Quebec consciously opts for a 10% lower wage increase than characterizes ROC). Then, suppose that Quebec strikes its new currency, say the dollard (after Dollard des Ormeaux) which will be pegged at 1 to 1 with the Canadian dollar. Finally, assume that for an indefinite period Quebec runs a "currency board" rather than a Bank of Quebec where, by definition, the dollard is backed up, dollard per dollar, by Canadian dollars (or gilt-edge Canadian dollar assets). After the dollard is well established, the currency board can become a full-fledged central bank.

Several implications derive from this. First, if Quebec is going to introduce a separate currency, this is the way to do it (or some equivalent variant) because a) it latches on to the Canadian currency in terms of price stability (although, admittedly the dollard could still be devalued), b) it minimizes transactions costs because the dollard exchanges 1 for 1 with the Canadian dollar and c) it effectively (internally) devalues the Quebec currency by 10% vis-à-vis the Canadian and the U.S. dollars and there is *nothing* that ROC can do (i.e. ROC cannot devalue against the dollard) because Quebec is really, via a currency board, just "using" the Canadian currency. Second, over the longer term, FTAs and a separate Quebec currency should allow the Québécois to play their trump card, namely a quasi Japanese/continental-European style economic structure within the North American environment. However, the third implication is the most important. Whatever the longer-term prospects, the transition period for Quebec without an economic and monetary union could well be devastating. For example, it is easy to imagine that an acrimonious break-up will result in shareholders of "national" companies (e.g., Via, Air Canada, C.P., Bell, some of the chartered banks) insisting on immediate headquarter transfers. There is only so much that the Caisse de dépôt can do and there has to be a threshold beyond which the economic fallout will sap the momentum of Quebec's entrepreneurial class. In a very real sense, they may not be able to get there from here.

Prior to concluding this section, there is one important caveat. If the Canada-U.S.-Mexico talks succeed and then the resulting NAFTA broadens to encompass (beginning with, say, Chile) parts of South and Central America, then the sovereignty dynamic changes. Assuming that the resulting Community of the Americas begins to resemble the EC both in its confederal nature and in the emergence of the U.S. dollar as the single currency, then a "latching on" to the Community by an independent Quebec becomes much more feasible.

This caveat aside, my overall conclusion is that Quebec will not go. But ROC could force Quebec out. To this I now turn.

III. ROC Won't Push Quebec Out

As noted earlier, the "bon voyage" movement is alive and well in ROC. However, this is so because in large measure there has as yet been no focus on, let alone analysis of, the implications for ROC of a Quebec exit. I will not provide this analysis but what I shall do is draw from an earlier paper (1991d) and outline what I believe to be a not-unrealistic scenario from an Ontario perspective. An Ontario focus is not as narrow as it might initially appear. To be sure, Alberta and B.C. also underwrite ROC financially, but these economies are far more subject to cyclical swings than is diversified Ontario. Phrased differently, Ontario, not the far west, is the driving and integrating force in ROC.

From this perspective, the "have-not" provinces must now be rethinking their future. The most important factor here is the near $10 billion Ontario deficit for 1991-92 and the cumulative $35 billion dollar deficit over the next four years. Much of the ROC "bon voyage" movement is predicated on the assumption that Ontario will continue to play the role of ROC "paymaster" in terms of maintaining the system of interregional transfers. Moreover, this view does not take adequate account of the fact that 1991 Ontario is hollowing out and "bleeding" at the borders (an issue that will be dealt with later). This is the backdrop for a potential Quebec exit.

Suppose Quebec does go. How does this impact Ontario? The first concern is that neither the FTA nor the Autopact will likely remain intact. At the very least, the FTA has to be "re-opened" to allow for the fact that it is now a trilateral rather than a bilateral agreement. Jack Valenti and Carla Hills have already signalled their desire and intention to press the cultural dossier. In terms of the Autopact, if Ontario can no longer "deliver" the Quebec market the safeguards will obviously be ratcheted downward. Second, some portion of Quebec-Ontario trade will be disrupted. The expectation might be that Quebec would come out of this distinctly second best since the net migration of people and headquarters would clearly be towards Ontario. (Indeed, it is not difficult to conjure up scenarios where Ontario is also inundated by migrants from Atlantic Canada, particularly since the cuts in federal transfers in the last two Ottawa budgets leave the future of social programs in these provinces in considerable doubt.) Nonetheless, this disruption of trade will be costly to Ontario. Third, if Quebec's economic situation deteriorates this will, of necessity, reflect on Ontario, and ROC generally, in terms of credit ratings in international markets. This is especially the case since Canada's debt will remain the official liability of ROC. With $35 billion of debt to float over the next four years, Ontario is obviously very vulnerable here. Now fold into this picture of a deteriorating Ontario economy the demands that will emanate from the rest of the ROC provinces. Accordingly, fourth, the six (non- Quebec) have-not provinces will clearly expect that Ontario (and B.C. and Alberta) will continue to underwrite interregional transfers, including equalization. Fifth, all other provinces and particularly Alberta and B.C. will presumably want some checks and balances to offset Ontario's 50 per cent of new Canada's population - either some version of a triple E Senate or the divying up of Ontario into at least two and preferably three provinces.

At what point do Ontarians move aggressively to pursue their self interest? The data from Horry and Walker (1991, Tables 3.7 and 3.8) indicate that "net" transfers out of Ontario are not far from $1,000 per Ontarian, or roughly equal to Ontario's $9.7 billion forecast deficit for fiscal 1991-92. An additional $2 billion flows out through the operations of UI. If, as I believe, a Quebec exit will be a negative-sum game for both parties (at least for a substantial transition period) these interregional transfers will be even more draining on Ontario. Moreover, the notion that Ontario would accede to a triple-E Senate is surely far-fetched. (The same reasoning should, from my vantage point, also apply to the other "have" provinces. Why would the three have provinces, with roughly 75% of the population of ROC, transfer 2/3 of the votes in an upper chamber to the have-not provinces?) I have no qualms asserting that Ontario would not accede to this. Beyond this, the internal politics of ROC will be very divisive - private-sector Ontario will clearly want to re-establish close economic links with private-sector Quebec, which will not go down well in the far west. Nor will Ontario's attempt to negotiate higher domestic-content requirements as a way of preserving the value of the Autopact to Ontario.

Some of these issues will be elaborated later. For present purposes, the message is clear, however. If ROC maintains its political integrity in the face of a Quebec exit, it will be a very different ROC. Specifically, Ontario will be faced with the choice, given its fiscal position and the transitional problems on the economic front arising from the rending of the nation, of maintaining its role as interregional paymaster or maintaining its tax base (from southward hemorrhaging). My hunch is that, with the support of B.C. and Alberta, it will choose the latter. Phrased somewhat differently, it is far from axiomatic that the nine- province ROC which will arise from the rending of Canada will bear much resemblance to the Canada of 1991. More to the point, the underlying message of this paper is that this self-interest/societal-interest trade-off is coming to the fore whether or not Quebec exits.

By way of a conclusion to this section, ROC will begin to have second thoughts with respect of the "bon voyage" movement when some of these implications become more apparent. Intriguingly, however, given the momentum of the movement, the recognition that Quebec might not go may well trigger among Reformers and others a desire to "disentangle" somehow in order that Quebec issues are not always centre-stage. But this is exactly what Quebec wants!

With this as backdrop, I now turn to a set of forces that will, in my view, have every bit as much influence on the Canada of the millennium as will the Meech and post-Meech influences. This analysis begins with a brief discussion of the implications of globalization.

IV. Globalization and the FTA[2]

As already alluded to, globalization and the telecomputations revolution is transforming important aspects of the traditional role of governance in nation states. In a sense, national governments are finding themselves at the same time both too large and too small for some of the emerging challenges. In terms of the latter the shift from multinationals (which are subject to host country constraints) to transnationals (which are not, as reflected in the "national treatment" provision of the FTA, for example) has effectively internationalized production and constrained the powers of nation states. One already noted consequence is that national welfare states which were meshed with "national" production economies are being rethought everywhere, in light of production going international. More generally, national governments will increasingly find that activities that used to be undertaken at the nation-state level will now have to be passed "upwards", partly as countervail to the globalizing transnationals. Relatedly, as mobility increases, "standards" will progressively come to be set at a supranational level. The BIS capital-adequacy rules for financial institutions (adhered to now by at least a dozen countries) are a case in point. This trend towards international regulation, international standards and confederal or EC-type arrangements is bound to intensify.

At least two other forces are transferring power *downwards* from nation states. The first relates to the fact that the telecomputational revolution is empowering citizens both in terms of access to information and the ability to process it. While this is inherently decentralizing, it complicates old-style governance at all levels, not just the national level. A second, perhaps more intriguing point, is that globalization is spanning the world through a network of "international" cities. These international cities (Montreal, Toronto and Vancouver for Canada) are the critical national nodes in the global communications and trading networks, i.e. the essential cultural and economic "connectors" outward from Toronto to Frankfurt and New York and inward to Kingston and Kitchener.

The dilemma here for Canadian federalism is obvious: these cities are "constitutionless" (although recently Metro Toronto has suggested that, in any reconstituted Canada, Toronto, Montreal and Vancouver ought to acquire provincial status). They are creatures of their respective provincial governments. But they will soon become much more influential. This poses rather unique problems because, for example, Saskatchewan's global city is not in the province and the Maritimes' international city is (arguably) not even in the country. This again poses a constraint on the role and influence of national, even provincial, governments.

I shall limit myself to only two implications from all of this. In the face of a diminished role in the economic, regulatory and even cultural sphere for national governments, citizens will increasingly view "sovereignty" as the ability to have some influence on how they live and work and play. One can argue whether or not the level of government to deliver this is the international city or the provincial government or the local government, but under our federal system it is clearly not the national government. Indeed, will there be much left of "sovereignty" in the millennium other than distinct societies?

The second implication is that the traditional link between economic policy and social policy is being severed. Nations will find it progressively more difficult to use the allocative mechanism for distributional purposes (e.g. tariffs, marketing boards, cross-subsidization for telephones). At one level, this implies that the old centralization-decentralization debate is now far less relevant. If economic policy is increasingly influenced by factors beyond the nation state, it becomes much less important, internally, which level of government controls these levers. At another level, distributional concerns will become more complex and contentious because they have to be delivered, increasingly, via the tax-transfer system. (Note that this is part and parcel of the earlier point that the internationalization of production has created problems for welfare states.) The essential integrating link here is that in a progressively knowledge-intensive world an emphasis on developing human capital is emerging as appropriate economic policy *and* social policy. More on this later.

In a sense the FTA is best viewed as a specific example of increased integration or globalization. One aspect of the FTA merits highlight because it plays directly into the later analysis relating to the future of Canada's social policy infrastructure. Specifically, the political economy of Canada's east-west transfer system will come under increasing scrutiny in the context of north- south integration (which the FTA will enhance, but was in any event inevitable). In particular, Ontario's much-heralded "magnanimity" in terms of existing regional transfers has, in my view, always contained a healthy dose of "Ontario first". As long as Canadian trade flowed largely east-west, with Ontario the principal north- south conduit, the second (and future) round spending impacts of these regional transfers generally came to rest somewhere in Ontario. Under full north-south integration for all of Canada's regions, this may no longer be the case. Some of the erstwhile regional payments imbalances with the centre will, now, shift south with the result that the second-round impacts of regional transfers may no longer come to rest in Ontario but rather in North Carolina or California. At a political level, this will surely erode support for such transfers, particularly the ones that privilege "place" rather than people. I should note in this context that I view equalization as falling under the rubric of a "people" transfer. However, it too will be subject to considerable rethinking.

This may or may not be viewed as decentralizing, but what is clear is that our tradition of sheltering various regions of the country from market forces is going to become progressively more difficult both economically, politically and perhaps "legally" under the FTA.

That these forces will impact on Canada is obvious. However, there are also some *internal* policy-driven forces that are reshaping our federation, with or without Meech or post-Meech. To these I now turn.

V. Deficit Shifting and Social Policy Infrastructure

During the FTA election, Canadians made it very clear that much of what they valued came under the general rubric of social policy infrastructure - regional sharing, medicare, other national programs and the fact that citizens wherever they may live ought to have relatively equal access to these key social-policy ingredients of being Canadian. As a result of the last two federal budgets, this infrastructure is now in shambles:

• The equalization ceiling[3] has now become binding, with the result that for fiscal year 1989-90, actual payments were over a billion dollars beneath entitlements.
• The growth in federal cash transfers under the 50-50 shared-cost Canada Assistance Plan (welfare) has been capped at 5% for the three have provinces (Ontario, Alberta and British Columbia).
  The EPF ceiling which used to be escalated at the rate of nominal GNP growth was scaled down to GNP-2% in 1986 and further to GNP-3% in 1989. The combined effect of the last two budgets has been to freeze the ceiling over the 1990-95 period, albeit with an allowance to take account of population growth (about 1% per year). The net result is that the cash component of EPF transfers will fall to zero for Quebec perhaps as early as the mid 1990s and for the other provinces early in the next decade.[4]

There are many interpretations that can be placed on these developments. One (which some might view as the Ottawa position, although I do not want to speak for Ottawa) is that federal- provincial transfers should not be exempt in any belt tightening, particularly since even with these cuts overall federal-provincial transfers are still expected to grow by 3.7% per year from 1991-92 to 1995-96 in comparison to a 3.4% growth per annum for all other federal spending. (1991 Federal Budget, p. 18.) In terms of the individual programs, different sorts of rationales for restraint can be made. Consider equalization. One of the principal reasons why the ceiling became binding was that during the 1983-89 period not only was Ontario's tax base growing rapidly but so were its tax rates, both of which fed into a mushrooming of equalization to the have-not provinces and triggered the application of the ceiling. In terms of the Canada Assistance Plan, part of the rationale for the 5% limit on CAP transfers to the three have provinces has to do with the fact that the most rapid growth was occurring in these provinces, and particularly in booming Ontario. For their part, the poorer provinces could not come up with their own share to trigger an equivalent share from Ottawa. Therefore, the 5% limit effectively begins a process of "equalizing" CAP. While this may well be "politically correct", it certainly is at odds with the initial rationale of the program and, more importantly, bites dramatically on a province like Ontario where welfare payments have increased by roughly $1.5 billion over the recent period (with more to come) and where the province is now entitled to only 5% growth of its existing CAP transfers rather than to 50% of this dramatic increase. Indeed, had Ontario known that Ottawa would unilaterally alter CAP, would it have mounted its new welfare legislation in the present form?

The point here is that these are all *federal* programs and can be (and are!) altered at will and without notice[5] by Ottawa.

These changes in federal-provincial transfers can also be viewed from an entirely different perspective. The most general comment here would be along the following lines: something very dramatic must have gone wrong with overall macro policy in the 1980s when, via the GST and high interest rates and exchange rates, Ottawa first precipitates and exacerbates a "made in Canada" recession and then responds by pulling the plug on the federal- provincial transfer system which is, in effect, the provinces' social policy "safety net".

The implications of this will be many and far reaching. Let me begin with a personal observation. Many Canadians, or at least many non-Quebec Canadians, believe that Canada is already very decentralized, probably too decentralized. There are plenty of comparative "ratios" across federations and trends within Canada that can "support" such a claim. My view is, however, that a country can hardly be called decentralized in an effective sense when in one fell swoop Ottawa can undermine the fiscal positions of *all* the provinces. And the worst of the provincial fiscal crunch is yet to come.

A second, and related, observation is that we will finally begin to see some effective decentralization. Provinces have the choice of raising taxes to place their existing social programs on a sustainable basis or of altering these "national" programs, or most likely some of both. All options represent decentralizing moves. Intriguingly, in recognition of this, Ottawa has responded in its 1991 budget with two rather internally inconsistent initiatives or proposals. The first is that, with respect to the established or national programs, Ottawa will attempt to implement its own version of the "golden rule": it will stop supplying the gold, but it has no intention to stop making the rules. Good luck! The second is that it will entertain the notion that the ROC provinces be given rate-and-bracket-structure freedom in terms of the operations of the provincial component of the shared personal- income-tax system. This is clearly a defensive move because even before the 1991 budget some provinces were seriously contemplating following Quebec's lead and establishing their own, separate, personal income tax systems. Nonetheless, the result is again decentralizing in that it will not only allow greater fiscal flexibility to the provinces but it will also give them a greater say in the distribution of income via the tax system.

The third implication is that this series of federal cutbacks has driven a wedge, as it were, between the views of individual Canadians and provincial governments. Citizens are not aware of the niceties of the federal-provincial financial interface so that when they see provincial program cuts or provincial attempts to mount user fees they tend to appeal to Ottawa without any recognition that these initiatives were presumably triggered by federal budget trimming. On the other hand, all provincial governments and especially provincial treasurers are fully aware of the constraints that the federal government has put them under, so much so that several provinces are asking for greater control including equalized tax point transfers.

The final and related implication is that this erosion of the principles underlying fiscal federalism is influencing the on-going constitutional debate. Specifically, I think that the poorer provinces will be reluctant to sign on to any reconstituted Canada without some new agreement on the fiscal federalism front. In particular, any move towards increased decentralization will not find favour with the have-not provinces unless some new federal- provincial sharing rules are put in place. On the one hand, this is only to be expected. Yet on the other, if the result is to "re- create" the present interprovincial and interregional transfer system, the net result will be to ignore the "economic-space imperative" referred to in the introduction. Now that I have clearly broached a subjective, as distinct from a more descriptive, approach, I want to focus on my own views on Canada's social policy infrastructure.

A. Subjective View of Our Social Policy Railway

Ottawa is correct in maintaining that provincial transfers must share in the deficit-trimming exercise (although this sets aside *why* Ottawa did not move toward fiscal prudence much earlier!). However, the approach was clearly wrong. Cuts as massive as the deficit shifting incorporated in the last two federal budgets must have a longer lead time so that provincial treasurers can accommodate these changes.

There is another reason why some slowing down in transfer growth is essential. Canada has become a veritable transfer state. We equalize all provinces' revenues up to the Five-Province Standard (or close to it, depending on the operations of the ceiling). But we do not stop here. We have equalized or regionalize the operations of unemployment insurance (via variable entry requirements, regional benefits and a special program for fishermen). The resulting regional transfers are enormous - the ratio of UIC benefits to contributions for Atlantic Canada range from 1.67 in Nova Scotia to 4.16 in Newfoundland (Courchene 1991b). Anyone who doubts that this has had absolutely disastrous implications for the long-term viability of citizens and regions alike must consult the Report of the Newfoundland Royal Commission on Employment and Unemployment (1986). My personal experience is that even Ministers of the Crown of Atlantic Provinces talk openly of the hopelessness of breaking away from the 10-week job syndrome, since community pressure to "rotate" work has become effectively institutionalized. Intriguingly, some of these officials are now ready to contemplate some "decentralization" of UI on two counts. First, it is inconceivable that the respective provinces would end up creating a system as distortive and anti-development as that which Ottawa has designed for them. Second, and relatedly, if the poorer regions are ever to move away from dependence, a program as significant as UI must be integrated with, not against, other provincial development initiatives.

But the problem goes well beyond this. As noted, the Canada Assistance Plan has now been "equalized", since the growth of these federal transfers to Alberta, B.C. and Ontario in the depth of this recession can only grow by 5% annually. No limits are placed on the growth of CAP payments in have-not provinces. However, even this is viewed as inadequate: the "horizontal equity" advocates among us argue that the appropriate approach is to extend equalization to include "needs". Phrased differently, equalization that focusses only on the revenue side is inadequate: it must encompass the expenditure side as well. Transferred to the Canada Assistance Plan, this means, for example, that the per cent of federal sharing should be a function of the incidence of welfare. And so on across other spending categories.

This flies in the face of the economic challenge facing Canada. It may have made sense in the prosperous 1950s and 60s when Canada was living off the cushion of resource rents. It makes no sense (even on equity grounds) now that Canada must fight to maintain or rather regain its competitive position in the emerging global economic order. Essentially, this is a policy framework that puts "place" before "people". Regional wages, on a weekly level, are not very far off national levels, but the "stand alone" exchange rate for a separate Atlantic Region would surely not be more than 70¢ with respect to the existing Canadian dollar. This is part and parcel of the Allaire Report's argument to the effect that Canada is "not working" economically. What the Allaire Report should have also said was that Quebec's influence in the corridors of power was a major reason why Canada became so accommodating to its have-not regions.

This harks back to the opening paragraphs of this paper and Quebec's altered perception of itself in the federation. Thanks to its economic revival in the 1980s this province is now treated in a more-or-less "neutral" manner in terms of the overall federal tax-transfer system. This will have major implications for the political geography of our nation since Quebec will, in my view at least, increasingly tend to side with the "have" provinces, not the "have not" provinces in terms of interregional distribution.

Reverting to the discussion of regional transfers, it is instructive to focus on the thrust of the recent Throne Speech and its emphasis on competitiveness. One of the principal features of the Throne Speech is to enhance the internal common market. By this, Ottawa has in mind the striking down of high-profile impediments like the provincial beer fiefdoms, provincial purchasing preferences and the like. However, *by far* the most destructive impediments to competitiveness and to the processes of interregional adjustment are the *implicit* bariers, namely those barriers that distort the optimal distribution of people by distorting not only the incentives to migrate but as well the incentives to acquire human-capital skills (House Report, 1986). This aspect of the internal common market issue is *entirely absent* from the Throne Speech because Ottawa has fully bought into the notion of itself as a redistributive institution. In my view, any and all attempts to increase our overall productivity as a nation by wiping out beer monopolies will be a Pyrrhic victory since our underlying policies are and have been catering so much to "place" prosperity that we have engendered the conception that the have-not provinces have a "quasi-legal" right to maintain their populations at "Canadian average" standards of living.

Nonetheless, the impact of the recent federal budget cuts in the transfer area have been marvellously salutory. The Maritime provinces have finally been forced to think in terms of rationalization across their three provinces. The only notable initiative in this area thus far has been the decision by New Brunswick to hire a Nova Scotia company to produce

New Brunswick licence plates. But this is at least a beginning. The potential for reaping economies of scale is surely very significant in terms of, for example, rationalizing the university sector, medicare, the hydro grid, government purchasing, tax harmonization, greater control of UI (including some temporary continuing interregional subsidies). These directions are essential and, assuming we back away from the existing distortions in the transfer system, rather inevitable. Interprovincial cooperation and integration will also characterize Canada West.

The point of all of this is that the current definition of Canada as a transfer economy needs to be put to bed. This is *not* to say that the transfer system must become mean and lean (à la USA). Quite the opposite is true. But the future of the transfer system must be one where Ottawa a) treats individual Canadians as equals, wherever they reside and b) backs away from policies that go well beyond this and have tended to bestow privilege on "place" at the expense of "people". As a result, both place and people have all too frequently become marginalized, and increasingly dependent on a system that perhaps could be rationalized in the context of a resource-rent, tariff-protected economy but cannot be rationalized in the modern Canadian economy which is increasing open internationally and cannot afford to spend monies in, or on, areas that effectively serve to *decrease* incentives for human capital formation.

In terms of federal net spending benefits (outflows minus inflows) for 1988, the Atlantic provinces "gain" to the tune of roughly $3,500 per capita for New Brunswick to over $4,500 per capita in PEI (Horry and Walker, 1991, Table 3.7 and 3.8). Manitoba and Saskatchewan are not that far behind either. Alberta leads the way in terms of the three "have" or "contributing" provinces. However, in terms of overall dollar flows the roughly $1,000 per capita for Ontario corresponds to an outflow not far off $10 billion. I am not suggesting that such calculations have much to commend them in terms of assessing who benefits from the Canadian federation. However, they do provide a convenient backdrop to the following section, namely the range of implications that arise from the recent Ontario budget.

VI. ONTARIO'S QUIET REVOLUTION

A. Ontario and Social Policy

Ontarians always viewed themselves as the core of a distinct society - Canada. In a sense, it has always been easy for Ontarians to be "Canadians first" because their size and dominance in the federation typically meant that federal legislators had to put Ontario's concerns uppermost. Relatedly, there was little reason for a strong Queen's Park because Ontarians and particularly Ontario business "had" Parliament

Hill. However, as I have elsewhere noted (1989, and Chapter 1, this volume) this cosy relationship began to fragment over the last decade, indeed perhaps since the first oil shock which alerted Ontarians to the fact that their comfortable and privileged position within Canada could be challenged. Apart from a few "victories" (e.g. lowering the NEP on the West) much of the recent period has led to a perception among Ontarians that the province has lost its rightful place in the corridors of power. Added to this perception is the reality that the Mulroney Tories have forged a Quebec-West axis and, from all appearances, are about to try it again.

The result has been the emergence not only of a radically different Ontario but an Ontario that from all appearances is in the process of profoundly altering major aspects of the institutional fabric of the nation. It would be wrong to argue that this Ontario challenge has the same immediacy or crisis attached to it as the Quebec challenge, but what is clear, I think, is that the two will begin to interact in ways that will have important and perhaps dramatic implications as we count down to any 1992 Referendum.

One of the areas where this is most evident is social policy. In *What Does Ontario Want?* (1989, and Chapter 1, this volume), I suggested that Ontario was on the verge of becoming Canada's social policy leader (and in a sense embarking on its own Quiet Revolution). With the recent Ontario budget, there is no longer any doubt. Moreover, what appears to be in the offing is a major divergence in provincial social policies. Most provincial treasurers reacted to the recession and to Ottawa's budgets with cuts and freezes of their own. Not Ontario. Whether Ontario is really gambling its economic viability in pursuit of social goals will be addressed later. For the present, attention focuses on what it means to have Ontario as Canada's social policy leader. As long as Quebec was in the forefront or, earlier, Saskatchewan, there was little pressure on Ottawa from the other provinces. New Brunswick, for example, might find a Quebec or Saskatchewan initiative intriguing, but if finances did not permit mounting a similar program, that was the end of it. With Ontario in the lead, however, the nature of the game changes. The issue will become one or all of regional disparities, introducing a "needs" component to equalization and equality of opportunity - essentially section 36 of the Constitution - and the focus will be on Ottawa to ensure that all citizens have the same rights and opportunities as Ontarians.

But this is occurring at the same time that the existing federal-provincial fiscal interface is effectively in shambles and, of course, in the same time frame as the Quebec challenge. How can or will this be resolved and with what trade-offs? At one extreme is a full levelling-up of provincial finances or, alternatively, a complete unwinding of the federal restraint initiatives on the provincial transfer front. At the other extreme is a complete reworking of fiscal federalism where Ottawa abandons attempts to privilege "place" eliminating all interregional (e.g. UI) or federal-provincial (Canada Assistance Plan) "concessions". Within this approach all sorts of options are possible - allowing EPF transfers to fall to zero, replacing CAP transfers and child benefits with a single generous transfer to children ($3400 is what is being touted), eliminating all federal-provincial transfers except for an overarching equalization program accompanied by a further transfer of tax points. There is an additional appeal to this approach from Ottawa's vantage point. It is difficult for the federal government to achieve "visibility" with, and to exercise account-ability over, these federal-provincial transfers. Direct transfers to persons are far more effective on this score - hence the discussion of the shift from CAP to direct payments to children. Moreover, this type of transfer also plays well in terms of linking individual Canadians economically and symbolically to their national government.

Neither of these extremes is likely to be wholly adopted let alone implemented in the time frame dictated by the Quebec challenge. How-ever, as noted earlier it would appear the case that some version of the latter scenario is the only one consistent with coming to grips with the economic-imperative aspect of our on-going societal crisis. Nonetheless, it is equally clear that the have-not provinces will press for the former, and in particular they may use this as a bargaining chip in the context of renegotiating federalism. Before one devotes too much time attempting to sort this out, it should be noted that the stabilization/economic policy implications of the Ontario budget are probably more important that those relating to social policy.

B. The Ontario Budget and Stabilization Policy

In one fell swoop, Ontario has unwound the fiscal/monetary rebalancing that was accomplished with the 1991 federal budget and the Bank/Finance accord on inflation targets. This represents the second time in recent years that Ontario has compromised overall macro stabilization. The first occurred over the Ontario 1983-89 boom when the province decided to "spend" rather than "save" its fiscal dividend and in the process served to overheat its already booming economy. The result was that the Bank had to ratchet up interest rates (and exchange rates) and in the process engaged the rest of the country in fighting what was Ontario's inflation. This time around, Ontario has compromised the credibility of the new inflation targets.

None of this should be surprising to those who are following devel-opments in the European Community and particularly the EC's prepara-tions for a single European bank and single currency. The Europeans recognize fully that if the EuroFed is to be successful in achieving price stability, this will mean that there have to be limits to the deficits that member states are allowed to run. Even the Allaire Report recognized as much when it discussed a potential ROC-Quebec monetary union.

More to the point, Ontario's deficit has made it imperative that Canada put some semblance of order into its conduct of overall stabilization policy. My preference now that we have the FTA in place has been to opt for fixed exchange rates with the U.S. along with federal-provincial coordination (or guidelines) on the fiscal front (1990g and Chapter 6, this volume). This is, in effect, the European solution and recently even Sweden has also decided to tie its currency to the EMS. Others, like Laidler (1991), take the lead from the Allaire Report and argue for a restructuring of the Bank of Canada - an independent board of directors which would increase the independence of the Bank but would also serve to "govern the Governor".

The point is that we have witnessed a better part of a decade where the Bank and Finance were engaged in a costly duel. Now that this has finally been sorted out at the federal level it appears that the Bank will have to take on the provinces, or at least Ontario. An integral element in regaining our competitive edge must be a set of guidelines for the conduct of stabilization policy on the part of all players and there is some urgency that these be put in place soon.

Surely Ontario recognizes this as well. So why has it launched itself into a near $4,000 per person increase in debt over the next four years? I shall attempt to shed some light on this question in the context of assessing the impact of the Ontario budget on the province's economic viability.

C. The Ontario Budget and Economic Viability

Over the last two years the Ontario economy has been a disaster area. High interest rates and an overvalued dollar were taking their toll in terms of manufacturing plants, let alone jobs. None of this was helped by the fact that Ontario taxes have risen sharply in recent years. Cross-border shopping has reached dramatic proportions, perhaps triggered by an anti-GST mentality. Then came the 1991 federal budget which (along with the 1990 counterpart) represented a not-very-disguised attempt at unloading much of the federal deficit onto the provinces. Presumably, Ottawa anticipated that the provinces would pass much of this restraint on to the provincial economics, in the name of competitiveness. But in this overall context, Ontario interpreted "competitiveness" to mean little other than buying into the American Creed (or apparently so, since I am not privvy to official Ontario thinking). Phrased somewhat differently, Ontario refuses to go the "low- wage/low-tax/low redistribution" route. Presumably, its sights are set on replicating the social democratic economies of

Europe which are "high wage/high tax/high transfer" and which tend to embody a close working relationship among business, labour and government. Perhaps aspects of Quebec Inc. were influential as well. No doubt, however, some of the deficit was meant to counter what Ontario perceived as a wholly inappropriate macro stance at the federal level.

Presumably, it was a combination of things including the tariff and the cushion of growth from abundant natural resources that allowed us to become a high-wage country in the first place. But to do this in the context of the FTA must mean that we dramatically enhance productivity. On this score, a comparison table in the Ontario Budget (1991, p. 97) reveals that Ontario a) had a much lower productivity growth than G7 nations over the last decade, b) had a 0.1% average annual *decline* in real wages over the decade (the U.S. fared worse here) and c) experienced a 5.2% average annual increase in unit labour costs (well above any other G7 nation). Thus, the challenge is daunting.

Equally daunting will be any attempt to replicate a European- style social democracy in Ontario. However, if Ontario wants to flex its muscle on this front then the first task for an Ontario government (particularly an NDP Government) is to get corporate Ontario on side. This is a tall order, made even more difficult by virtue of the fact that, unlike Quebec, big business in Ontario tends, apart from the banks, to be foreign owned. Yet the budget went essentially in the opposite direction - not only did it cater to labour and more generally the NDP constituency but it did so in a way that increased the costs of doing business in Ontario and this is apart from the fact that there are major tax increases coming along shortly.

The question thus becomes one of whether Ontario is putting its tax base at risk? As Table 1 indicates Toronto is already a very high-cost city. The Ontario Treasurer's promise of a $500 million tax hike in the near future will make the comparison even worse. At what point will the on-going southward shift of economic activity become a wholesale migration?

It is in this sense that Ontario may well have embarked on an economic strategy that is unsustainable. One possibility here is that market forces, domestic and international, will trigger, à la Mitterrand, a sharp about face in Ontario's strategy. While some backtracking is, I think, inevitable Ontario will probably begin to pursue alternative avenues. For example, the province will likely come to the realization (as did the Allaire Report) that Canada is no longer working economically and what is required is nothing less than a societal commitment in the direction of knowledge intensity, skills development, high-value added production and the like. However, this implies a full integration of social and economic policy which in turn implies either that Ontario fights for some version of a national strategy or, failing that, it begins to demand more powers on the economic front. In either case, Ontario will begin to assert itself more aggressively in the federation. Going on nothing more than sheer speculation, my hunch is that it will indeed opt for more powers. In particular, if the province moves to integrate social and economic policy it will presumably want to accomplish this integration via the personal-income-tax system. Perhaps the rate-and-bracket-structure freedom proposed in the 1991 federal budget is sufficient in this regard (rather than a separate income tax à la Quebec) but it will not take long for Ontario to request the extra 16.5 tax points (16.5 percent of the federal income tax) that Quebec now has. Moreover, while Ontario will presumably always support a significant redistributive role for Ottawa I also think that a strong emphasis on human capital formation by Ontario would carry with it the implication that people, not place, are uppermost.

I readily grant that one can construct other scenarios where Ontario would push for greater centralization. This is certainly the case in the area of ensuring the free mobility of goods, services, labour and capital across provincial boundaries. But I have convinced myself, at least, that apart from obvious areas like the economic union Ontario will begin to speak with a louder voice.

D. Resumé

The 1991 Ontario budget is truly a watershed document. Over a four year period, it will effectively double Ontario's net debt - from 35 to 70 billion. No part of Canada is unaffected by its implications. It challenges the federal macro authorities approach to inflation targetting. It creates a wedge in the nature of the social envelope across provinces and at the same time creates the perception if not the reality for the have-not provinces that Ontario may no longer be able to play its same role as paymaster for the transfer system. It severely complicates the "bon voyage" movement because a weakened Ontario economically may well be a "strong" Ontario politically in terms of pushing Ontario first concerns in the context of any break-up. The implications for Quebec are, to me at least, confusing. On the one hand, the Ontario Budget hardly contributes to making Canada a "winner" economically and it certainly will, after the four years, make Quebec-Ontario debt comparisons much more favourable to Quebec (although not that far off in per-capita terms). On the other, Quebec's efforts in the direction of getting its public finances in better order may well begin to pay off in terms of attracting business, now that Ontario will doubtless establish itself as the high-tax jurisdiction.

What is of most concern, however, is what it does to Ontario. There is, of course, some value to the Keynesian pump-priming thrust of the budget. However, when the basic cost-price structure is out of line (albeit due to macro policy), much of the second- round impact of pump-priming will simply spill across Ontario's borders. Of more concern is what will happen to Ontario's economy and tax base. If this begins to migrate south, the projected deficits will correspondingly ratchet up. As noted, I think that the die has now been cast for Ontario to become a more active player on the economic front. Moreover, the province will be forced to jettison its "social policy only" agenda and to move toward an integration of social and economic policy. It is instructive to remember that the so-called entrepreneurial dynamism of the 1980's in Quebec was essentially a product of the policies of the post-Referendum P.Q. Once launched along this road, it is difficult to turn back - if anything, the Bourassa Liberals built upon, not recoiled from, the policies of the Parti Québécois. Phrased differently, this prediction of direction does not turn on political philosophy, although admittedly the NDP are more likely to trigger the initial launch.

The underlying message is, however, that the implications of Ontario budget have become key factors is our constitutional debate. At the same time, these same implications have also heightened concerns relating to the economic-imperative aspect or prong of the initial Quebec challenge. Thus, the constitutional/political and economic imperatives are now fully joined.

VII. CONCLUSION

Essentially, the conclusion is contained in the series of "bullets" in the introductory section. However, a few summary observations are probably warranted. The first is that some further decentralization of powers is inevitable. Canada is simply too large and its economic regions are too diverse (much more diverse than the U.S. regions) to run everything with a single vision emanating from the center, particularly when the center has been and presumably will continue to be distribution oriented. Second, Ottawa will be in charge of maintaining the economic union. As the Europeans are demonstrating, this is a very powerful instrument and will, accordingly, maintain a powerful federal presence. But the role of the centre must speak to Canadians in political terms as well as economic terms. The Charter helps here. What else is needed, however, is some version of a social policy charter or set of principles that applies to all Canadians and a transfer system adequate to this task. I have already suggested that converting aspects of the federal-provincial transfer system to a system of direct transfers to individuals is a likely direction. In other words, the most likely outcome is a rebalancing of powers.

However, I doubt that it is instructive, let alone possible, to attempt to work out a new, compartmentalized, division of powers. The world no longer works this way. Thus, my third point is that it may be useful to turn to the concept of concurrency with provincial paramountcy (CPP). Let me illustrate this with the proposed education initiative in the recent Throne Speech. Ottawa has quickly pulled back from its original assertiveness and it now suggests (Delacourt, 1991) that all provinces will be able to pull out of any federal initiative on education and they will get financial compensation. (Presumably the costs of so doing would be the inefficiencies on the administrative side, which could be substantial). This is concurrency with provincial paramountcy. It would have the virtue that, first, it allows Ottawa to legislate in an area of provincial jurisdiction. Second, since opting out is possible, Ottawa would ensure that it would not just impose its own will on the issue, given the outcome would then be predictable. Rather the incentives are appropriate in the sense that consultation with the provinces would be inevitable. Finally, not all areas would be placed under CPP, but my list would be larger than most.

As a fourth summary comment, let me focus on a federal "proposal" that is clearly inappropriate. This is the apparently "soon-to-be-announced" (according to the lead story in a recent Financial Post) National Securities Commission which would effectively take away the regulation for securities from the provinces. I am sympathetic to the view that if we were to start a country afresh, we would not place control over securities at the provincial level. But the fact is that the system works. Indeed, one could mount a reasonably convincing case that we have the second most efficient securities market (after the Americans). Moreover, the international securities commissioners certainly have confidence in us since they placed their executive office in Montreal! Setting aside the critical issue that this is one of the "initiatives" referred to earlier that is likely to rend the nation, where are the gains to come from since the result will be duplication, entanglement, continuous court challenges and the like, given that the provinces would still retain aspects of this role. And in true redistributive style, one of Ottawa's first initiatives would likely be to open up an exchange in Halifax to "balance off" the other five. To be sure, there are some problems that do arise because of provincial jurisdiction and these must be sorted out. But the perspective needed at this point in time is to fix the things that do not work rather than the things that do.

Fifth, assuming that the transfer system shifts from place to people, the likely result will be substantial initiatives in Canada West and Canada East in terms of rationalization and cooperation: they, not Ottawa, will have to assume responsibility for "place prosperity".

Were I to continue along these lines, I would end up essentially describing my "reconstituted federalism" model. (The Community of the Canadas). This would be counterproductive since it would take the focus away from the core of my current paper.

My final comment harks back to the title. Were we Canadians somehow to put the country back together again without addressing the economic imperative (i.e. political renaissance and economic denouement) it would in all likelihood be a short-lived "victory". Yet, this is where our focus was in the immediate post-Meech period and, unfortunately, may still be. However, once we address as well the economic-imperative aspect of the Quebec Challenge the possibilities of reconstituting a viable Canada increase very substantially. The message in this paper is that these economic aspects can no longer be ignored - the unwinding of the federal- provincial social-policy infrastructure and the dramatic implications of the Ontario budget have literally forced ROC to integrate the political/constitutional and the economic elements. Canada 1992 is no longer primarily about arriving at a Quebec/ROC accommodation. To be sure, this dimension remains but it does so in the context of a pan-Canadian challenge. In the paper I suggested that it is quite possible that Ontario could find common cause with Quebec on many issues. However, once this new societal debate broadens we are probably in for a lot of surprises in terms of "linkages".

When all is said and done Canadians may not end up brewing a veritable political *and* economic renaissance, but at least we are now mixing the right ingredients.

Table I

The amount a Canadian employer must pay
a worker earning $100,000 in the U.S. to transfer to Canada
and maintain the same standard of living

Transfer From	To Toronto	To Montreal	To Calgary
New York	$144,500	$117,850	$120,550
Chicago	159,075	134,300	135,125
Houston	204,550	184,100	179,225

NOTE: We have assumed the employee is a married person whose spouse does not work, who has two children and is a home-owner.

   • U.S. dollars throughout.
   • Social programs are ignored.

Source: Brown and Gimbert (1991).

Endnotes

*   It is a pleasure to acknowledge the comments of and conversations
     with my colleagues John McDougall and Art Stewart. As is the case
     with all of my writings in this general area, discussions with Tom
     Kierans are an essential ingredient.

1.   This section as well as the one which follows are a précis of
     aspects of my C.D. Howe monograph (1991d).

2.   This section draws from Courchene (1991d and 1990b, and Chap-
     ter 5, this volume).

3.   The ceiling on equalization payments operates so as to ensure that
     total entitlements of all provinces do not grow more rapidly from the
     1987-88 base year than the growth of GNP from the 1987 calendar
     year. If the entitlements pierce the ceiling, actual equalization
     payments are reduced by an equal amount per capita until the point
     where they are consistent with the ceiling.

4.   Quebec receives 16.5 more "tax points" than the other provinces. Of
     these, 8.5 are associated with the EPF program. The other nine
     provinces receive an equivalent amount in terms of a cash transfer. In
     a year or two the value of the overall tax point transfer for Quebec will
     exceed the ceiling. It is not clear what then happens. Will Ottawa
     attempt to decrease Quebec's cash transfer from other programs? If
     so, Quebec will view this as a taking back "its" tax points. If Ottawa
     does not "tax back" this excess then all the provinces will request these
     tax points. The value of an equalized tax point is about $900 million.

5.   This may not be true for equalization in the sense that the provinces
     could mount a court challenge based on the Section 36 wording. The
     CAP challenge, now before the Courts can only deliver a temporary
     victory for the provinces since Ottawa *can* alter this program after
     appropriate "notice". Essentially, what is before the courts is the
     nature of this "notice" period. Nonetheless, a provincial victory here
     would be worth more than a billion dollars to Ontario.

6.   Obviously, Canada could not have escaped this recession. However,
     despite the boost we received from the FTA, we went into recession
     well before the U.S. (not after, as should have occurred if the macro
     policy was even "neutral" rather than perverse).

9. In Praise Of Renewed Federalism

There are probably as many visions of what a renewed federalism might look like as there are Canadians. And over the next year and a half there may be nearly as many proposals. My distinct preference is for what I have called "The Community of the Canadas" (Chapter 3 above). Here, however, I do not want to argue for any particular model. Rather, I want to focus on the incredible variety of instruments that are available for redesigning the Canadian federation. I also want to do something clearly un-Canadian by celebrating past accomplishments in terms of just how creative and adept we were (and still can be!) as a federal nation living and working within the existing Constitution.

Some reflection on aspects of these past achievements is an appropriate way to start. First, Canada was able to undergo vast swings in terms of decentralization and centralization without much, if any, change to the *Constitution Act, 1867*. Thus, there was centralization during wartime, then decentralization during the prosperous 1960s and early 1970s, then renewed centralization for the next decade. Decentralization now seems to be where we are headed - or, perhaps more correctly, rebalancing - once more.

Second, Canadians have been innovative in a great number of areas. Several examples come to mind. The initial equalization program was a product of ordinary federal legislation. It became such a hallmark of Canadian federation that the principle was enshrined in the *Constitution Act, 1982*. Saddled with a Senate that was potentially powerful but that lacked the moral authority to exercise this power, Canadians developed "executive federalism" - at the apex of which is the First Ministers' Conference - which allowed some way of bringing provincial input to decisions at the center and vice versa. My colleague Ed Safarian (1980) refers to executive federalism as Canada's "contribution to the art of federalism." To be sure, executive federalism has fallen on hard times recently, particularly in the Meech Lake process, but this merely implies that it is time to become creative again.

Third, Canadians are pioneers in the development of parliamentary democracy: the Charter of Rights and Freedoms was introduced within a parliamentary framework. The Charter is, in my view, a remarkable achievement in its own right.

Fourth, rather than change the formal allocation of powers, Canadians have used the intergovernmental transfer system to change *de facto* powers. An emphasis on unconditional grants enhances provincial powers, while conditional grants and the use of the spending power increase federal authority. In the process, so- called national programs were created - provincially run programs in health and social assistance that became "national" by virtue of their portability, accessibility, lack of residency requirements, and the like.

Fifth, Canadians also did some rather mundane but important things, such as formally changing the division of powers between the federal and provincial governments. For example, constitutional amendments gave old age pensions and unemployment insurance to the federal government. Somewhat more creatively, the public pension system was made "concurrent with provincial paramountcy" - a concept that I will feature later - which meant that Quebec could initiate its own pension plan and which made it possible for ROC to allow Ottawa to mount the Canada Pension Plan on behalf of non-Quebecers.

Sixth, Canadians have always found ways to allow for diversity. In this context, the most creative instrument has been "opting out". Quebec controls several program areas that the other provinces have left to Ottawa. Along similar lines, Quebec has its own personal income tax (PIT), while ROC has a shared PIT with Ottawa. Here is a case where allowing Quebec to "opt out" also allowed ROC to have a far more harmonized system than if Quebec were required to remain in.

There are many other examples of ways in which Canadians have been innovative in addressing their constitutional and institutional needs, but by now the point should be obvious. Canadians have displayed a rare genius in accommodating their political structure to internal and external forces. Moreover, it is important to recognize that most of these innovations *did not require a formal constitutional amendment,* even though they affected the *de facto* division of powers between Ottawa and the provinces.

The challenge Canadians now face is once again to call on this innate ability to adjust institutions to emerging needs. To some degree, this challenge can be met by deploying the current array of instruments more creatively. What is encouraging, however, is that further novel instruments are coming to the fore.

Among the most promising of these new instruments is "concurrency", which would allow both levels of government to legislate in certain areas. Canada's Constitution, unlike that of many other countries, has very few concurrent powers. Yet almost all policy areas end up *de facto* being concurrent.

One approach to concurrency is to associate it with provincial paramountcy. "Concurrency with provincial paramountcy" (or CPP for short) is the principal operational instrument driving my "Community of the Canadas". It would give Quebec access to more powers while still allowing Ottawa to legislate in these areas. Quebec wants greater control of culture, for example, but it appears to be quite satisfied with such national institutions as the research councils and the National Film Board, so it likely would accept federal legislation in these areas.

Under CPP, the other provinces would be entirely free to rebalance, to decentralize, or to centralize - the same freedom they would have if Quebec left the federation, but without the economic costs of such an exit. Moreover, section 94 of the Constitution could come into play here. Essentially, this allows the non-Quebec provinces to coordinate (or "to pass up" to Ottawa) their powers in the general area of property and civil rights. According to Frank Scott, section 94 was included so that, in a more favorable political climate than that of 1864-66, it would afford an easy way for closer integration of the non-Quebec provinces (LaSelva, 1983). In tandem, CPP and section 94 allow "symmetry" - or equality of the provinces - in principle and "asymmetry" in practice.

Effectively, the PIT is concurrent. Ottawa controls its own part, while the provinces' part is really operated under CPP. At any point, any province can follow Quebec's lead and set up its own personal income tax. In a way, the RCMP operates under CPP as well: in terms of provincial policing, the provinces can opt to "hire" the RCMP or, if they wish, follow the lead of Quebec and Ontario and establish their own provincial police forces.

There is another powerful instrument that, while not new, might also play a key role this time around - namely, the economic union. If decentralization in some areas is inevitable, an enhanced economic union, perhaps run through the Senate, might act as an appropriate counterweight.

As emphasized above, much can be done without touching the Constitution. For example, one of the key points in the Allaire Report is that the structure of the relationship between the federal government and the Bank of Canada ought to be changed to make the Bank more independent. David Laidler (1991) has recently addressed the pros and cons of developing for Canada a variant of the U.S. Federal Reserve approach, which would strengthen the independence of the Bank but which would also constrain the power of the governor of the Bank by strengthening the role of the directors of the Bank in policymaking. This may or may not be desirable, but the federal government need only pass the necessary legislation to bring it about; it does not require a constitutional amendment.

Finally, but not exhaustively, the *Constitution Act, 1982* provides a mechanism for amending the Constitution that does not require ratification by unaffected provinces. Specifically, section 43 of the act reads as follows:

An amendment of the Constitution of Canada in relation to any provision that applies to one or more, but not all, provinces, including

a) any alterations to boundaries between provinces, and
b) any amendment to any provision that relates to the use of the English or the French language within a province,

may be made by proclamation issued by the Governor General under the Great Seal of Canada only where so authorized by resolutions of the Senate and House of Commons and of the legislative assembly of each province to which the amendment applies.

The most ardent advocate of section 43 as the key to unlocking the constitutional impasse is probably Patrick Monahan of Osgoode Hall Law School. Monahan (1990) argues that this section is "the only realistic prospect for accomplishing constitutional changes to accommodate Quebec under the existing legal procedures." He goes on:

Under section 43, it is possible for the federal Parliament and a single provincial legislature to enact an amendment without reference to the other provinces. Such an amendment must be limited to constitutional provisions that apply to "one or more, but not all, provinces." This somewhat limits the scope of any possible amendment utilizing this procedure. But it is noteworthy that a clause along the lines of the "distinct society" clause might have been enacted on the basis of the section 43 procedure.

This possibility is reflected in the "Final Communique" issued by the First Ministers' Meeting on the Constitution, signed on 9 June 1990. The June 1990 agreement proposed a constitutional amendment that would have recognized that "within New

Brunswick, the English linguistic community and the French linguistic community have equality of status and equal rights and privileges." The proposed amendment would also have affirmed the "role of the legislature and government of New Brunswick to preserve and promote the equality of status and equal rights and privileges of the provinces' two official linguistic communities." In short, this proposed amendment tracked in fairly precise terms the "distinct society" clause in the Meech Lake Accord, with the exception that the amendment would have specified that it applied within New Brunswick alone. What is significant is that the June 1990 agreement specifically provided that this amendment would be enacted under the section 43 procedure, with only New Brunswick and Canada required to approve resolutions (p. 35).

Not all analysts would be as optimistic as Monahan in terms of the potential role for section 43, but it clearly enhances the range of available instruments in a significant way.

While not in any way downplaying the magnitude of the post- Meech Lake societal challenge, it is equally important not to downplay the way in which the constitutional game has been played in the past nor to underestimate the incredible flexibility of the instruments that are available. There is, in my view, ample scope and flexibility to fashion a renewed federalism that will be first- best economically, politically, and constitutionally for both Quebec *and* ROC. There certainly is a way if there is a will.

References

Aitkin, H.G.J. (1959) *The State and Economic Growth* (New York: Social Science Research Council).

Armstrong, Christopher (1981) *The Politics of Federalism: Ontario's Relations With the Federal Government, 1867-1942* (Toronto: University of Toronto Press.

Aubin, Benoit (1988) "Quebec Unveils Financial Deregulation Plan" *Globe and Mail* April 13, p. 34.

Bastien, Richard (1981) *Federalism and Decentralization: Where Do We Stand?* (Government of Canada: Ministry of Supply and Services).

Bell, Daniel (1987), "The World and the United States in 2013" Daedalus, vol. 116, No. 3 (summer).

Boothe, Paul and Richard Harris (1991), "Alternative Divisions of Federal Assets and Liabilities", in Robin Boadway, Thomas Courchene and Douglas Purvis (eds.) *Economic Dimensions of Constitutional Change* (Queen's University: The John Deutsch Institute For the Study of Economic Policy), vol. 2, pp.

Breton, Albert (1985) "Supplemental Statement", in Royal Commission on the Economic Union and Economic Development Prospects for Canada, *Report*, vol. III, (Toronto: University of Toronto Press), pp. 486-526.

Breton, Albert (1990) *Centralization, Decentralization and Intergovernmental Competition*, The 1989 Kenneth R. MacGregor Lecture (Queen's University: Institute of Intergovernmental Relations).

Cairns, Alan (1979) "Recent Federalist Constitutional Proposals: A Review Essay" *Canadian Public Policy*, Volume 5, pp.348-365.

Cairns, Alan (1984) "The Politics of Constitution Making: The Canadian Experience" in K. Banting and R. Simeon (eds.) *Redesigning the State: Constitutional Change in Historical Perspective* (London: Macmillan).

Cairns, Alan C. (1990) "Constitutional Minoritarianism" in Ronald Watts and Douglas Brown (editors), *Canada: The State of the Federation, 1990*, (Kingston: Institute of Intergovernmental Relations, School of Policy Studies), pp.

Canadian Bankers' Association (1990), *The Right to Compete?* (February).

Carmichael, Edward A. (1988) "Tax Reform: The Impact on Government Finances" in E.A. Carmichael (ed.), *Tax Reform: Perspective on the White Paper*, (Toronto: C.D. Howe), pp. 75-86.

Chandler, Mark (1990) "Ontario and Canada in a Global Economy. Can We Compete?" Treasury Division, Royal Bank of Canada, presentation to State University of New York.

Chrétien, Jean (1980) *Securing the Canadian Economic Union in the Constitution*, (Ottawa: Ministry of Supply and Services Canada).

Cloutier,Laurier (1986) "Les patrons sont maintenant aussi populaires que les chefs religieux" *La Presse*, Montréal, December 4, p. D.l.

Constitutional Committee of the Quebec Liberal Party (1991) *A Quebec Free To Choose* (January 28). This has come to be known as the "Allaire Report", after the Committee's chair, Jean Allaire.

Cook, Ramsay (1986) *Canada, Quebec and the Uses of Nationalism* (Toronto: McLelland and Stewart).

Côté, Marcel (1990) "Canada's Constitutional Future: A Viable Option" mimeo (Montreal: Secor).

Courchene, Thomas J. (1984a) "The Political Economy of Canadian Constitution-making: The Canadian Economic Union Issue" in *Public Choice*, vol. 44, pp. 201-294.

Courchene, Thomas J. (1984b) "The Canada Health Act and Federalism" in William Watson (ed.), *Report of the Policy Forum on Medicare in an Age of Restraint*, (Queen's: John Deutsch Institute).

Courchene, Thomas J. (1987a) *Les offrandes des Rois mages: Etat providence ou Etat providential?* (Montreal: C.D. Howe Research Institute).

Courchene, Thomas J. (1987b) "Entrepreneurship: A Mind of State" Working Paper 87-F03, Robarts Centre for Canadian Studies, York University.

Courchene, Thomas J. (1987c) "Meech Lake and Federalism: Accord or Discord?" Working Paper 87-F02, Robarts Centre for Canadian Studies, York University.

Courchene, Thomas J. (1988a), "Tax Reform: Impact on Individuals" in E.A. Carmichael (ed.), *Tax Reform: Perspectives on the White Paper*, (Toronto: C.D. Howe), pp. 11-48.

Courchene, Thomas J. (1988b) "The Free Trade Agreement: Reflections of a Market Nationalist" Working Paper 88-S01, Robarts Centre for Canadian Studies, York University.

Courchene, Thomas J. (1988c) "Social Policy and Regional Development" in John Crispo (ed.) *Free Trade: The Real Story,* (Toronto: Gage), pp. 135-147.

Courchene, Thomas J. (1989) *What Does Ontario Want?* (York University: The Robarts Centre for Canadian Studies) and *this volume.*

Courchene, Thomas J. (1990a) "Towards the Integration of Social and Economic Policy", in Bruce Doern and Bryne Purchase (eds.), *Whither Ottawa? Canadian Public Policy in the 1990s,* (Toronto: C.D. Howe), pp.

Courchene, Thomas J. (1990b) "Global Competitiveness and the Canadian Federation", paper prepared for the University of Toronto Conference, Global Competition and Canadian Federalism", and *this volume.*

Courchene, Thomas J. (1990c) "Reflections From Meech Lake" in *Econotes,* The Newsletter of the John Deutsch Institute for the Study of Economic Policy (Vol. 3, No. 1).

Courchene, Thomas J. (1990d) "The Tragedy of the Commons", forthcoming paper from the School of Policy Studies, (Queen's University: School of Policy Studies).

Courchene, Thomas J. (1990e) "Mon pays...C'est l'hiver". Plenary paper prepared for the All-European Canadian Studies Conference, "Canada on the Threshold of the 21st Century" October 24-27, The Hague, mimeo (Queen's: School of Policy Studies).

Courchene, Thomas J. (1990f) "Rethinking the Macro Mix: The Case for Provincial Stabilization Policy" in Robert C. York (editor), *Taking Aim: The Debate on Zero Inflation,* (Toronto: C.D. Howe Institute).

Courchene, Thomas J. (1990g), "Zero Means Almost Nothing: Towards a Preferable Inflation and Macroeconomic Policy", *Queen's Quarterly* vol. 97, No. 4 (Winter), pp. 543-561, and *this volume.*

Courchene, Thomas J. (1990h) "Grappling with Mobility: The Role of the State as a Regulator of Financial Services", in Diane Wilhelmy and Pierre Coulombe (eds.) *Penser Globalement, Think Globally.* Proceedings of the 42nd Annual Meetings of the Institute of Public Administration of Canada, (Toronto: IPAC), pp. 299-330, *in this volume.*

Courchene, Thomas J. (1990i) "How About Giving Natives a Province of their Own", *Globe and Mail* (October 18), p. A25, and *this volume.*

Courchene, Thomas J. (1991a), "Crumbling Pillars: Creative Destruction or Cavalier Demolition?" forthcoming in a Fraser Institute Conference Proceedings on Deregulation and Reregulation.

Courchene, Thomas J. (1991b), *The Community of the Canadas,* Reflections/Reflexions No. 8 (Queen's University Institute of Intergovernmental Relations). An earlier version of this paper is part of the "expert witness" volume of the Bélanger- Campeau Report. Also in *this volume.*

Courchene, Thomas J. (1991c), "Reflections On Canadian Federalism: Are There Implications for European Economic and Monetary Union". A paper prepared for the European Commission, mimeo (Queen's: School of Policy Studies).

Courchene, Thomas J. (1991d), *In Praise of Renewed Federalism.* Canada Round Series, vol. 2, (Toronto: C.D. Howe Institute).

Courchene, Thomas J. (1991e) *Forever Amber,* Reflections Paper No. 6 (Queen's: Institute of Intergovernmental Relations), and in David Smith, Peter McKinnon and John Courtney (eds.) *After Meech Lake: Lessons for the Future*, (Saskatoon Fifth House Publishers), pp. 33-60, and in *this volume.*

Courchene, Thomas J. (1991f) "Canada 1992: Political Denouement or Economic Renaissance" in Robin Boadway, Thomas Courchene and Douglas Purvis (eds.) *Economic Dimensions of Constitutional Change,* (Queen's: The John Deutsch Institute for the Study of Economic Policy), pp.45-69, and in *this volume.*

Courchene, Thomas J., John D. Todd and Lawrence P. Schwartz (1986), *Ontario's Proposals for the Canadian Securities Industry* (Toronto: C.D. Howe Institute).

Courchene, Thomas J. and Arthur E. Stewart (1991) "Personal Income Taxation" in Mel McMillan (ed.), *Provincial Finances: Plaudits, Problems and Prospects*, (Toronto: Canadian Tax Foundation), forthcoming.

Courchene, Thomas J. and John N. McDougall (1991) "The Context for Future Constitutional Options" in Ronald L. Watts and Douglas M. Brown (eds.) *Options for a New Canada*, (Toronto: University of Toronto Press), pp. 33-52.

Courtis, Kenneth (1992), "Reflections on the Japanese Keiretsu" in Thomas J. Courchene and Arthur E. Stewart (eds.) *Quebec Inc. II: Financing Innovation* (Kingston: School of Policy Studies).

Coyne, Deborah (1987) Testimony before the Special Joint Committee of the Senate and House of Commons on the 1987 Constitution Accord. Committee Hansard, Issue No. 14, (August 27).

de Vries, Rimmer and Gerald Caprio (1986), *World Financial Markets* (New York: Morgan Guaranty Trust).

Delacourt, Susan (1991), "Education Plan Not Mandatory, Bouchard Says", *The Globe and Mail* (January 25), p. 1.

Drucker, Peter F. (1986) "The Changed World Economy", *Foreign Affairs* (Spring), pp. 3-17. Note that the page references to this article relate to Drucker's 1987 book *The Frontiers of Management,* (New York: Harper and Row).

Drucker, Peter F. (1987) "The Changing Multinational", chapter 4 of Drucker's *Frontiers of Management*, (New York: Harper and Row), pp. 61-65.

Drucker, Peter F. (1989) "The New World According to Drucker", *Business Month,* (May), pp. 48-59.

Eden, Lorraine and Fen Osler Hampson (1990), "Clubs are Trump: Towards a Taxonomy of International Regimes", Working Paper 90-02, Centre for International Trade and Investment Policy Studies, (Carleton University: Norman Patterson School of International Affairs).

Energy Options (1988) *Energy and Canadians into the 21st Century,* (Ottawa: Ministry of Supply and Services).

Fortier, Pierre (1989), "Reform of Financial Institutions: Where Are We And Where Are We Going" Address to the Canadian Club of Montreal (February 13).

Fortin, Pierre (1989) "Credit Crunches and Wage Dynamics: A R e v i - sion of the Canadian Phillips Curve, 1957-1987", mimeo, (University of Quebec at Montreal: Centre for Research on Economic Policy).

Fowke, Vernon C.L. (1952) "The National Policy - Old and New", *Canadian Journal of Economic and Political Science* vol. 18, no. 3, (August), pp. 27-86.

Friedrich, Carl J. (1968) *Trends of Federalism in Theory and Practice,* (New York: Praeger).

Gotlieb, Allan (1990) "Remarks on Globalization" in Douglas Brown and Murray Smith (editors), *Canadian Federalism: The Global Economic Changes,* (Kingston: Institute of Intergovernmental Relations and the Institute for Research on Public Policy), forthcoming.

Grossman, Larry (1980) "Constitutional Renewal Requires a Canadian Common Market" in *Policy Options* (September/October), pp. 9-11.

Grossman, Larry (1981) *Interprovincial Economic Cooperation: Towards the Development of a Canadian Common Market* (Toronto: Ministry of Industry and Tourism).

Hay Management Consultants (1986) *Opinion Leader Research Program* (Toronto).

Hudon, Raymond (1983) "Quebec, The Economy and the Constitution" in Keith Banting and Richard Simeon (eds.) *And No One Cheered: Federalism, Democracy and the Constitution Act* (Toronto: Methuen) pp. 133-153.

Jacobs, Jane (1980) *Canadian Cities and Sovereignty Association.* The XVIIIth Massey Lecture Series, (Toronto: Canadian Broadcasting Corporation).

Janisch, H.N. and R.J. Schultz (1989) *Exploiting the Information Revolution: Telecommunications Issues and Options for Canada,* (Montreal: The Royal Bank of Canada).

Johnson, David R. (1990) "The Zero Inflation Target: Do Wilson and Crow Agree?" *Canadian Public Policy/Analyse de politique* XVI, vol. 3 (September), pp. 308-325.

Kapstein, Ethan (1989), "Resolving the Regulator's Dilemma: I n t e r - national Coordination of Banking Regulations" *International Organization* vol. 43, No. 2 (Spring), pp. 323- 347.

Laidler, D.E.W. (1991) *How Shall We Govern the Governor: A Critique of Governance of the Bank of Canada,* (Toronto: C.D. Howe Institute).

LaSelva, Samuel (1983) "Federalism and Unanimity: The Supreme Court and the Constitutional Amendment", *Canadian Journal of Political Science* XVI.4 (December), pp. 757-770.

Laughren, Floyd (1991), *1991 Ontario Budget* (Toronto: Ministry of Treasury and Economics), (April 29).

Leyton-Brown, David (1985) *Weathering the Storm: Canada-US Relations, 1980-83,* (Toronto: C.D. Howe Institute).

Manfredi, Christopher (1990) "The Use of United States Decisions by the Supreme Court of Canada Under the Charter of Rights and Freedoms", *Canadian Journal of Political Science* XXIII:3 (September), pp. 499-518.

McNish, Jaquie (1990) "Rate Hedges Beginning to Worry Bank of Canada", *Report on Business (Globe and Mail)* Tuesday, May 22, p. B1 and B4.

Milne, David (1986) *Tug of War: Ottawa and the Provinces Under Trudeau and Mulroney,* (Toronto: James Loriman and Company).

Milne, David (1991) "Equality or Asymmetry: Why Choose?" in Ronald L. Watts and Douglas M. Brown (eds.) *Options For A New Canada* (Toronto: University of Toronto Press), pp. 285-308.

Monahan, Patrick (1990) *After Meech Lake: An Insiders' View,* Reflections No. 5, (Queen's University: Institute of Intergovernmental Relations).

Morton, Peter (1990) "Canada Risks Procurement 'Shutout'", *Financial Post* (September 5), p. 5.

Mundell, Robert A. (1990) "The Overvalued Canadian Dollar", *L'Actualité économique* (June).

Newfoundland Royal Commission on Employment and Unemployment (1986) *Building on Our Strengths,* (St. John's: Queen's Printer). This is generally referred to as the House Report after the Commission Chair, Douglas House.

Ohmae, Kenichi (1990) *The Borderless Economy: Power and Strategy in the Interlinked Economy,* (New York: Harper Business).

Ontario Ministry of Community and Social Services (1988) *Transitions,* Report of the Social Assistance Review Committee, Toronto.

Ostry, Sylvia (1990) "Economic Factors and Impacts" in Diane Wilhelmy and Pierre Coulombe (eds.) *Penser Globalement, Think Globally.* Proceedings of the 42nd Annual Meetings of the Institute of Public Administration of Canada, (Toronto: IPAC), pp. 3-13.

Paquet, Gilles (1987) "Entrepreneurship canadien-français: mythes et réalities" *Transactions of the Royal Society of Canada* (Toronto: University of Toronto Press) pp. 151-178.

Pepin, Jean-Luc (1985) "Closing Address" in John Lennox (ed.) *Se Connaître: Politics and Culture in Canada* (Toronto: Robarts Centre for Canadian Studies), pp. 111-117.

Petrella, Ricardo (1990) "Facteurs et impacts sociaux et culturels" in Diane Wilhelmy and Pierre Coulombe (eds.) *Penser Globalement, Think Globally.* Proceedings of the 42nd Annual Meetings of the Institute of Public Administration of Canada, (Toronto: IPAC), pp. 14-39.

Petter, Andrew (1991) "Comments on the *Constitution Act, 1982*", in Richard Simeon and Mary Janigan (eds.) *Toolkits and Building Blocks: Constructing a New Canada,* (Toronto: C.D. Howe Institute), pp. 47-8.

Porter, Michael (1990) *The Competitive Advantage of Nations,* (New York: The Free Press).

Quebec Liberal Party Constitutional Committee (1980), A New Canadian Federation (Montreal: Quebec Liberal Party).

Recent Innovations in International Banking (1986) Basle: Bank for International Settlements.

Royal Commission on the Economic Union and Development Prospects for Canada (1986) *Report,* (Ottawa: Ministry of Supply and Services).

Royal Trust Corporation (1989), *Responsibility and Innovation: Toward a Framework for Financial Services* Background paper submitted to the Senate of Canada.

Safarian, A.E. (1980) *Ten Markets or One? Regional Barriers to Economic Activity",* (Toronto: Ontario Economic Council).

Scott, Frank R. (1977) *Essays on the Constitution,* (Toronto: University of Toronto Press).

Senate of Canada (1986), *Towards A More Competitive Financial Environment* Sixteenth Report of the Standing Senate Committee on Banking, Trade and Commerce (Ottawa: Senate of Canada).

Senate of Canada (1990), *Canada 1992: Toward A National Market in Financial Services* Eighth Report of the Standing Senate Committee on Banking, Trade and Commerce (Ottawa: Senate of Canada).

Sheppard, Robert (1991) "Public Opinion in Passing Them By", *The Globe and Mail* (March 27), p. A19.

Simeon, Richard (1972) *Federal-Provincial Diplomacy: The Making of Recent Policy in Canada* (Toronto: University of Toronto Press).

Simeon, Richard and Ian Robinson (1990) *State, Society and the Development of Canadian Federalism*, vol. 71, Studies commissioned by the Royal Commission on the Economic Union and Development Prospects for Canada, (Toronto: University of Toronto Press).

Simpson, Jeffrey C. (1980) *The Discipline of Power* (Toronto: Personal Library Publishers).

Simpson, Jeffrey (1987) "Choosing the Lesser of Two Evils", *The Globe and Mail*, (October 9, editorial page).

Smiley, Donald V. and Ronald L. Watts (1986) *Interstate Federalism in Canada* research volume 39 (Royal Commission on the Economic Union and Development Prospects for Canada) (Toronto: University of Toronto Press).

Special Joint Committee of the Senate and the House of Commons (1987) *The 1987 Constitutional Accord*, (Ottawa: Queen's Printer).

The Task Force on Canadian Unity (1979) *A Future Together: Observations and Recommendations.* This is generally referred to as the Pepin-Robarts Report, after its co-chairs (Ottawa: Supply and Services Canada).

The Economist (1990), "Finance: French Banks' German Model" *The Economist* (August 4), pp. 61-2.

Treasurer of Ontario (1980) "Equalization and Fiscal Disparities in Canada" Background paper to the *Ontario Budget, 1980* (Toronto: Government of Ontario).

Treasurer of Ontario (1981) "Renegotiation of Federal-Provincial Fiscal Arrangements: An Ontario Perspective" Background paper to the *Ontario Budget, 1982* (Toronto: Government of Ontario).

Treasurer of Ontario (1982) "Fiscal Federalism in Canada: The Record to Date, and The Challenge Ahead" Background paper to the *Ontario Budget, 1982* (Toronto: Government of Ontario).

Trudeau, Pierre (1980) Transcript of the Opening Remarks to the First Ministers Conference on the Constitution, September 8- 12, (Ottawa: Document 800-14/083).

Trudeau, Pierre Elliott (1980) *Transcript of the Opening Remarks to the First Ministers Conference*, Ottawa, (September 8-12).

Western Finance Ministers (1990) *Economic and Fiscal Developments and Federal-Provincial Fiscal Relations in Canada.* A report of the Western Finance Ministers submitted to the Western Premiers' Conference, Lloydminster, Saskatchewan, (July 26- 27).

Whyte, John (1990) "The Impact of Internationalization on the Constitutional Setting", in Diane Wilhelmy and Pierre Coulombe (eds.) *Penser Globalement, Think Globally.* Proceedings of the 42nd Annual Meetings of the Institute of Public Administration of Canada, (Toronto: IPAC), pp. 468-481.

Wilson, Michael H. (1991), *The Budget* (Ottawa: Department of Finance), (February 26).

World Commission on Environment and Development (1987) *Our Common Future.* This is generally referred to as the Brundtland Report, (Oxford: Oxford University Press).

Wylie, Torrance (1990) "Multinationals versus Transnationals", in Thomas J. Courchene (ed.) *Quebec Inc: Foreign Takeovers, Competition/Merger Policy and Universal Banking*, (Kingston: Queen's School of Policy Studies), pp. 26-27.

Ziegler, Dominic (1990) "Capital Markets Survey: Stormy Past, Stormy Future", *The Economist,* (July 21), pp. 1-28.

Zysman, John (1983), *Government, Markets and Growth: Financial Systems and the Politics of Industrial Change* (Ithaca: Cornell University Press).